GLOBAL ECONOMIC STUDIES

THE TRANSFORMATION OF ASIA IN A GLOBAL CHANGING ENVIRONMENT

GLOBAL ECONOMIC STUDIES

Additional books in this series can be found on Nova's website
under the Series tab.

Additional E-books in this series can be found on Nova's website
under the E-book tab.

ASIAN ECONOMIC AND POLITICAL ISSUES

Additional books in this series can be found on Nova's website
under the Series tab.

Additional E-books in this series can be found on Nova's website
under the E-book tab.

GLOBAL ECONOMIC STUDIES

THE TRANSFORMATION OF ASIA IN A GLOBAL CHANGING ENVIRONMENT

BERNADETTE ANDREOSSO-O'CALLAGHAN

AND

PETER HERRMANN

EDITORS

Nova Science Publishers, Inc.
New York

Library of Congress Cataloging-in-Publication Data

The transformation of Asia in a global changing environment / editors, Bernadette Andreosso-O'Callaghan, Peter Herrmann.
    p. cm.
 Includes bibliographical references and index.
 ISBN 978-1-61470-873-5
 1. Financial crises--Asia. 2. Global Financial Crisis, 2008-2009. 3. Globalization--Economic aspects--Asia. 4.   Asia--Economic conditions--21st century.   I. Andriosso-O'Callaghan, Bernadette, 1959- II. Herrmann, Peter, 1955-
  HB3808.T73 2011
  337.5--dc23
                                       2011028024

Published by Nova Science Publishers, Inc. ✛ New York

CONTENTS

LIST OF FIGURES

LIST OF TABLES

LIST OF CONTRIBUTORS

Bernadette Andreosso-O'Callaghan is Jean Monnet Chair of Economics and Director, Euro-Asia Centre, Kemmy Business School, University of Limerick, Ireland.

Duncan Freeman is a Researcher at the Brussels Institute of Contemporary China Studies, Belgium.

Gerry O'Hanlon, S.J., is a staff member of the Jesuit Centre for Faith and Justice and Associate Professor of Systematic Theology at the Milltown Institute, Dublin.

Joern-Carsten Gottwald is a Lecturer at the School of Asian Studies, University College Cork, Ireland a Professor of Geopolitics at the Rouen Business School, France.

Dr Louis Brennan, is an Associate Professor within the School of Business at Trinity College, Dublin, Ireland. He is also Director of the Institute for International Integration Studies at Trinity College and a Fellow of Trinity College.

Niall Duggan is a Research Associate at the School of Asian Studies, University College Cork, Ireland.

Nicholas McIlroy is a Scholar and post-graduate research student in the School of Business in Trinity College, Dublin.

Orla Bothwick .is a Researcher at the Euro-Asia Centre, Kemmy Business School, University of Limerick, Ireland.

Dr Paul Gillespie is a columnist and leader writer for The Irish Times; he is also a Lecturer at University College Dublin's School of Politics and International Relations.

Peter Herrmann teaches comparative social policy, social economy and welfare economics at the University of Eastern Finland, Department of Social Sciences and University College Cork, School of Applied Social Studies. He is also corresponding to the Max-Planck Institute of Foreign and International Social Law and Social Policy, Munich.

Tomoko Oikawa is a Researcher at the Euro-Asia Centre, Kemmy Business School, University of Limerick, Ireland.

Yantao, Bi is President of the World Society for Strategic Communication, and Director/Associate Professor at the Center for Communication Studies, Hainan University, Haikou, China.

ACKNOWLEDGMENTS

The collection of chapters included in this book arose from an international workshop held at University College Cork (UCC) in November 2009.

Without the support of the Institute for Chinese Studies (UCC), of the Asian Studies Ireland Association, and without the unbounded commitment of the contributing authors, to whom we are immensely grateful, this publication would not have been possible. Special thanks go to Dr. Joern-Carsten Gottwald and to Professor Fan Hong for their continuous support throughout the entire research project.

We are greatly indebted to the different referees, in particular to Professors Guilhem Fabre and Bruna Zolin for their invaluable help, and also to Frank O'Callaghan for his precious work on the proof reading stage of the manuscript.

LIST OF ABBREVIATIONS

ADB	Asian Development Bank
AFTA	ASEAN Free Trade Area
APIBF	Asia Pacific Irish Business Forum
ASEAN	Association of South East-Asian Nations
APT	ASEAN+3, i.e. ASEAN, China, Japan and South Korea
BOK	Bank of Korea
BBS	Bulletin Board System
CDFs	Contracts For Difference
CDOs	Collateralized Debt Obligations
CST	Catholic Social Teaching
CEO	Chief Executive Officer
CCP	Chinese Communist Party
CCTV	Closed-Circuit Television
CNNIC	China International Network Information Center
CPC	Communist Party of China
CPI	Consumer Price Index
CSO	Central Statistics Office (in Ireland)
EAS	East Asian Summit
EUROSTAT	EU Statistical Office
FAO	Food Agriculture Organization
FDI	Foreign Direct Investment
FTSE	Financial Times Stock Exchange
GAA	Gaelic Athletic Association
GAPP	General Administration of Press and Publications (in China)
GDP	Gross Domestic Product
GNIB	Garda National Immigration Bureau (in Ireland)
GNP	Gross National Product
ICT	Information and Communication Technologies
IIT	Intra-Industry Trade
IMF	International Monetary Fund
INSEE	Institut National de la Statistique et des Etudes Economiques
IT	Information Technology
ISP	Internet Service Provider
KAMC	Korean Asset Management Corporation

LCDs	Liquid Crystal Display Devices
MERCOSUR	Mercado Común del Sur
MII	Ministry of Information Industry (in China)
MNE	Multi-National Enterprise
MOFCOM	Ministry of Commerce (in China)
MOFSTAT	Ministry of Statistics (in China)
MPS	Ministry of Public Security (in China)
MSS	Ministry of State Security (in China)
NEF	New Economics Foundation
NESC	National Economic and Social Council (in Ireland)
NESDO	National Economic and Social Development Office (in Ireland)
NPLs	Non-Performing Loans
OECD	Organization for Economic Cooperation and Development
ODI	Outward Direct Investment
PLC	Public Limited Company
PRC	People's Republic of China
R&D	Research and Development
RMB	Renminbi
SAFE	State Administration of Foreign Exchange (in China)
SARFT	State Administration of Radio, Film and Television (in China)
SITC	Standard International Trade Classification
SME	Small and Medium-Sized Enterprise
SNS	Social Networking Services
SNU	Seoul National University
TASC	Think Tank for Action on Social Change (in Ireland)
UN	United Nations
UNCTAD	United Nations Conference on Trade and Development
USD	US Dollar
USSR	Union of Soviet Socialist Republics
WTO	World Trade Organization
WWII	World War II

INTRODUCTION

Bernadette Andreosso-O'Callaghan and Peter Herrmann

The current global environment is profoundly marked by an economic crisis that started manifesting itself most startlingly with the collapse of the US Lehman Brothers bank in the Autumn 2008, and that, at the time of writing, sill does not show any signs of abating.[1] It is, therefore, a crisis which, according to the very etymology of the word ('krisis' in ancient Greek) suggests a turning point, or a radical break, with the past. Although this turning point happened at a specific point in time, it is important to note that scholars from various disciplines and also from different political strands had been sending out warnings about the lack of sustainability of the system, in particular with respect to economic development in the strict sense, to the global and regional division of labour and wealth, and to its increasing socio-cultural viability. Since the focus of this book is on Asia, we also use, as a point of departure, the Chinese expression for crisis (危机, *wei ji*) which is a combination of two characters: danger and opportunity. Consequently, this book proposes to study the current economic global settings with reference to these two meanings of the word crisis, and to analyse the extent to which the current crisis might lead to a (profound) transformation of the world (economic) system, and in particular of the Asian system. The focus of this book on Asia stems from a simple assessment of geo-political economic history, which saw the economic centers of gravity shift from the Mediterranean basin to the Low Countries and Great Britain in Europe, to finally reach the North American region during the first part of the 20th century, a region that may have to cede its economic leadership role to Asia in the years to come.

For the Western economies, and in particular for the European Union (EU) countries, the current crisis is indeed reminiscent of the 1929 'Great Depression' and of its consequences. First of all, the 1929 world crisis led to the acknowledgement that the world economic center of gravity had irremediably and incontestably shifted to the USA. Although spectacular economic growth during the 19th century had enabled the USA to overtake Great Britain as the main world industrial power in the 1880s (Cameron and Neal 2003), it took the western

---

[1] Some (optimistic) commentators do claim that if we have not already left the bleak valley of economic downturn, we nevertheless have at least overcome its deepest point, and are already facing the harbinger of another bright "future business as usual".

economies another few decades to officially acknowledge the economic supremacy of the USA; this was eventually done at the 1944 Bretton Woods Conference (in New Hampshire), when the US dollar became recognised and accepted as the new world reserve currency. Within the USA itself, it took four years (1929 to 1933) for a number of radical institutional reforms to be devised and implemented in response to the Great Depression. The *New Deal* administration brought a number of fundamental reforms, a *transformation* of the capitalist system with, in particular, the enactment and enforcement of the Glass Steagal Act of 1933.[2] In the labour market, the 1929 crisis gave birth to an important transformation of US labour relations (Aglietta, 1976). These complex changes brought a mutually-interwoven cause-effect 'relationality' (the term 'relationality' being used in order to emphasise that, though we are dealing with causal relationships, these have to be understood as dialectically interwoven: what is cause of something is at the same time the effect of what it causes). Of special importance are the far-reaching changes of the following four factors

- the mode of production, including not least a change of the technological foundation
- the social and socio-political structuration, commonly[3] characterised by the catchwords 'post-Fordism', 'post-modernism' and 'governance'
- the international hegemonic structures
- the hereupon-based new orientations of economic governance and business management.

Given the many striking similarities between the 1929 and 2008 crises, (their common geographical origin - the USA - ; their diffusion effects spreading to other regions of the world, in particular the EU; their intensity; and their devastating effects in terms of growth, unemployment and public finances), it is tempting to infer that the current crisis, will, in the course of time, lead to a number of *transformations*. We believe that these will be along the lines of the concept of 'systemic change' by going beyond the mere 'adaptations' of individual rules and rulings. A number of questions spring to mind, such as: to what extent does the current crisis reveal the inherent contradictions of the current world capitalist system that, although increasingly allowing Far-Eastern countries to carve out power positions, is still dominated by the traditional patterns of Western hegemony? To what type of readjustment of the global economic structure will the crisis lead to? Does the crisis change the global investment environment? Is this a critical juncture in terms of Asia-Western, and in particular, Asia-EU relations?

The various chapters in this collection attempt to provide some answers to these fundamental and complex questions. They will do so by focusing on a region that learned some 'lessons' from the 1997 economic crisis, a crisis that was regionally confined to some Asian countries. As a result of these 'lessons', Asia is today relatively sheltered from the devastating effects of the current crisis, and the region shows some encouraging signs of resilience, making the region attractive in the eyes of businesses and policy makers alike.

---

[2] Designed to control speculation, which was one of the very root causes of the 1929 crisis, the Act was enacted in reaction to the collapse of a large share of the US banking system after 1929. By introducing the separation between commercial banks and investment banks, the Act was aimed at protecting bank depositors. The act was abrogted in 1999 under the Clinton Administration.

[3] And commonly open to misinterpretation.

Whereas the second part of the book encompasses Asian national case studies, the book starts with three chapters dealing with theoretical and ethical issues. These are presented from a Western perspective, given that the current crisis is grounded both in Western economies and Western economic theoretical thinking, and these first three chapters set the scene.

In Peter Herrmann's chapter on 'Globalization', we are reminded that globalisation is neither an economic process alone nor an economic process with effects on socio-cultural patterns of reproduction and social development. Rather, it is a process that is concerned with the very core of the entire mode of production as an entity of accumulation and regulation. The decisive point in the process of globalisation – distinguished from the process of internationalisation, international cooperation etc., already known for a long time - can according to this approach be seen in the fact that we are now confronted with a conscious and 'planned' mechanism of 'relationality'. Going beyond the division of labour, globalisation is about new hegemonies, going beyond coercive power and the development of new patterns of accumulation and regulation. The second chapter by Bernadette Andreosso-O'Callaghan borrows from an economic epistemology approach. By asking whether the current crisis is the symptom of a 'systemic failure' rather than a simple regulatory mechanism of temporarily-failing markets, the author dissects the neo-classical economic theory, - which forms the essence of the theoretical basis nurturing the current crisis –, and explores the extent to which this theory can be classified in the Marxian group of ideologies. The chapter concludes with suggestions of a way out of the crisis; in particular, it calls for an exit from economic ideology, and for a reconciliation of economic science with European and Asian philosophies and theologies, leading to new premises upon which a new paradigm can emerge. The way theology can enlighten the scholar eager to devise a new economic paradigm is an issue taken up in the following chapter by Gerry O'Hanlon. By using a Christian perspective, the third chapter of the book is aimed at indicating grounds for realistic hope that an alternative and more humane economic model may be sketched and implemented. By first questioning the standard measures of economic growth as a criterion for success, the author outlines the major elements of a new model in which: banks and financial markets would be socially responsible; economic activities would center on greater equality and sustainability; culture would adopt the common good as its dominant influence; and the political system, transformed by a religious voice, would sustain and institutionalize these dominant values.

These three contributions, taken either in isolation or together, show that the current situation can only be fully understood if economic, cultural as well as political factors are taken into account together, and moreover, if they are seen as a relational entity. This is of special relevance when it comes to current debates on crisis management and proposals on how to find answers to the current challenges. A fundamental shortcoming of many proposals is that they focus on only one aspect of the crisis. This began by characterising the current crisis purely and solely as a financial crisis: a crisis of the financial system, of financial management, a credit crunch etc. – factors that should not be dismissed, but which are only part of a wider reality. Another interpretation focused on the property market and the naïve view was that the overheating of the US-housing market – tsunami-like –caused the global crisis. The chain of isolated arguments continued, finally reaching arrays that are entirely external to the economic realm, by suggesting, for example, greed and human misbehaviour as the reasons behind this crisis. Indeed, it is tempting to refer to a quote in Karl Marx's

'Capital', where in a footnote of the chapter on the *Genesis of the Industrial Capitalist*, he refers to T.J. Dunning, a British trade unionist as follows:

> 'Capital is said by a Quarterly Reviewer to fly turbulence and strife, and to be timid, which is very true; but this is very incompletely stating the question. Capital eschews no profit, or very small profit, just as Nature was formerly said to abhor a vacuum. With adequate profit, capital is very bold. A certain 10 per cent will ensure its employment anywhere; 20 per cent will produce eagerness; 50 per cent, positive audacity; 100 per cent will make it ready to trample on all human laws; 300 per cent, and there is not a crime at which it will scruple, nor a risk it will not run, even to the chance of its owner being hanged. If turbulence and strife will bring a profit, it will freely encourage both. Smuggling and the slave-trade have amply proved all that is here stated (T. J. Dunning, l.c., p.36)' (see Marx, 1867; 1963 edition: page 1224).

In the same line of thinking, another quote by Harvey contends that:

> '[t]ese "consuming classes" represent "consumption for consumption's sake" and exist as a kind of mirror image to the "accumulation for accumulation's sake" that prevails among the productive capitalists' (Harvey, 1982/2006: 92; see also 90 f.).

This is, in some ways, just another expression of the contradictions of the system. This system contains not only the antagonist relationship between the *bourgeois* and the proletariat, but also a multitude of contradictions within the *bourgeoisie* itself, as one contradiction here is the contradiction between the bourgeois and the *citoyen* (citizen); another contradiction is that between an accumulation-oriented and a consumption- oriented part; between hoarding and debauchery and prodigality. Boccara (2011), importantly, brings these different aspects together, speaking of a *modèle anthroponomique* and outlining the importance of going beyond technical changes, also going beyond changes in regulating power relationships. It can be summarised as the need to be concerned with the mode of societal integrity rather than looking for mechanisms of social integration.[4] This suggests a fundamental and radical change: another *renaissance*, a step not to post-modernity but to something that is positively defined, in its own right, rather than by reference to something that preceded it. This is an alternative to the easy way in which changes are made at a surface level, which are purely cosmetic, and are there only to maintain the same system (the 'future business as usual' syndrome). The third way, incrementalism, lies somewhere between the two; it actually limits itself to technical alterations and adaptations though claiming to be making fundamental (*i.e.* systemic) changes. The very fundamental question –outside of the realm of this book – has to concern the definition of the 'turning point': (How) can we define the reach of system change, *i.e.* where can we speak of a turning point that fundamentally changes the accumulation regime with its reference to an at least temporarily specifically-defined or organised relationship of production and consumption, and the way each of them and also their relationships are organised, including the respective mode of regulation, *i.e.* the institutional and normative mechanisms that serve as a framework for the accumulation regime and regulate in particular the relevant social relationships.

Pointing at only one aspect of internal and external socio-economic mechanisms and their interplay, we can refer to Chandler's findings, with regard to processes of centralisation and

---

[4] See also Herrmann (forthcoming).

decentralisation. Chandler (1962) points out that increasing centralisation in the societal domain goes hand in hand with decentralising management structures; considering Norbert Elias's understanding of the process of civilisation, we could possibly speak of a process of 'civilising (the) capitalist enterprise (system)'. All this could well be considered as important enough, and even more so as complex enough, to deserve its own publication. The reason for mentioning it here was only to provide the reader with a background that may be of interest as a kind of guideline or framework when reading Part 2. The chapters look at different facets, important in their own right, but finally only comprehensible when seen as part of a package: the shift within and of the system of global or globalising capitalism – a system that fumbles for new accumulation regimes and new modes of regulation – nationally and globally. This is, of course, of some special relevance to Asian countries and some sectors within these countries, and the transformation is a twofold one: the transformation from a developing country's economy to a developed capitalist economy, and the development from a capitalist economy, as we know it, to a new – and at this stage - somewhat open system.

In chapter 4 (of Part 2), Duncan Freeman deals with the topical issue of Chinese outward direct investment (ODI) policy and with its reaction to the crisis. The author notes how China's ODI increased substantially after the Chinese government adopted its "go global" policy in 2001, and how its growth rate slowed down dramatically with the advent of the current crisis, in the background, however, of falling ODI flows worldwide. The author's main argument is the ambivalent reaction by both Chinese investors and the Government. On the one hand, there are positive factors at play such as a relatively healthy macroeconomic situation in China, large foreign exchange reserves and reduced transaction costs. On the other, these positive factors need to be weighted against an increased uncertainty and higher risks (both at world level), as well as the still-inexperienced attitude of Chinese investors who tend to follow an asset-seeking strategy. The author concludes that official policy documents suggest that the government did not adopt a definitive policy that focused on the exploitation of opportunities during the crisis. In chapter 5, Bi Yantao deals with the increasing power of information and communication technology (ICT) in transforming the Chinese cultural and political landscape. The author sees the ICT sector as being a 'revolutionary' force in China, leading to a 'virtual struggle' between the ruling and the ruled. The author shows the dual effect of ICTs: on the one hand, ICTs empower citizens, and on the other, the authorities use censorship and information manipulation as means to lessen the potential destabilising impact of ICTs on the Chinese political scene. The Chinese case is explored further in the following chapter by Jörn-Carsten Gottwald and Niall Duggan. The authors analyse the ways in which China's socialist market economy has been affected by the crisis, and the possible threat to the stability of the Chinese system. In chapter 7, Orla Bothwick examines the impact of the 2008 global economic crisis on the South Korean economy, an economy that managed to avoid a prolonged recession. She presents an overview of some key economic indicators and of government policies pursued, so as to highlight the classic V-shaped recovery that has occurred in the economy. She investigates whether the lessons learned from the 1997 Asian currency crisis furnished Korea with the appropriate tools allowing the economy to bounce back quickly from the 2008 crisis. In Chapter 8 on the supposed demise of *keiretsu* in Japan, Tomoko Oikawa examines how the Japanese *keiretsu* has been managing through the current crisis. Although the Asian crisis had already signalled the changing relationships in, and diminishing influence of, *keiretsu,* the author shows that the participating enterprises in *keiretsu* have been developing closer information exchanges between them, as a response to the crisis. As a result, the Japanese *keiretsu* is evolving into a more complex network of relationships, with an increasing number of enterprises in the network, and leaving the principles of *keiretsu* untouched. These principles are essentially core values in Japanese society. Chapter 9 by Louis Brennan and Nicholas McIlroy proposes a bilateral approach by investigating the impact of the global crisis on Sino-Irish trade, investment, and human flows. The authors start by reviewing the main theories of international trade, and by analysing the Sino-Irish trade, investment and human flows from the mid-2000s onwards. This data analysis shows similar pre-crisis trajectories for both countries, and their subsequent divergence in the wake of the crisis. The authors also examine the differing responses of China and Ireland to the crisis using a network and government-level perspective. They describe Irish and Chinese migrant networks in China and Ireland respectively, and outline their relevant spheres of activity within the host community. Finally, in Chapter 10, Paul Gillespie concludes the book with a global inter-regional perspective. The chapter highlights the relatively less traumatic impact of the current crisis on Asia (and in particular on East-Asia), compared to the financial crisis of the late 1990s, and the learning process that helped the Asian economies to engage in selective regional cooperation, and to strengthen their role in the worldwide capitalist system since the late 1990s. The author suggests a number of reasons why the 1997-8 economic crisis stimulated Asian regionalism more so than the 2008-9 one; in particular, the changing role of China and its increasing interest in taking global rather than regional action is mentioned. According to the author, the current crisis has led to a more outward orientation of Asia, and this change in geo-political relations leads to a more multi-polar world and to a new configuration of power in Asia itself. Although it is impossible to predict what will happen in the decades to come, the author notes that there is ample room for conflict in the emergence of such multi-polar systems. The chapter concludes by highlighting the crucial stabilising role that Asia can play in the decades to come, in terms of its capacity to act, whether in terms of economic space, provision of public goods or in relation to sovereignty.

REFERENCES

Aglietta, Michel. (1976). *Régulation et Crises du Capitalisme – L'expérience des Etats-Unis.* *Paris* : Calman-Lévy.

Boccara, Paul (2011). *La Crise Systémique : Une Crise de Civilisation – Ses Perspectives et des Propositions pour Avancer vers une Nouvelle Civilisation,* Pantin: Fondation Gabriel Péri.

Cameron Rondo and Larry Neal (2003). A Concise Economic History of the World, 4th Edition, Oxford: Oxford University Press.

Chandler, Alfred D. (1962). *Strategy and Structure*, Cambridge, Mass: CUP.

Harvey, David (1982/2006). The Limits to Capital; London/New York: Verso.

Herrmann, Peter (ed.) (forthcoming*). All the Same – All Being New. Basic Rules of Capitalism in a World of Change;* Amsterdam: Rozenberg.

Marx, Karl (1867) *Le capital,* Huitième Section, Chapitre XXXI, La Genèse du Capitaliste Industriel, pp.1211-24, Paris: Editions Gallimard, Bibliothèque de la Pléiade (1963 edition).

PART 1: THE 2008 ECONOMIC CRISIS –
Economic Context and CULTURAL SETTING

In: The Transformation of Asia …   ISBN: 978-1-61470-873-5
Editors: B. Andreosso-O'Callaghan and P. Herrmann   © 2012 Nova Science Publishers, Inc.

Chapter 1

GLOBALIZATION REVISITED

Peter Herrmann

ABSTRACT

The present chapter looks at globalization, taking up different classical issues as they had been raised especially by world systems theory. These are applied in order to shed some light on the current developments. Seeing globalization in a wider historical perspective is not seen as matter to develop a long-term perspective in hindsight (the question posed since when we can speak of a world system). Rather, at the centre we find a proposal to frame and methodologically and theoretically underpin current debates by presenting an approach that allows us to systematically analyze the current shift that is strengthening Asia's and in particular the PRC's role in the world system.

1. INTRODUCTION

Revisiting globalization is not a matter of looking for different interpretations of current processes. Instead, we have to question the concept of globalization if understood as mainly a matter of internationalization – in economic and other terms. Equally problematic is the understanding of globalization as generalized enforcement of capitalism – capitalism is per definition 'global' and had been since its beginning striving for open borders and at the same time for protective measures. The actual question is more one of determining the development and positions within a complex structured and developing world system – looking at economic and political patterns alike. The transformation of Asia and Europe then appears as part of a wider development of a global action agenda.

A more fruitful enterprise can be seen by drawing attention to two factors, namely:

- the concept of hegemony, going much beyond coercive dominance,
- the guiding question that looks into the character of actual capitalism, *i.e.* the specific mode of production and accumulation regime.

Against this background, we can see the major meaning (*i.e.* character) of current globalisation as shift in the pattern of global power distribution, thus as well as a shift of the culture of capitalism.

Beginning with presenting a definitional framework, the importance of the concept of hegemony will be highlighted. This delivers the foundation for analyzing and assessing the changing character of capitalism by looking at the development of the accumulation structure and the linked international and global patterns of division of labor.

2. GLOBALIZATION – A DEFINITIONAL OUTLINE

The usual reference for globalization is the breaking down of borders. This may refer to establishing a new (kind of) colonialism, and it may also be seen as a matter of dissolving nation states, establishing 'open spaces' or establishing a seedbed for new powers.

We find this in theories on the increasing power of regional institutions as for instance the EU, global institutions like the United Nations (UN) or global institutional settings like the International Monetary Fund (IMF) or World Bank or the regular Summit meetings. However, in all these cases we find another pattern shaping in one way or another, the pattern of real development and its interpretation: we barely find the stance of suspension of power. Even the emphasis of governance, let alone its claim of involving all 'stakeholders' into processes of analysis, decision-making, implementation and evaluation are about overcoming power.

It is suggested to put the following matters at the core of globalization:

- the reordering of territorial borders and in particular the redefinition of regions,
- the reordering of the division of labor and distribution of power,
- the changed role of culture.

The latter point deserves some brief explanation. The reason for seeing culture as a major point is not that part of behavior is culturally determined and plays for instance a role in maintaining a culturally defined take on factory discipline.[1] The actual reason is that production or an economy is a complex socio-political process in which accumulation regimes and modes of regulation closely interact. So, it seems to be more appropriate to speak of the new culture of capitalism rather than the culture of new capitalism – the latter being suggested by Richard Sennett in his book with the same title (Sennett, 2006). And rather than a blurring of borders into liquid modernity (Bauman, 2000), we are confronted with a redefinition of the old borders of and within modernity.

This is important when it comes to issues that are frequently mentioned: the openness and the matter of 'breaking borders' by studying abroad, looking for trade opportunities versus looking for peripheralization, colonialism and shifting orders.

This is based on the assumption that the economic process is not a matter of wealth, in a narrow sense, and its distribution (Marshall, 1890/1895[3]), but one of production. So

---

[1] Though the latter should not be underestimated as we see many businesses returning to their countries of origin due to difficulties with producing abroad, for instance publishers, who have printed journals in India. Quality issues and also problems of timing are mentioned as reason for relocation, not the costs.

production is not reducible to the technical process of construction but has to be seen in its processuality, ranging from manufacturing/construction which is in itself a matter of consumption, having a distributive character and being a matter of exchange. In this light, both local/regional and power distribution is very much concerned with the 'order of production'.

In this light we have to emphasize the process character of globalization itself – the sometimes at least implicitly suggested finality: a globalised world is then somewhat deceiving. This deserves more attention not least by looking at different perceptions as they can be seen in terms used in current discussions. For instance, the Korean highly politicized term used in this context – 體化, 일체화 (*Il-Che-Hwa*) – translates into 'making one body' and suggests a move towards leveling, abolition of differences and apparently a move to homogenization.[2] The French term, *mondialisation*, suggests a 'generalization' by way of merging into a 'common standard' towards the bottom – it is also a process of assimilation, but has at the same time a terminological emphasis of something positive: a new world order, though in a colonializing way by way of a secular trend of the diffusion of the socio-political culture of the centre, thus a move from the bottom of the new world order. Still, all such concepts suggest some kind of finality. The suggestion here is focused on the shift towards a new global order which may merge into a temporary new quasi-equilibrium but not in the actual suspension of borders.

3. HEGEMONY

It is as well about the order of things as matter of hegemony. As a general definition we can take that from Antonio Gramsci. He sees it as:

> 'domination' and as 'intellectual and moral leadership'. A social group dominates antagonistic groups, which it tends to 'liquidate', or to subjugate perhaps even by armed force; it leads kindred or allied groups. A social group can, and indeed must, already exercise 'leadership' before winning governmental power (this indeed is one of the principal conditions for winning such power); it subsequently becomes dominant when it exercises power, but even if it holds it firmly in its grasp, it must continue to 'lead' as well.
> (Gramsci, Antonio, 1971: 57)

It is important to fully acknowledge that the concept of hegemony goes far beyond the idea of establishing and maintaining a coerced order. Though coercion can be part of it, the actual points are two dimensions of 'supremacy' that allow developing hegemony as a non-coercive relationship. The one is 'systemic', the other subject oriented. In the words of Giovanni Arrighi (1994/2002: 29):

> World hegemonies as understood here can only arise if the pursuit of power by states in relation to one another is not the only objective of state action. In fact, the pursuit of power in the inter-state system is only one side of the coin that jointly defines the strategy

---

[2] I am very grateful for detailed information given by Youngsoo Yook, Leiden/Seoul.

and structure of states qua organizations. The other side is the maximization of power vis-à-vis subjects.

However, one has to be careful with the suggestion of a synonym like supremacy as – looking for instance at the French language, this might well point towards domination, leadership, *supériorité*, *toute-puissance*, so a rather determinist notion – these notions cover only one side of the coin.

Anyway, taking together what had been mentioned before with what had been said on globalization, we arrive at the important conclusion that:

> [c]apitalism has been able to flourish precisely because the world-economy has had within its bounds not one but a multiplicity of political systems.
> (Wallerstein, 1974: 348)

Then processes of globalization are primarily processes of shifting 'balances' of social territories, concerned with the question of who does what within the chain and who gets which kind of results?

4. CHANGING CAPITALISM: PRODUCTION AND ACCUMULATION

This system is based on economic and political division of labor. In this light we can grasp globalization not least by referring to different forms of differentiation, borrowing from Niklas Luhmann the three forms: segmentary, stratificatory and functional differentiation. However, I argue against Luhmann that we are not concerned with different historical stages but with different societal mixes of differentiation. In other words, it is not about the historical development from segmentary to stratificatory to functional differentiation. Instead, we are dealing with different mixes of these three forms of differentiation.

This makes sense only if we see it as instrument. In the following different dimensions are suggested to make sense of developments of the mode of production and the accumulation regime.

The Postfordist Shift

Looking at the common interpretation of more recent changes, the most common approach is the proposed shift from Fordism to Postfordism – and it is notable that the latter stage is very much caught in its determination by overcoming Fordism rather than presenting itself as an entirely new stage. Still, this may be very well positively acknowledged if we take for instance the confrontation provided by Bob Jessop, looking at the *Keynesian Welfare National State* and the *Schumpeterian Workfare Post-National Regime* (Jessop, 2002). Jessop (2000: 173) characterizes the *Keynesian Welfare National State* as one where market and state form a 'mixed economy' typology; it is *Keynesian* in the sense that the economy is a closed economy where full employment and demand management prevail; it is *national* in that the national scale has relative primacy and it is a *welfare* state in that it includes income redistribution. On the other hand, the current situation is seen as a *Schumpeterian Workfare Post-National Regime* and it is defined in the following way: its Schumpeterian nature stems from the fact innovation and competitiveness as well as supply-side policies interact in an open economy; its 'workfare' aspect derives from the fact that this type of regime subordinates social policy to economic policy, that downward pressure is placed on 'social wages' and that it attacks welfare rights. It is *post-national* in that scale is 'relativized' and it is a regime charcterizd by an increased role of governance mechanisms to correct both market and state failures (Jessop, 2000: 175).

Importantly, we are not simply dealing with economic systems as accumulation regimes but with modes of regulation, implying a wide range of different socio-political components.

Overcoming Tributary Societies

Before coming back to this, it is worthwhile to look at two more fundamental distinctions. The first is concerned with, on the one hand tributary, on the other hand market-exchange systems. Samir Amin defines the first as tributary societies.

> According to Amin, pre-capitalist societies are characterized by differentiation of the principal source or authority because of what he has called the 'central' or 'peripheral' nature of the tributary society under consideration. The 'central' or 'peripheral' character in pre-capitalism can be found in the area of the dominant authority, that is to say, in the State (power) and in ideology (cultures, religions), whereas the 'central' or 'peripheral' character of a capitalist formation is located in the area of the economy. In this sense, Amin has defined feudalism not as a specific mode of production but as a specific – peripheral – form of tributary society.
> (A Brief Biography, 1992).

Characterising is not least that:

> the ideology of the communal modes, spanning the long transition from primitive communism to the development of class and state society, is of a qualitatively different nature. Here the essential content of the ideology is in a strict relationship of extreme dependency on nature (a result of the weak development of the productive forces) and the still embryonic character of the classes and the state.
> (Amin, 1989: 23)

In contradistinction, the contributory system is understood by Samir Amin's view on capitalist societies. He states:

> The reproduction of precapitalist social systems rests upon the stability of power (which is the basic concept defining the domain of the political) and of an ideology that endows it with legitimacy. In other words, politico-ideological authority (the 'superstructure') is dominant at this point. ...
> Capitalism inverts the order of the relationships between the realm of the economic and the politico-ideological superstructure.
> (ibid.: 2)

It is in this context that Amin takes a developmentalist perspective from where he elaborates his view on centre-periphery relationships, proposing

> to distinguish the completed central forms from the uncompleted peripheral ones. (ibid.: 7)

The Process of Production

A further level of distinction can be seen in the 'sectorial structure', *i.e.* in the way in which value is actually created. This establishes a reference to the orientation (and their mix) on production, refining, (enhanced) reproduction, service provision, commodity exchange and financial systems. This obviously goes beyond the most commonly used division between primary, secondary and tertiary sector – importantly as it looks at the steps of mediation. These areas are especially important as it is exactly here, (i) where systematic transformations take place and (ii) the 'culture of capitalism' – and its crisis – is actually emerging and crystallizing. And it is here as well that major structural moments of the economy are shaped in concrete terms, not least the choice between indigenously self-sufficient, export-orientation or import orientation economy.

Capturing the socio-cultural meaning of economic developments and changes thus means taking a three-dimensional space for reference:

1. mode of societal production (accumulation regime plus mode of regulation)
2. mode of societally constituting distribution, and
3. mode of producing and defining value.

On the surface level, this seems to be primarily concerned with econometrics rather than being seen as a matter of the macro-economic setting. However, the meaning goes far beyond this. At least it is worthwhile to raise as question if and in which way specific 'econometrics' of the economy translate into (un)certain 'econometrics of life'; the first time I considered this, was a study on third-level education, undertaken together with Deirdre Ryan. In that work, we talked about:

> life regime, defined as combination of factors regarding the individual, locating to the physical and social environment which can be reproduced over time despite conflictual tendencies
> (Herrmann and Ryan, 2005: 48)

and mode of life:

> as an ideological and psychological constellation of various and complex set of norms which can secure the individuals' integration into the capitalist circle of reproduction.
> (ibid.)

It is worthwhile developing this in an interdisciplinary perspective, and ask for instance as well for the possible psychological meaning of living in a strongly export oriented society in comparison with either living in a strongly import-oriented society or a society that is self-sustaining. And we can see the importance of the latter pattern as well in many Asian countries, for instance in the policy of autarkism that prevailed for some time in the People's Republic of China (PRC).

From here we can locate a field of societal patterns – surely only in a somewhat ideal-typical manner but at least providing a heuristically useful stepping stone.

5. Territoriality and the Split of Production

Looking at the relationship in the perspective of world-systems theory, we recognize two overlapping circles. The first one is concerned with 'space' – surely this means always social space but it should be recognized as well in its rather straightforward meaning of territories and their relationship. This can be seen as a multi-layered relationship that can be idealized as presented in Figure 1.11.

This has to be linked with a second level of centre-periphery relation that refers to the different elements of the process of production and can be presented in the later Figure 1.2.

It is undisputed that the different levels are overlapping – and also that we are facing permanent minor shifts throughout history. And equally undisputed is the fact that we have a global standard by which no country persists over a long time within any pure pattern. However, we find nevertheless, specific patterns dominating, demarcating the various regional and country-specific patterns of the division of labor on the international arena.

Underlying is the secular trend of shifts between the different elements of the productive process – in several ways connected to the long waves à la Kondratieff. However, it is a trend of shifts between elements, but not of overcoming of elements. Postindustrial societies can be characterized as such only to the degree to which they manage to utilize peripheralized (or we may say relocated) industrialism.

Segment 1[3]

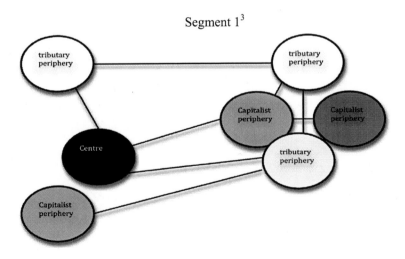

Figure 1.1. (Continued).

---

[3] Though the figure suggests identical segments this should not be taken literally – they can be very different, although they are structurally the same.

Segment 2

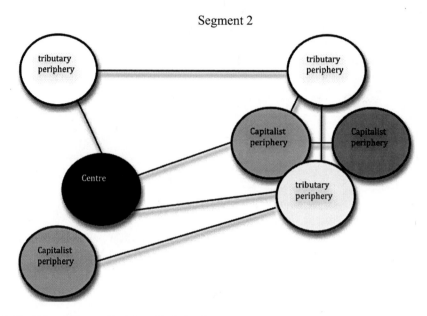

Figure 1.1. Traditional Centre-Periphery Relation I.

And finance-capitalism can only prevail for a short period as such; it is doomed to fail when financial speculation is actually really getting independent of the relocated productive forces. To put it differently, wealth can only be for a short time expressed in art works. As soon as David's beauty turns into individualized pleasure, accedes to greed, the firm marble from which David is build, adjourns in the same waves in which Narcissus drowned.

And now we can come back to the centre-periphery metaphor. The problem arises if and when we find a peculiar shift in the relation between the centre-periphery relationship: the power moves away from the productive forces, towards the fictive centre of fetish-based finance values.

Centre	Semi-Centre	Intermediary	Semi-Periphery	Periphery
manufacturing	refining	utility-service	exchange	information and financial service
pre & emerging capitalism	industrial capitalism	developed capitalism	hyper-capitalism	'casino- or finance capitalism'
dominance of utility value	strict dependence of exchange value on utility value	in tendency, decoupling of exchange value from utility value; separation of the realization of the utility value from the immediate action of the 'end-user'	complete interspersion of the fetish character of commodities	idealiter complete decoupling of money as fetishised value from any real-value

Figure 1.2. Traditional Centre-Periphery Relation II.

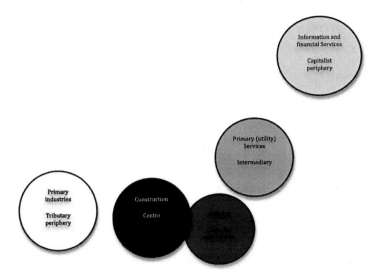

Figure 1.3. Centre-Periphery Relation in Developed Industrial Capitalism/Hyper-Capitalism.

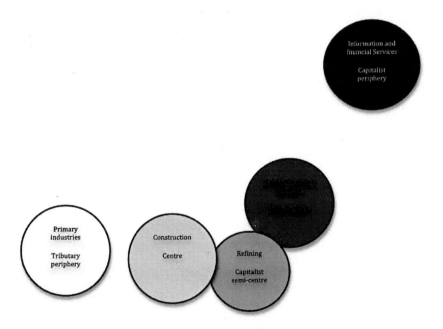

Figure 1.4. Centre-Periphery Relation in Casino- or Finance Capitalism.

We can see such periods as twofold reversion: on the one hand – and economically – we are confronted with the de-productivation of wealth production; on the other hand – and politically – we are concerned with the orientation on 'wealth' production rather than 'value' production. In the latter case, wealth is understood as accumulated economic standard (for instance the growth of GDP); and value is understood as pure exchange values – fetish of its foundation. It is important that we can now explain as well the so-called greediness: not being a matter of moral decay, but instead being a matter of de-valuation of production following the same mechanism as we can find the devaluation on international currency markets.

This is visualised in Figure 1.33 and Figure 1.4. The actually interesting aspect is that from here we can have a new view on finance capitalism and equally on new governance.

The 'new prince' – as undemocratic patronage, in the best case led by virtue, in the worst case being a simple dictator, and in a mystified case being part of deception under the cover of postmodernist governance – develops in this form as paradox: it is the overwhelming power that is now shifting towards the financial sector that supports on the one hand the development of 'pure individualism' which seems to be detached from the productive sphere, indulging in consumerism and 'princedoms' (Herrmann and Dorrity, 2009); however, it is on the other hand exactly this pattern of pure individualism that underlies the emergence of a new productivism: as matter of legitimation and also as matter of actual production everything now requires commodification although it is in many cases the commodification of the un-commodifiable: emotions are commodified via branding products (even if it is under the name of 'junk de luxe') in a similar frivolous way as privation (e.g. in form of workfare or the form of reality-tv). Only one thing remains caught in tradition: the story of 'prince and beggar' remains a fairy tale.

6. AN ATTEMPT FOR COMPARISON

Keeping this problematic aside, and also bearing in mind that we are actually talking only about differences within the global capitalist economy, we can look with a broad brush at a comparative confrontation in the following way (reduced to the two regions Asia and EUrope, and knowing that these are internally hugely differentiated). This is depicted in table 1.1.

All this qualifies as well the view on the concept of developmental welfare states. Rather than looking at this concept as such, to the question presented here is concerned with the underlying idea of a linear development – as for instance in suggestions to overcome the crisis simply by regaining economic growth – within the limits of measuring growth as matter of the development of GDP.

The one point in question is directed to the need of qualifying growth beyond measuring GDP; much work has been done already (this reaches from for instance the rather shallow, since the eclectic approach brought forward by the European Commission under the title 'Beyond GDP' and equally the rather complex approaches as they are developed under headings as 'Human Development', 'Human Security' and the like),[4] and there is a remaining lack of clarity of the systematic and strategic dimension of a much needed shift that goes in a thorough way beyond the eclectic compilations and also beyond its more or less rigid link to regional backgrounds and that is finally not bound into the traditional economic paradigms.[5]

The other point in question is that the quality of growth is very much a matter of the kind of the economic system. This cannot be explored in detail. However, if we look simply at the data of growth rates of GDP (or even if we take other strictly economic figures), we do not get any information on from where this growth comes exactly, given the existence of non measurable activities such as household work and voluntary work.

---

[4] On the discussion of different approaches see for instance Gasper et al. (2008).
[5] For instance, it is rather obvious that the Human Development approach is a "child of underdevelopment". And it is also obvious that the capability approach is principally attached to classical economics – going beyond without contemplating about the need of transcending this approach.

To name one example, it surely makes a difference if growth is based on stable and quality work, if it includes investment in sustainable infrastructure, including social investment or if not. Part of this will be taken up again later.

Table 1.1. Asia – Europe: Tentative Comparative Outlook

Asia	EUrope
MODE OF SOCIETAL PRODUCTION Large scale industrial production according to Fordist rules, and adapting post-Fordist techniques. Adapting Fordist patterns as well in the area of IT-industries Maintained family business structures – literally but as well in terms of management methods – securing integration via collectivist-paternalist systems	MODE OF SOCIETAL PRODUCTION Post-Fordist with an increasing number of small enterprises with a semi-independent status. Dominant niche production and high-end refining on large production scales Increasingly searching for new methods of governance in politics and economics in order to establish more open structures, reflecting the demeaning of territorialism
MODE OF SOCIETALLY CONSTITUTING DISTRIBUTION To large extent family oriented and clientelist systems (this can mean as well orientation along different lines of community led services). Supporting somewhat community-based integration	MODE OF SOCIETALLY CONSTITUTING DISTRIBUTION Highly institutionally-contributory systems, linked into 'market solidarities'. Subsequently individualist understanding of social provision
MODE OF PRODUCING AND DEFINING VALUE Production and refining oriented, this includes including service delivery into this chain.	MODE OF PRODUCING AND DEFINING VALUE Highly financial market driven, gaining a partial and temporary independences from immediate production spheres

In a condensed way this is reflected by the shifts of the welfare system of China – and on this occasion it is more appropriate to speak of shifts in the welfare culture. In the following, a brief overview is given in respect to the Chinese urban and the rural areas. What changes is not simply a formal or institutional setting, but these changes are based upon and lead towards fundamental changes of the mind sets of both the recipients and the providers alike (Guan, 2008). With this reference, I want to look not primarily at the patterns of change, but more at two other issues, namely (i) the foundation on which perceptions are based and (ii) the specific input into the emerging global order.

The point of departure for further consideration is not least the idea of a strong path-dependency not in terms of institutions but in terms of 'ideological' or 'socio-cultural life hegemonies'. Hsiao-Hung Chen points for instance on some moments characterizing the situation in today's PRC:

> Urban workers employed in the SOEs enjoyed the fullest welfare of all. Patterned after the Russian model, urban labourers of SOEs, in a sense, were treated as 'labour aristocrats'. The welfare needs of rural residents, by contrast, were taken care of by their Communes before the latter were abolished. For instance, in 1981 when the commune

system was still functioning, 71 per cent of all Chinese were covered by medical services. But this proportion had declined to 21 per cent by 1993 (World Bank 1997 a).

The 'enterprises' in China, especially the SOEs, were acting as an all-encompassing 'unit', whereby not only the 'full employment' of all their workers was guaranteed but also 'from cradle to grave' welfare was delivered.

The socialist idea of 'to perform according to one's ability, to each according to his need' cultivated the 'eating from the same big pot' atmosphere, which was detrimental to work incentives and motivation. As a result, there was likely to be much 'redundant labour' in the SOEs. With the advent of the reform, a new type of distribution – distributing according to one's work' – was introduced.

(Chen, 2003: 52 f.; with reference to World Bank, 1997)

From personal communication with the author it is possible to add that only part of it has to be seen as matter of socialist history; she underlines that much of it has to be attributed to more general aspects of Chinese or even Asian culture. Though Ireland is definitely not socialist or Confucian or anything else that is frequently seen as characterizing (part of) Asia, it may well be based on a somewhat similar way of 'bonding' in economics: contract-oriented business relationships and bonding-culture in business are tensions that may well find the same solution in both traditions in favor of the latter.

An important aspect shown in both the presentation by Xinping Guan (see below) and Hsiao-Hung Chen has to be seen in the different ways of understanding social integration. It is here very much based on two foundations – and independent of the level of support -: first it is about an egalitarian principle, and second, its highly collectivist claim. It is important though to see that this can be actually not only linked into the communist system but equally into traditional Asian value systems – on other occasions certain orientations that can be seen as very specific individualist amalgamation with the natural and social environment has been proposed (Herrmann, 2009: 171 and 230). One may see this as self-denial and subordination or one may it also see it as a matter of striving for a harmonious and integrated relationship with the environment. The concept of 'social harmony' which is frequently brought forward by colleagues from different countries in Asia is an important issue in this context.

Shifting Borders: Towards a New Mode of Societally Constituting Distribution

With all this we face a paradox in the current situation: speaking of globalization means that we are not simply concerned with blurring borders. Instead, we come back to the quote alluded at above, namely:

Capitalism has been able to flourish precisely because the world-economy has had within its bounds not one but a multiplicity of political systems.
(Wallerstein, op.cit: 348)

This means as well that we face new forms of territorialization. We have to keep in mind:

that the territorial state emerged concurrent with the deterritorialization of political economy and geographical imagination
(Steinberg, 2009: 468)

Territorialization is then part of the process of centre-periphery structuration and looks for the attribution of specific moments of the productive process to different regions and countries – the nearness to raw material and other resources is only one point in question. To the extent to which one may speak of production regimes[6] they can be roughly specified as systems of manufacturing, of consumption, of distribution and exchange.

7. Shifting Borders: Developing a New Mode of Societal Production

In this light it is also important to look at the consequences of the recent developments. We can take China as an example where the reforms have been introduced as part of the China's full and conscious entry into global capitalism. Referring to Xinping Guan, we see as achievements:

> A long term economic development and the increase of income per capita
> Decline of poverty rate (by both market reform and the public actions)
> Higher living quality and better provisions in education, health, etc. for most of Chinese people
> (op.cit., slide 14)

However, the problems are equally obvious:

> Higher inequality (The growing Gini Coefficient)
> 'Absolute poverty' still remains, while 'relative poverty' increases
> Social protection of the vulnerable groups has been relatively in decline as a result of the government's social expenditure, especially in health care, etc.
> Inability to solve the social problem caused by urbanization and rural labor migration
> Latent problems in the future 'ageing society'
> (ibid.: 15)

Broken Harmony – A Shift in Power, Expectations and Perceptions

The two main challenges that should be mentioned are the overlap of 'economic cultures' in two ways. On the one hand, we find the consequences of the – though partly weakened – ongoing dominance of the US-system. Actually the term is problematic as I do not mean the dominance of the Northern American nation state but I am talking about the American dream: an individualist, entirely entrepreneurized society. We can see this for instance reflected as well in the distribution of the country of origin of degrees. There is for instance evidence that we find a rather strong influence from the US on Taiwanese studies in sociology and social work, whereas we find a strong European influence when it comes to legal studies (Herrmann, 2009: 82)

On the other hand – and somewhat interwoven – we find a more 'internal shift', though locked into the global processes: the relationship between the different elements of the

---

[6] Using the understanding of production as it had been presented above.

productive process – manufacturing, consumption, distribution and exchange – is changing. At least as a working hypothesis it is worthwhile to assume that one of the major issues is the fact that large parts of the Western economy, namely in the manufacturing sector – broke away – a process that took place over decades and had been somewhat hidden behind exceptional conditions.[7] Be it as it is, even the new global pattern – finance capitalism and knowledge and service societies – are at least in their current form still industrial societies. This means as well that a – though altered – manufacturing demand has to be served.

In this way, we find a somewhat new division of labor and dimension to globalization: the reordering of the meaning of tributary systems.

Social Harmony or Social Quality – An Attempted Outlook

We can put this in a global context, not least by looking for the changes of a historical perspective – again looking at the change of the culture of global capitalism.

In this context usually shifts of locations of power and the change of the balance of power between states are highlighted. This is insofar misleading as it suggests the traditional nation state as point of reference.

Equally misleading is another notion that we meet occasionally, though not as frequent nor elaborated: such an approach suggests that nation states are not relevant anymore and we are now dealing with a shift of power towards indefinable, diffuse power amalgamations; Bauman speaking of 'Liquid Modernity' (Baumann, op.cit.) – surely a paradoxical approach and surely contradicting the approach mentioned before.

Here we propose to look for the new mode of integration – not simply continuing the traditional notion of the nation state nor looking for the solution in disintegration. This can only take the form of briefly pointing out the different forms of 'values' which should be put forward.

This links into different views on what a 'social and sustainable development' should be about. And apparently it is nowhere contested that we are at this stage talking about some kind of 'global capitalism'. Any other developmental path seems currently out of reach. Different views may be brought forward under catchwords as Human Development Approach, Capability Approach, Social Quality and Quality of Life Approach.

Leaving the discussion of these approaches aside, the following presentation wants to draw attention to the social quality approach – it had been recently presented on the 3rd OECD World Forum on 'Statistics, Knowledge and Policy'. Charting Progress, Building Visions, Improving Life (27-30 October 2009 in Korea), an approach that had been very much appreciated by the Organizer of that conference, stating that 'it shows good balance between good conceptual analysis and practical implementation, and the approach has built more reliable indicators and contributed to the better policy-making. It is, without question, at the forefront of OECD's visionary initiative' (from the statement of the evaluation committee).

At the core of the present approach is the orientation on different understandings of how everyday's life is actually produced and reproduced. The social dimension is surely a

---

[7] For instance due to the conditions after WWII which created particularly favourable conditions for satisfying the backlog demand and for building up an emerging export-lead industry in several core countries of what is now the EU.

'supportive framework'. However, rather than being primarily seen as such, the more important factor is that the social is a constitutive and constituting factor.

It is the dialectical relationship between biographical and societal development within the dialectically related reference frames of communities and institutions that permanently constitutes the social. This requires that we have to look at the 'raw material' of such a production – crucial parts of it have been outlined above in the attempt to outline the hegemonic patterns of varying centre-periphery relationships.

At this stage it is surely no more than an outline – but in this way it may well serve to provide a new framework for further analyzing the differences and similarities, and as well the divergences and convergences as matter of a revisited globalization.

CONCLUSION

It should be clear from the foregoing that current shifts of globalization are not simply a matter of shifting political power relationships. Rather, more important are shifts in the underlying economic patterns of accumulation regimes from where modes of regulation develop now in a national and global system of complex world systems. It would be fallible trying to reduce the current shifts simply on changing political power distribution or to see them as a consequence of a successful growth strategy. Both political power shifts and successful growth are bound to a fundamental shift which is potentially the emergence of a new accumulation regime. It will be important to observe if this development departs more or less fundamentally from the existing regime, if it only means a 'logistic' shift from resources and power between regions or if it is actually about a move back, allowing 'new princedoms' to emerge.

REFERENCES

A brief biography, 1992: A brief biography of Samir Amin – former director of the United Nations African Institute for Economic Development and Planning; 3; in: Monthly Review, Sept. http://findarticles.com/p/articles/mi_m1132/is_n4_v44/ai_12663251/pg_3/ - 12/11/2009 7:19 p.m.

Amin, Samir, 1989: Eurocentrism; New York: Monthly Review Press

Arrighi, Giovanni, 2002: The Long Twentieth Century. Money, Power, and the Origins of Our Times; London/New York: Verso: 1994/2002: 29f.

Bauman, Zygmunt, 2000: Liquid Modernity; Cambridge/Oxford/Malden: Polity.

Chen, Hsiao-Hung, 2003: Paradigm Shifts in Social Welfare Policy Making in China: Struggling between Economic Efficiency and Social Equity; in: Catherine Jones Finer [ed.]: Social policy reform in China: views from home and abroad; Aldershot: Ashgate, 51-68; here: 52 f.

Gasper, Des/van der Maesen, Laurent/Truong, Thanh-Dam/Walker. Alan, 2008: Human Security and Social Quality: Contrasts and Complementarities; The Hague: Institute of Social Sciences.

Gramsci, Antonio, 1971: Selection from Prison Notebooks; London: LawrenceandWishart.

Guan, Xinping, 2008. Social Protection in China – Reform and Development in the Background of marketization, globalization and urbanization. *Presentation during the 33rd Global Conference of ICSW, Tours, France 2008:* slides 5, 7; http://www.icsw.org/doc/P2_Guan_Eng.ppt - 11/11/2009 3:25 p.m.

Herrmann, 2009: *Social Quality. Looking for a Global Social Policy. Attempting an Approximation to the Analysis of Distances of Social Systems;* Bremen: Europaeischer Hochschulverlag.

Herrmann, Peter and Dorrity, Claire, 2009: Critique of Pure Individualism; in: Dorrity, Claire and Herrmann, Peter [eds.]: Claire Dorrity: *Social Professional Activity – The Search for a Minimum Common Denominator in Difference;* New York: Nova Science: 1-27

Herrmann, Peter and Ryan, Deirdre, 2005: Education – Just Another Commodity. Exposing the Rhetoric of «Human Capital» in the Light of Social Quality, in: Herrmann, Peter [ed.]: *Utopia between Corrupted Public Responsibility and Contested Modernity. Globalisation and Social Responsibility;* New York: Nova Science: 43-60.

Jessop, Bob, 2000: From the KWNS to the SWPR; in: Gail Lewis/Sharon Gewirtz/John Clarke (eds.): *Rethinking Social Policy;* London et al.: Sage publications: 171-184.

Jessop, Bob, 2002: The Future of the Capitalist State; Cambridge: Polity Press.

Marshall, Alfred, 1890/1895[3]: *Principles of Economics. Vol. I;* London: Macmillan and Co.

Sennett, Richard, 2006: *The Culture of New Capitalism;* New Haven/London: Yale University Press.

Steinberg, Philip E., 2009: Sovereignty, Territory, and the Mapping of Mobility: A View from the Outside; in: *Annals of the Association of American Geographers;* 99(3), 467-495.

Wallerstein, Immanuel, 1974: *The Modern World Systems I;* San Diego: Academy Press.

World Bank: 1997: China 2020; Development Challenges in the New Century; Washington DC: World Bank. (http://www-wds.worldbank.org/external/default/WDSContentServer /WDSP/IB/1997/09/01/000009265_3980625172933/Rendered/PDF/multi0page.pdf; 17/03/2011 7:54 a.m.)

Xinhua, 2009: National Human Rights Action Plan of China (2009-2010); in: *China Daily; November 11th, 2009;* Updated: 2009-04-13 15:08; http://www.chinadaily.com.cn/china /2009-04/13 /content_7672483_5.htm - 11/11/2009 4:04 p.m.

In: The Transformation of Asia …
ISBN: 978-1-61470-873-5
Editors: B. Andreosso-O'Callaghan and P. Herrmann © 2012 Nova Science Publishers, Inc.

Chapter 2

ECONOMIC CRISES, NEO-CLASSICAL THEORY AND PARADIGMATIC CHANGE

Bernadette Andreosso-O'Callaghan

ABSTRACT

Because of its magnitude and breadth, the first economic crisis of the third millennium – which is primarily a western economic crisis - invites one to analyze whether the crisis is a simple regulatory mechanism of temporarily failing markets or whether it is the symptom of a more severe type of failure, that of 'systemic failure'.

Since the current economic system is rooted in western-based neo-classical economic theory (and in neo-liberalism), this chapter will first elucidate the difference existing between economic crises and business cycles; it will then explore the extent to which neo-classical theory can be classified in the Marxian group of 'ideologies'; it will finally suggest a durable way out of the crisis which implies first an exit from economic ideology (from neo-classical thinking) by borrowing from European and Asian philosophy and theology, as well as the building of a new economic paradigm. The chapter argues in particular that crises are not inherent to all economic systems and that economics ought to reconcile itself with philosophy for the elaboration of premises upon which a new paradigm can emerge.

INTRODUCTION

The current economic outlook in the European Union, the USA and, to a lesser extent, Asia invites one to ask the following question: can the current economic crisis - which is primarily a western economic crisis - be seen as a simple regulatory mechanism of temporarily failing markets or is it the symptom of a more radical and severe break, of a failing system (in which case one would refer to the wording 'systemic failure')? Doubts about the potential of capitalism to survive beyond a certain time limit were already expressed by non Marxist economists such as Schumpeter (1943). Since any economic system is grounded on an economic theory, and since contemporary capitalism is based on neo-classical economic theory, this chapter will attempt to answer the fundamental question posed above by analyzing the extent to which neo-classical economic theory and neo-liberalism are flawed and are incompatible with long-term economic growth; in particular, it will discuss whether the neo-classical theory ought to be classified as belonging to the group of ideologies rather than as being classified as a science (Section 2). A third section will discuss the implications of the current crisis for the field of economic epistemology and it will suggest some avenues for the delineation of a new economic paradigm. Insights from Chinese philosophy and from European theology will tentatively be used for that purpose. Before we delve into these issues, we will clarify the important distinction existing between an economic crisis and an economic cycle (Section 1).

1. ECONOMIC GROWTH, BUSINESS CYCLES AND CRISES

From a historical perspective, economic growth in post-war agrarian societies has been characterized by a sequence of growth periods, followed by contractions or recessions, in short, by a number of business cycles.[1] Building on the work of various scholars, such as the 14th century thinker Ibn Khaldun who, by depicting the cyclical nature of human civilisations, is regarded as one of the precursors of the business cycle theory, and also of Kondratiev (1935), Joseph Schumpeter (1939) distinguished between three categories of business cycles: Kitchin cycles based on a periodicity of 40 months (Kitchin, 1923); Juglar cycles spanning between 7 and 10 years (Juglar, 1862), and Kondratiev cycles of 50 years length, with the longer cycles encompassing cycles of shorter duration (three Kitchin cycles for one Juglar cycle and six Juglar per Kondratiev). Whereas Kitchin business cycles are short term periodical movements of economic activity with disequilibria explained by time-lags in information available to firms, Juglar and Kondratiev business cycles are of a wider magnitude since they refer to long cycles of several years or several decades. According to Schumpeter (1911), although business cycles are inherently part of the process of economic growth and development, economic crises *do not* belong to the essence of economics. For Schumpeter (1911), crises are merely the amplification of a phenomenon which is inherent to economic growth: economic depression.

Consequently, a distinction needs to be made between business cycles and crises. Borrowing from the insights developed by the French regulationist school (Aglietta, 1976), economic crises occur in the case of failing economic systems ('systemic failure'). Economic systems are seen by this school as open systems in that interactions between the different parts of the system (in our specific case under analysis, between the banking sector and other economic agents within and across countries) involve feedback effects, or regulatory mechanisms that allow the system to go back to equilibrium. The system is viable as long as it operates at equilibrium or in the vicinity of equilibrium *via* feedback or retroactive effects. If however, fundamental *equilibria* are violated over a long period of time, - for example in the case of the US economy, persistently high current account deficits have to be financed by

---

[1] The capitalistic system centered on investment and growth in manufacturing activities – as opposed to agricultural activities - can be traced back to the end of 16th century Europe. By the late 19th century, this industrial-based system diffused to most of the countries in the world, including to those spared by colonialism such as Meiji Japan (Wallerstein, 1996). For more on the development of capitalism in Japan, the interested reader can refer to Itoh (1990).

high capital account surpluses (in part via borrowing) -, the regulatory mechanism (banking sector) cannot restore equilibrium and the whole system is condemned to change radically. For Wallerstein (1996), crises do occur in the case of 'historical systems'. Such systems are unsustainable given the exacerbation of inner contradictions which are too important to allow any regulatory mechanisms to set in. The only possible outcome is a radical break (rupture or crisis) which invites radical policy change and the shift to a new capitalistic system.

In the eyes of Wallerstein (1996), 20th century Western capitalism – and in particular post WWII capitalism – is one such system nurturing many contradictions; the Soviet economic system would be another one. Western capitalism needs here to be understood as epitomizing the systems of the USA and the UK, which have been emulated in other parts of the world, in particular within European Union countries and further afield. For example, in Japan and China, general traits of western capitalism (such as the 'financialization' of capital) have been combined with specific characteristics of 'Asian capitalism' such as a greater involvement of the state in economic and social affairs, when compared with an average EU country. The existence of radical breaks has led several scholars, from various schools of thought, to refer to the current crisis as a manifestation of a systemic failure, *i.e.* a failure affecting the entire economic system, including but not limited to its finance component (Kotz, 2009; UNCTAD, 2009). Since 20th century Western capitalism is fundamentally rooted in neo-classical economic thinking, and since the current crisis mirrors a case of systemic failure, it might thus be legitimate to question the validity of the theoretical framework underpinning this capitalistic system; in particular, to what extent can we say that the neo-classical theory is an ideology? Beyond their many differences, the Western capitalist and Soviet capitalistic systems may therefore combine a common fundamental feature: their grounding on fragile theoretical frameworks, perhaps on ideology, an issue to which we now turn.

2. To What Extent Is the Neo-Classical Economic Theory an Ideology?

2.1. Science *versus* Ideology

Science evolves from the known to the unknown. The observation of mere facts allows the scientist to state a number of premises. Starting with a number of known premises, an adequate reasoning will allow the scientist to reach several conclusions. In contrast, ideology proceeds backwards, by going from the conclusions (which are known) to the premises (unknown). In some ways, for the ideologist, the reasoning and/or scientific demonstration is constructed in such a way so as to justify the phenomenon under study.

In Marx and Engels (1932), ideology refers to ideas and conceptions drawn from different fields such as politics, law, metaphysics and religion. The authors stress that different epochs are marked by different 'ruling ideas', which are ultimately those of the 'ruling class'. In the authors' words:

> "The class which has the means of material production at its disposal, has control at the same time over the means of mental production [...]. The ruling ideas are nothing more than the ideal expression of the dominant material relationships, [...]; hence of the

relationships which make the one class the ruling one, therefore, the ideas of their dominance" (Marx and Engels, 1932: 64).

Clearly, a primary goal of ideology is to legitimize the existence of hegemonic forces and to allow these forces to perpetuate themselves. Ideology is therefore the direct expression of 'class' interests, for it is founded on the interests of a specific group (of a class, of a clan, in any case of a minority). The ultimate objective of ideology is therefore to allow an economic and political system, that serves the interests of a specific group, to reproduce itself.

To demonstrate the opposition existing between science and ideology, Leroux (1999) analyzes the premises, methodology and conclusions reached in the works of Joseph Schumpeter and Friedrich von Hayek, over time, as two edifying contrasting examples.

In Joseph Schumpeter's work (1911, 1939, 1943), Leroux (1999) shows that the central premise is constant, - innovation is the cause of evolution and the entrepreneur is the human vector of innovation - , but that the conclusions reached evolve over time, in line with the maturity of the author's work. Indeed, whereas in his *Business Cycles*, Schumpeter (1939) concludes that the Great Depression will not lead to a collapse of the capitalist system, in his 1943 work Schumpeter acknowledges the contradictions inherent in capitalism and its inevitable replacement with Socialism. This suggests that the work of Schumpeter dos not follow any prescribed or fixed idea (any ideology), but rather that it based on a scientific methodology. By contrast, Hayek's thought (1931, 1944, 1979) is characterized by a remarkable stability in the conclusions reached in his various works all along his life, independently of the specific historical context in which he wrote (Leroux, 1999). His immutable conclusion is that government intervention in economic affairs is counterproductive or even harmful. This constant conclusion is reiterated during a long period spanning from the Great Depression to the 1970s, in spite of the changing nature of his premises (which went from being economic, then axiological, and finally anthropological).

Following these lines of reasoning, can it be argued that the neo-classical economic theory is an ideology?

2.2. The Limits of the Neo-Classical Economic Theory

Economic policies in the western economic system preceding the 2008 crisis drew heavily from the teachings of neo-classical theory, an economic theory that emerged during the 1870s in Europe, in reaction to socialist and Marxist ideas. Using some concepts developed by classical economists such as Bentham's utility theory (Bentham, 1789), and refuting at the same time other concepts and laws developed by the same classical school (such as Ricardo's labor theory of value), the primary intention of neo-classical economists was to reform the field of economics by using mathematical tools. It was believed that mathematics would raise economics to the level of other sciences, such as physics, from which economics indeed borrows a number of concepts. It was under the influence of Hume (1751) that Bentham (1789) developed his utility theory. According to Hume (1751), human sciences must be founded on experimental methodologies; the delineation of a philosophical and economic system must rest on the simple observation of facts, rather than, as previously, on prescriptive Christian values. With the advent of the industrial revolution in Europe, the time was ripe for the 'scientification' of economic theory, and, consequently, the measurable - and therefore scientific and objective - concept of utility became widely accepted.

Neo-classical economic theory is best represented by the work of three main scholars: Stanley Jevons (1871) and Carl Menger (1871) who both used and expanded on the concept of marginal utility, and Léon Walras (1874) who developed general equilibrium theory. Of critical importance to these authors was the necessity to demonstrate again the main conclusion reached by classical economists, *i.e.* the benefits arising from governmental non-interference in economic affairs, by using however substantially different methodologies to those of the classical economists. In particular, before he published his work on general equilibrium theory, Walras wrote in 1860 against the ideas of the French socialist Joseph Proudhon, in which he clearly stated his objective of building a new economic theoretical framework (the general equilibrium framework) that would invalidate the arguments of the socialists. This was a clear response to Proudhon's 1846 publication in which the socialist author highlighted a number of contradictions inherent to the then existing economic system, contradictions that explained poverty and social injustice (Proudhon, 1846).

The fact that this new Walrasian framework (published in 1874) makes extensive use of mathematics, led to its wide acceptance, for, as argued later by Perroux (1983: 62):

> "… the theory of general equilibrium based on the mechanics of market forces was repeated *ad nauseam* and expressed in terms of simple mathematics which gave it an aura of prestige in the eyes of the general public".

From the very outset, it can be seen that neo-classical economic theory was developed with clear over-riding conclusions in mind: governmental non-interference in economic affairs is the most efficient framework for resource allocation, and individual rights (as opposed to duties) are paramount. Its use of simple mathematical tools (linear algebra and differentiation) made this theory look 'respectable' in the eyes of non experts.[2] From this rather shaky beginning, making the theory an ideology rather than a scientifically constructed series of premises and of logically-inferred statements, we can add the numerous limits embodied in the very content of the theory. These limits go beyond the restrictive assumptions upon which the theory rests – a weakness that has been highlighted frequently (see in particular Deraniyagala and Fine, 2001) - , and encompass:

a) the vacuum surrounding the question of individual endowments (as the basis of the exchange in Walras' framework),

b) the arbitrariness of the utility concept, something that had been noted by Fisher (1892), the first mathematical economist in the USA, and

c) the conflict arising from the interaction of egocentric (supposedly rational and hedonist) individual agents.

---

[2] It is interesting to observe at this juncture that Augustin Cournot was in fact the first economist to make extensive use of mathematical tools in the field of political economy (Cournot, 1838). Since Cournot's work defended protectionism, his 'Recherches' published in 1838 were totally ignored and overshadowed by the free-trade dogma defended in France at the time by Jean-Baptiste Say and his acolytes. Cournot epitomized a disappearing type of scholar, common in 18th century Europe: he was a mathematician, a philosopher as well as an economist.

These three weaknesses highlight the inability of the 'homo oeconomicus' concept to help us understand ethical norms (Sen, 1987). It is clear that value judgments are at the core of decisions made with respect to: individual endowments; the measure placed on individual utilities; and the process of utility maximization by hedonistic agents. As long as these decisions are made by individual agents acting independently and for their own sake, conflict is likely to arise.

2.3. From Neo-Classical Economic Theory to Neo-Liberalism: Further Ideological Fine Tuning

After WWII, and therefore after the short-lived experiment represented by Keynesian policies necessitated by the Great Depression, a new boost was given to neo-classical thinking with the advent of neo-liberalism.

From a theoretical viewpoint, neoliberal advocates (grouped in the 1970s under the label 'new economists') claim their roots in classical economic theory and see themselves as being well embedded in neo-classical economic thinking. For example, they find their inspiration in Adam Smith's 'invisible hand' concept (forgetting that Smith did advocate state intervention in certain areas), as well as in Léon Walras' general equilibrium theory (neglecting the fact that Walras's *Deus ex Machina*, as the economy-wide auctioneer, inspired central planning in the USSR and in other authoritarian regimes). In terms of methodology, the school stresses positive empirically-based studies using mathematical tools (*inter al.* econometrics), which again ought to confer these studies with an 'aura of prestige'.

The work of Hayek, which as we have seen above, is perfectly tainted with ideology, backed the take-off of the new economists' school in the 1970s. Born in the Chicago school of economics, with Milton Friedman's writings at its centre, the school's ideas diffused from the United States and led to the adoption of neo-liberal policies in many countries of the world, - including Deng Xiaoping's People's Republic of China -, and starting with Pinochet's Chile of the 1970s which was then used as a laboratory case (Gowan, 2009). With the fall of the Berlin wall in 1989, and the concomitant collapse of the Communist bloc, the teachings of the school were strengthened and they led to quasi universal further political and economic opposition to state intervention and to Keynesianism. The economic policies nurtured by the school aimed at minimizing governmental interference in economic affairs and at maximizing the private business sector. Transferring part of the control of the economy from the public to the private sector, leads, according to this school of thought, to a more 'efficient' government and it improves the economic performance of the nation as a whole. This resulted in the well-known array of policies such as: privatization of state-owned enterprises; deregulation (except for regulations justified on safety, environmental and consumer protection grounds); trade liberalization and liberalization of the capital account (by removing capital controls); tax reform, skewed in favor of capital and to the detriment of labor and households; and the 'financialization' of capital, by repealing the Glass Steagal Act in the USA in particular.

It is clear from this broad spectrum of policies that the focus is primarily on the primacy of economic individual *rights* and that the role of the government should be confined to being a *moderator* of last resort in economic affairs.

Interestingly, when subjected to the test of whether neo-liberalism is a science (rather than an ideology, in light of what has been explained above), the test fails on two accounts. First, neo-liberalism feeds mostly on neo-classical economic theory, in spite of its many inherent flaws as noted above. Second, the school has been holding the same conclusions all along, that is: (i) state intervention in economic affairs distorts economic efficiency, and that the latter ought to be a primary goal of any economy; (ii) individuals' *rights*, which are paramount, should not be inhibited by *rules*. This is despite the fact that the premises used to arrive at such a conclusion have been varying. Depending on the case and author, the following have been highlighted, alternatively: Smith's invisible hand (to validate trade liberalization in GATT talks), Walras' equilibrium paradigm (to substantiate deregulation), a revived monetarism *á la* Friedman (to justify budgetary cuts in the social area), rational expectations theory and supply side economics (to defend tax cuts for investors).

It seems therefore that neo-liberalism belongs also to the Marxian category of ideologies. As stated above, ideologies serve the narrow purpose of a small group of individuals, of an oligarchy. In the EU (and the USA), this group comprises today a fringe of top bankers and financiers, some large investors as well as some politicians. Although very much permeating the economies of most western countries, this oligarchy can nevertheless be increasingly found in Asian countries. By analyzing the case of China, Fabre (2010) shows, for example, that land transfer for urban development purposes has led to considerable rent-seeking strategies resulting in 10 per cent of rural residents being landless and in an alarmingly increasing wealth inequality in the country. It is obviously in the interest of this group of rent-seekers to keep the current system in place as much as possible and to proffer palliative solutions to a host of marginalized individuals (such as the 2010 widespread increase in factory workers' wages) rather than more fundamental reforms. In the case of the pre 'lost-decade' capitalist development in Japan, Itoh (1990) shows how the internationalization of Japanese capitalism through a decisive turn in economic policy in 1980-81 in line with Thatcherism and Reaganomics aggravated many of the post oil shock disequilibria. In particular, and apart from the 1985 Plaza Accord, the mid-1980s will be remembered for the unprecedented speculation on land prices in Japan.[3] In both the Chinese and Japanese cases, an increasing western style capitalism, where speculation was allowed free reign, served the narrow interests of the ascending ruling minority.

3. IMPLICATIONS OF THE CRISIS FOR THE FIELD OF ECONOMIC EPISTEMOLOGY

There have been indeed two main responses to the 2008 crisis: one is to deliberately minimize the seriousness of the disequilibria by suggesting palliative solutions so as to prolong the economic system as much and as far as possible, so as to preserve the interests of the oligarchy. The second solution is to acknowledge the non-viability of the current economic system based on fragile theoretical grounds and to put forward a number of

---

[3] As recalled by Itoh (1990), in September 1987, the total price of land in Japan was estimated at Yen 1,800 trillion; this compared with Yen 412 trillion for the total price of land in the USA at the time, a country 25 times the size of Japan.

fundamental theoretical and policy reforms; this latter solution implies a departure from neo-classical theory and involves therefore a paradigmatic change.

3.1. *Statu Quo* and Palliative Measures: Short-Termism

The solutions proffered so far by the governments of the countries most hit by the current crisis (USA, EU), are a mixture of further tougher neo-liberal measures combined, interestingly, with temporary Keynesian-based measures. The latter include: (i) the various stimulus packages in a large number of countries such as the USA, Sweden and other EU countries, as well as in China and South Korea; (ii) and the cleansing of failed banks through nationalizations and recapitalization (in particular in Ireland and in the UK). In the former group of solutions falls an array of budgetary cuts hitting primarily health, education and social welfare payments. The banking sector, main source of all disequilibria, is given paramount importance to the detriment of firms, particularly the small and medium-sized ones, hampering investment and therefore growth. The idea behind these palliative measures is to 'reassure the markets', by correcting the large fiscal imbalances that are perceived by investors as inhibiting their potential return. The large budget deficits and the increasing debt/GDP ratios of both Greece and Ireland are reminiscent of the large fiscal and budgetary imbalances in Japan. In 2009, Japan's budget deficit was 7.4 per cent of GDP whereas its debt to GDP ratio surpassed 200 per cent, two macroeconomic performance indicators that failed nevertheless to undermine the markets. It is therefore obvious that the crucial issue is then less the size of the debt/GDP ratio *per se* than the ability of the country in question to *decouple* itself from the international financial markets and to internalize its debt (as in the case of Japan), a course of action denied to Greece, Ireland and to other euro-area countries through Treaty provisions[4].

These palliative measures, in particular the stimulus packages, did lead to rebounds in economic growth in countries such as France shortly after the beginning of the crisis. These were, nevertheless, short-term effects and they are insufficient to bring back business confidence over a longer period of time. A number of elements, such as the restrictive budgetary policies in the euro-area, below than expected growth rates in emerging countries (INSEE, 2010), combined with increased uncertainty in energy markets due to a number of social movements in the Arab world and to the March 2011 earthquake in Fukushima prefecture of Japan, lead to slower growth forecasts for 2011.

Beyond the fact that the oligarchy still seems to have an unconditional *belief* in the workings of the neoliberal system (perhaps because its obsession with private interests has subjected it to intense myopia), another reason for the faith in the old system and for these palliative solutions might be the expectations that growth, somewhere 'over there', will eventually trickle down to the USA and to the EU. The necessity to boost exports becomes therefore another common solution proffered by several crisis-hit governments. This solution suffers obviously from a logical stumbling block. First, it is impossible for all countries of the world to have positive current accounts, bearing in mind that the countries with positive current accounts at the time of writing are those that have been less affected by the crisis, and *vice versa*. Second, China, which has relied since the beginning of its open door policy on an

---

[4] TEU (Maastricht Treaty), Protocol on the Statute of the European System of Central Banks and of the ECB, Art.7.

export-led growth approach, has learned a valuable lesson from its relatively high exposure to the US market. As a consequence, through its 'decoupling' stance, the country now seeks to generate growth from within its own confines by putting some emphasis on domestic demand as opposed to foreign demand (ADB, 2009; Fabre, 2010)[5]. This lessens its likelihood to absorb further EU and US exports. This *état-de-fait* implies that the gradual geographical shift away from the USA as the main world economy and towards Asia (in particular China), in line with Braudel's model (Braudel, 1985) might not, against all odds, happen to the benefit of Western countries such as those in the EU.

It is clear that by not questioning the root causes of the current economic crisis, by only feebly acknowledging both the need for more regulation in financial markets and for better governance in the banking sectors, the solutions proffered so far to the crisis have not led to the effects expected by the different crisis-hit governments. These measures, including the stringent fiscal measures, are minor in the sense that they do not involve a substantial change in the workings of the current economic system, and in the sense that they do not bring a durable solution to the crisis.[6] They do not fundamentally challenge the essence of the very imperfect Western neo-liberal economic system.

3.2. Towards a Paradigmatic Change?

This sub-section is aimed at assessing the extent to which an exit from economic ideology, and in particular from a neo-classical based ideology can provide, through the delineations of fundamental reforms, a viable exit out of the crisis.

A first step with regard to the need to exit from ideology, and in particular from a neo-classical based ideology, is to break with '*a priorism*', to leave way to pragmatism, in other words, to avoid falling into the trap of a new ideology. The next task in the delineation of an ideology-free new economic paradigm involves defining a number of universally accepted principles (premises), as a starting point of this new paradigm, and transforming the old and irrelevant economic analytical tools. The new approach advocated here breaks with the rather convenient, albeit reductionist, opposition between those economists who think that economics is a hard science (positive, where rationality is a core element), and those who argue that economics is intrinsically normative (*i.e.* it formulates value judgements with an ethical dimension). This opposition has no *raison d'être*. The new approach in this chapter is Popperian in the sense that it assumes that value judgments can be subject to rational discourse, in the same way as fact judgments. Therefore, prescribing a value judgment, a moral norm to start with does not diminish the 'scientificity' of the paradigm. The new approach or paradigm aims therefore at going beyond the opposing trends between, on the one hand, the 'scientification' of economics inspired by the work of the Scottish philosopher David Hume (1751), and, on the other, the Aristotelian concept of virtue (founded on a cosmology of teleological inspiration) combined with the Christian notions of good (virtue), duty and charity (*i.e.* caring for the other rather than for oneself; see chapter 3 in this volume), notions that can also be found for example in Chinese philosophy. Indeed, the Chinese ethical

---

[5] On this idea of China as the most probable 'saviour' of the world economy, the interested reader can refer to Yeoh (2009).

[6] However, they might end-up posing a threat to this very system, given the risks they entail in terms of social justice.

concept of *gong* (public interest) denotes the idea of transcending the self; "all on earth is for the general public", wealth is despised and its storing for oneself is derisory.[7] As a result, the public interest becomes the fundamental principle of morality (Zhang, 2002: 312). Also, another core concept in ancient Chinese philosophy is *Yi Ti* (the whole) implying that all things can be considered one unit; this mirrors the idea of harmony between the parts and the whole (the body). Used in the context of the political body, *Yi Ti* implies that the wise ruler is entrusted with the task to secure first the welfare of its people.

It follows that the new paradigm brings us back to the Aristotelian tradition of cognitive empiricism and to a normative empirical approach. The logical way forward is, therefore, to prescribe a value judgment, a moral norm, which is justified epistemologically if and only if it is the result of the convergence *of interests of all parties* involved (as opposed to the sole interests of the ruling class in the neo-classical/neo-liberal model). The idea is one of impartiality between individuals, of a contractual approach *à la* Jean-Jacques Rousseau, of a harmony based on *Yi Ti*. To borrow again from an Asian perspective and as argued by Storm (2011), the morality books of the late Qing Dynasty (late 19th century) emphasised that charity and a sense of public ethics were necessary to oppose the effects of a sinful and decadent world.[8] This normative approach has to be guided by universal moral principles, for many of the moral normative statements embrace conditions of objective truths. For example, when one states as a premise that "all children ought to be provided with food and education", the ethical property of such a statement is independent from subjectivity since it can easily be unveiled through observation that well-fed and well-educated children are likely to form a less violent society, a more economically developed economy, and a more stable system.[9] This new approach also needs to go well beyond Pareto's efficiency theory, which has been the reference moral doctrine for economists and which, curiously, led to welfare economics in the 1930s.[10]

This implies introducing other principles such as equality, equity, charity and fraternity, in order to understand human actions and to determine the appropriate policy to develop (Sen, 1993; Grill, 1999).

In the last decade or so, the temptation has been to integrate considerations of equity and justice in neo-classically based mathematical models, using utility maximization as a core tool. This has implied, for example, the introduction of a social welfare function, with due recourse to the utility concept, to weighting coefficients of given individual utilities (Samuelson, 1977). The weighing coefficient is, for example, deducted from the degree of aversion to inequality by the individual who determines this social utility function. But how is it done exactly? Because of its loose tools (the degree of aversion to inequality is bound to vary widely across individuals in a very unequal society, with a low degree for those belonging to a ruling group if we assume that they are 'rational' agents, in the neo-classical

---

[7] See the Record of Rites 9, Evolution of Rites; the original text of the Record of Rites is credited to Confucius and it was later re-worked by several scholars during the Han Dynasty (206 BC – 220 AD).

[8] In these works, charity is a collective endeavour, and again self and society are interdependent parts belonging to a holistic world.

[9] The literature on the link between child well-being and economic well-being or economic development is prolific; the interested reader can refer to UNICEF (2009) for a recent analysis in the case of East European Countries.

[10] This is rather curious, for, as shown by Freund (1974) Pareto's work in the area of economics is fundamentally justified by the necessity to show that economics is a science; Pareto uses a positivist approach and highlights that society is but an aggregation of individuals. Note that for Wolfelsperger (1999: 183), Pareto's normative economics is merely a 'second best utilitarian ethic'; it is a variation of neo-classical utilitarianism.

sense), this way of introducing an ethical dimension in economic theory is 'more a formally elegant way to suppose that a problem is solved rather than a contribution to its solution' (Wolfelsperger, 1999: 181). It follows therefore that from a methodological viewpoint, the new paradigm involves the use of novel tools and, therefore, an emancipation from utility theory.

CONCLUSION

Whereas business cycles are normal and recurrent phenomena characterizing economic development and economic growth, economic crises are not inherent to all types of economic systems, but rather they occur in the case of capitalist systems nurturing inner contradictions that build up through time, and that become too important to be tackled through regulatory mechanisms. Twentieth century western capitalism is one such system. This system draws heavily from neo-classical economic thinking (a theory which is inherently flawed) and which belongs to the group of ideologies, the latter being the direct expression of class interests. Neo-classical economic theory, which found its roots in 18th century Britain with the work of David Hume and which established itself as a dominant theory in the 1870s, was allowed to nurture modern capitalism, and the theory was given a new impetus through the neo-liberal fine-tuning after the 1970s. This led, *inter alia*, to the well-known wave of ultra-deregulation in the financial markets and it gave free reign to speculative activities in traditionally sheltered markets such as food commodities and energy products. The solutions proffered to the 2008 crisis so far have only been palliative solutions. They consist essentially in the extension of a tougher neo-liberal agenda (cuts in public spending) and in the rescuing of an ailing banking system in some western countries (Ireland in particular). By tackling the problem of large fiscal imbalances (fuelled by *de facto* state aids in the banking sector) with growth inhibiting budgetary measures, many of the western economies are faced with increasing sovereign debt problems jeopardizing future growth prospects. Consequently, government bonds markets have become new lucrative places where to invest, pushing the yield prices of bonds to record levels.

The aim of these palliative measures is to prolong, as much as possible, the current economic system, until, it is hoped, a new capitalistic dynamism, centered on Asia (with China at its core), can emerge. In this way, the post WWII neo-liberal 'consensus' may be replaced with a new 'Beijing consensus'; this would imply a mere geographical shift *à la* Braudel of the slightly amended current capitalist system. The belief in a world economic system revived by Asia and in particular by China as the new engine of world economic growth is fraught with an undeniable limitation: an important lesson learned by China and by other Asian countries from the current crisis is that decoupling from the west is seen by these countries as the only way forward. This lessens the likelihood of positive trickle-down effects (in Europe) arising from China's rise in the future.

It follows that, for the western economies, the only way out of the crisis, and indeed the only way forward, is an exit from economic ideology and the delineation of a new normative economic paradigm based on principles of action that are both universally-accepted and subjected to rational discourse. A fundamental premise of this paradigm is that the new economic system ought to serve the interests of all the parties involved, as opposed to specific 'class' interests as in the case of the current system. In policy terms, this calls for the abolition of exorbitant economic rents drawn from speculative activities in the financial markets and this implies a substantial policy change in the western financial markets.

Only with such a new system, would it then be possible to envisage a world economic system where the economic complementarities between broad regions and countries of the world (including China) would allow a friction-less and harmonious exchange of goods, capital, people and information. This paradigmatic change is necessary, feasible and timely. It is feasible provided it emanates from the EU and the USA, champions of neo-liberalism, and it is timely since China is still today in a position to listen and to concede to some of the western demands.

REFERENCES

ADB. (2009). *The Asian Development Outlook - 2009 Update*. Manilla: Asian Development Bank.

Aglietta, Michel. (1976). *Régulation et Crises du Capitalisme – L'expérience des Etats-Unis*. Paris : Calman-Lévy.

Braudel, Fernand. (1985). *La Dynamique du capitalisme*. Paris : éditions Arthaud.

Bentham, Jeremy. (1789). *The Principles of Morals and Legislation* (2005 Edition). Boston: Adamant Media Corporation.

Cournot, Augustin. (1838) *Recherches sur les Principes Mathématiques de la Théorie des Richessses* (Œuvres Complètes, Tome VIII, 1980 Edition). Paris : Librairie J. Vrin.

Deraniyagala, S., and Fine, Ben. (2001). New Trade versus Old Trade Policy: A Continuing Enigma. *Cambridge Journal of Economics*, *25*(6), 809-25.

Fabre, Guilhem. (2010). The Twilight of 'Chimerica'? China and the Collapse of the American Model. In B. Andreosso-O'Callaghan and B. Zolin (Eds), *Current Issues in Economic Integration – Can Asia Inspire 'the West'?* (pp.53-74). Surrey: Ashgate.

Fisher, Irvin. (1892). *Mathematical Investigations in the Theory of Value and Prices* (1961 Edition). New Haven: Yale University Press.

Freund Julien. (1974). *Pareto*. Paris : Editions Seghers, Série Philosophie.

Gowan, Peter. (2009). American Primacy and Europeanist Responses. In: Nam-Kook Kim (Ed), *Globalization and Regional Integration in Europe and A*sia (pp. 9-20). Surrey: Ashgate.

Grill, P. (1999). L'épistémologie de l'éthique. In : Leroux, A., and A. Marciano (Eds), *Traité de philosophie économique* (pp.133-69). Bruxelles: De Boeck and Larcier.

Hayek, Friedrich A. von. (1944). *The Road to Serfdom*. London: Routledge Press.

Hayek, Friedrich A. von. (1931). *Prices and Production*, London: Routledge and Sons.

Hayek, Friedrich A. von. (1979). *The Political Order of a Free People* (Volume 3 - *Law, Legislation and Liberty – A new statement of the liberal principles of justice and political economy*). London: Routledge and Kegan Paul Ltd.

Hume, David. (1751). *An Enquiry Concerning the Principles of Morals*. (1998 Edition, edited by Tom L. Beauchamp). Oxford/New York: Oxford University Press.

INSEE (2010). *Note de Conjoncture*. Paris : Institut National de la Statistique et des Etudes Economiques, décembre 2010.

Itoh, Makoto (1990). *The World Economic Crisis and Japanese Capitalism*. London : The MacMillan Press Ltd.

Jevons, W. S. (1871). *The Theory of Political Economy* (Second edition, 1879). London : MacMillan and Co.

Juglar, Clément. (1862). *Des crises commerciales et leur retour périodique en France, en Angleterre et aux Etats-Unis*. Paris: Guillaumin.

Kitchin, Joseph. (1923). Cycles and Trends in Economic Factors. *Review of Economics and Statistics, 5* (1), 10-16.

Kondratiev, Nicolai, D. (1935). The Long Waves in Economic Life. *The Review of Economic Statistics*, November, *17*(6), 105-115.

Kotz, D.M. (2009). The Financial and Economic Crisis of 2008: A Systemic Crisis of Neoliberal Capitalism. *Review of Radical Political Economics*, Sept, *41*(3), 305-17.

Leroux, Alain. (1999). Idéologie et science. In: Leroux, A., and A. Marciano (Ed), *Traité de philosophie économique* (pp.17-43). Bruxelles : De Boeck and Larcier.

Leroux, A., and A. Marciano. (1999). (eds). *Traité de philosophie économique*. Bruxelles: De Boeck and Larcier.

Marx, K and F Engels. (1932). *The German Ideology*. International Publishers, New York, 1947. Moscow : Marx-Engels Institute.

Menger Carl. (1871). *Principles of Political Economy* (German Edition). Vienna: Wilhelm Braumüller.

Perroux, François. (1983). *A New Concept of Development – Basic Tenets*. Beckenham: Croom Helm.

Proudhon Joseph. (1846). *Système des Contradictions Economiques ou Philosophie de la Misère* (1850 Edition). Paris : Garnier Frères.

Samuelson, P. A. (1977). Reaffirming the Existence of 'Reasonable' Bergson-Samuelson Social Welfare Functions. *Economica, 44*(173), 81-88.

Schumpeter, Joseph A. (1911). *Theorie der wirtschaftlichen Entwicklung*. English translation 1934, *The Theory of Economic Development: An inquiry into profits, capital, credit, interest and the business cycle*. Cambridge, MA: Harvard University Press; Leipzig: Duncker und Humboldt.

Schumpeter, J. A (1939). *Business Cycles: A theoretical, historical and statistical analysis of the Capitalist process*. New York: McGraw-Hill.

Schumpeter, J. A. (1943). *Capitalism, Socialism and Democracy* (1976 Edition). London: Allen and Unwin.

Sen, A. (1987). *On Ethics and Economics*. Oxford: Blackwall Publishing Company.

Smith Adam. (1776). *An Inquiry into the Nature and Causes of the Wealth of Nations* (Reprinted 1976). Chicago: Chicago University Press.

Storm Carsten. (2012, forthcoming) Images and Frameworks of Collective Action in China. In : Royall, F., and B. Andreosso-O'Callaghan (Ed), *Economic/Social Exclusion and Collective Action in Europe and Asia* (53-67). Heidelberg: Springer Publishing Group.

UNCTAD. (2009). *Global Economic Crisis: Systemic failure and multilateral remedies*, Geneva, 19 March.

UNICEF. (2009) *Child Well Being at a Crossroads: Evolving Challenges in Central and Eastern Europe and the Commonwealth of Independent States*, Innocenti Research Centre, Florence.

Wallerstein, Immanuel. (1996). *Le capitalisme historique*. Paris : La Découverte.

Walras Léon. (1860). *L'économie politique et la justice - Examen critique et réfutation des doctrines économiques de M.P.-J. Proudhon.* Paris: Guillaumin.

Walras Léon. (1874). *Eléments d'Economie Politique Pure ou Théorie de la Richesse Sociale.* (1976 Edition). Paris : Librairie Générale de Droit et de Jurisprudence.

Wolfelsperger, A. (1999). L'économie normative comme éthique minimaliste. In : Leroux, A., and A. Marciano (Eds), *Traité de philosophie économique* (pp. 171-96). Bruxelles : De Boeck and Larcier.

Yeoh, Emile Kok-Kheng. (2009). *Towards Pax Sinica ? China's Rise and Transformation: Impact and Implications.* Kuala Lumpur: University of Malaya Press.

Zhang Dainian. (2002). *Key Concepts in Chinese Philosophy.* Beijing: Foreign Languages Press.

In: The Transformation of Asia …   ISBN: 978-1-61470-873-5
Editors: B. Andreosso-O'Callaghan and P. Herrmann   © 2012 Nova Science Publishers, Inc.

Chapter 3

THE GLOBAL CRISIS – A CHRISTIAN PERSPECTIVE

Gerry O'Hanlon

ABSTRACT

The aim of this chapter is to offer an analysis of the global economic and financial crisis from a Christian perspective. The methodology involves a conversation between theology and other human sciences that respects the proper autonomy of each discipline.

In a first section, the conventional wisdom around measuring economic growth as a criterion for success is questioned. The need for a new economic model is identified. The second section outlines the major elements of this new model - banks and financial markets that are more socially responsible; an economy that factors in greater equality and sustainability; a culture that adopts the common good as its dominant influence, a politics that can sustain and institutionalize this dominant value, and a religious voice in the public square that joins with other citizens in providing the kind of social capital which is needed to secure the required transformation of culture and politics. It is proposed that tackling the resistance in banking and financial sectors to caps on salaries and bonuses might be the kind of symbolic gesture that would give momentum to this kind of radical change. The third section describes one positive attempt, by the New Economics Foundation (NEF), to outline in the concrete what such a new economic model might look like. The fourth section engages more explicitly with the theological resources which recommend a model of principled pragmatism that must counter that commonsense bias which too easily favors the interests of the wealthy and powerful.

The aim throughout is to indicate grounds for realistic hope that an alternative, more humane economic model may be sketched and implemented.

INTRODUCTION

There is a new popular, as well as academic, interest in economics since the start of the global economic and financial crisis. The news is generally presented in the kind of way that encourages the general public to believe that if retail sales pick up, if 'consumer sentiment' is strong, if house prices are rising, and – the holy grail - if Gross Domestic Product (GDP) and

Gross National Product (GNP) register growth, then this is 'good' and we should all heave a little sigh of relief and, even, begin to feel a little happier.

But, suppose this is not so, suppose that the lesson of the recession is that we should not pursue a consumption-led, debt-fuelled economic model, then, in the words of a Sunday Observer article, 'is it time to ask if the traditional metrics of economic success – retail sales, house prices, even GDP growth – really point us in the right direction' (The Observer, 2010)? The topic of this chapter is a questioning of the apparent conventional wisdom that a return to 'business as usual', albeit with a bit of tinkering at the edges, is the correct way to proceed and it will propose an outline of elements of a counter-intuitive, alternative approach (O'Hanlon, 2009a). Perhaps the present crisis can persuade economists, bankers, Chief Executive Officers (CEOs) to rethink their positions in a more fundamental way: as the Reverend Jim Wallis, Evangelical founder of the Sojourners magazine and community in Washington DC, told a gathering of the great and powerful at Davos: 'You know, you all perhaps used to think that you don't have to bring values to bear because the invisible hand will take care of things and make things come out all right. But what happens when the invisible hand lets go of important things like the common good? Or even the values that are inside all of us?' (Wallis, 2010, 2)

With these objectives in mind, the topic will be approached from a Christian perspective. In his recent Social Encyclical, *Caritas in Veritate*, (2009), Pope Benedict XVI uses the notion of 'integral human development' to recall the teaching of Paul VI in *Populorum Progressio* (1967) and to face the new challenges of today. This Encyclical recalls to mind the many other concepts familiar from Catholic Social Teaching (CST) and Judaeo- Christian and religious thinking: the common good, subsidiarity, solidarity, preferential option for the poor, the universal destination of goods, and so on. The chapter will draw, mostly implicitly, on the vision and values emanating from this corpus of teaching.

This implicit approach is taken out of respect for the 'relative autonomy of earthly affairs' (*Gaudium et Spes*, Vatican II, 1965), to avoid imposing a theological or faith model without properly respecting the discipline of economics itself and the related human and natural sciences. Fortunately CST is bi-lingual: it operates from a faith perspective but adheres as well to the 'natural law', to human reason, confident that in the end there can be no contradiction between faith and reason.

The interdisciplinary approach taken in the chapters of this collection echo the words of Rowan Williams, Archbishop of Canterbury that this whole global crisis is a lesson that 'economics is too important to be left to economists' and that there is a role for 'awkward amateurs' in coming up with solutions (Williams, 2009). As responsible citizens, not to mention religious believers, none of us can abrogate our responsibility to help fashion a sustainable way forward.

In the first section, the conventional wisdom around measuring economic growth as a criterion for success is questioned. The need for a new economic model is identified. The second section outlines the major elements of this new model - banks and financial markets that are more socially responsible; an economy that factors in greater equality and sustainability; a culture that adopts the common good as its dominant influence, a politics that can sustain and institutionalize this dominant value, and a religious voice in the public square that joins with other citizens in providing the kind of social capital which is needed to secure the required transformation of culture and politics.

It is proposed that tackling the resistance in banking and financial sectors to caps on salaries and bonuses might be the kind of symbolic gesture that would give momentum to this kind of radical change. The third section describes one positive attempt, by the New Economics Foundation, to outline in the concrete what such a new economic model might look like. The fourth section engages more explicitly with the theological resources which recommend a model of principled pragmatism that must counter the commonsense bias which too easily favors the interests of the wealthy and powerful.

1. How Do We Measure Success?

'Our Gross National Product counts air pollution and cigarette advertising, and ambulances to clear our highways of carnage. It counts special locks for our doors and the jails for those who break them. It counts the destruction of our redwoods and the loss of our natural wonder in chaotic sprawl…yet the gross national product does not allow for the health of our children, the quality of their education or the joy of their play. It does not include the beauty of our poetry or the strength of our marriages, the intelligence of our public debate or the integrity of our public officials. It measures neither our wit nor our courage; neither our wisdom nor our learning; neither our compassion nor our devotion to our country; it measures everything, in short, except that which makes life worthwhile' (Robert F. Kennedy, Address at the University of Kansas, 18 March 1968).

Our usual measurement of economic success and progress is GNP or GDP. The point being made by Kennedy – and now increasingly by many economists and some politicians – is that this is a very partial, and on its own, a crude form of measurement.

First, it does not typically take into account hidden costs (the 'externalities' referred to by economists): so, for example, think of the real price of goods if the cost to the planet of carbon emissions was built in, or, at a different level, the cost to family life of excessively long commutes (the bane of so many families in Ireland as a legacy from our Celtic Tiger days). Different measuring tools are now being refined to take account of a wider range of factors – for example the UN Human Development Index (UN, 1990) factors in life expectancy at birth, educational attainment and income adjusted for different purchasing power in different countries; Sarkozy's Global Project (CMEPSP, 2009), with J. E. Stiglitz at the helm, measures 'well-being', with a combination of social and economic factors; and the New Economics Foundation in Britain have their Happy Planet Index (NEF, 2009), a measure of sustainable well-being, according to which, incidentally, Costa Rica ranks first, the UK 74th, Ireland 78th, the USA 114 – out of 143 nations![1]

Second, part of the thinking behind these new attempts to measure success more accurately is that while material progress is important, still it is not what is most important. The old truism that 'money isn't everything' is right. The ancients (e.g. Aristotle's notion of *eudaimonia,* happiness), our Western and Christian long philosophical and religious tradition, have always known that it is foolish to put excessive trust in money, and that the really 'good life', human happiness and flourishing, imply that 'integral human development' includes, but goes much deeper than, material possessions. There is a growing recognition that when basic 'needs' are met, when a modest amount of 'wants' or desires can be satisfied, when there is

---

[1] See Reynolds and Healy (2009).

an absence of glaring inequalities, then individuals and societies are likely to be happier than within any simple model of infinite economic growth.[2] Our more recent Western, Irish fixation of 'economism' (CST) has not been shared by all other cultures (one thinks, for example, of the sense of community in Africa, of harmony in Asia, the values of hospitality and gift-giving among Native Indians in the USA). The virtual axiom of orthodox economics that *more* is always better, and our obsession with the pursuit of individual gain as the route to happiness, are, viewed historically, 'a curious anomaly' (NEF, 2009: 14). There is a need to begin to outline the criteria for 'good growth', to view economic growth as an instrumental good in service of the deeper human good of a fully human life and development[3]: and in this context economic growth will be good when it leads to greater social justice and is environmentally sustainable, and it should continue to take a more material form in poverty-stricken societies, whereas in societies where an adequate standard of living is already attained it should take the form of an innovation or knowledge and service based economy.

Wallis (2010: 3), again, puts all this well: 'Let's get back to the new old values. So, "greed is good". No, enough is enough. 'It's all about me". No, we're really in this together. "I want it now". Well, let's call it the seventh-generation mind-set – which the indigenous people have – which is how you evaluate a decision today not by a quarterly profit-and-loss statement only, but by its impact on the seventh generation out. That's pretty rigorous criteria'. And, again, (idem, 2010: 4)): 'So we need a conversation that either goes deeper than or transcends politics. It's about: what kind of people do we want to be? We're buying things we don't need with money we don't have. My parents didn't do that. And yet a whole generation has been lured into that kind of behavior by a culture that says your self-worth is because of what you have, what you wear, how you look, your big-dog car, your big boat, your house, your second house, third house. This is how we define ourselves as human beings. And that is a spiritual problem, but it led to an economic breakdown'.

We are, then, faced with a profound dilemma: to resist growth is, according to conventional thinking, to risk economic and social collapse, whereas to pursue it is to endanger the ecosystem upon which we depend for our long-term survival and follow the kind of wrong path to well-being that our current recessionary experience has revealed. Given that a more integral notion of economic success seems to be putting down some roots in our public consciousness, what elements would be required for a corresponding new economic model?

2. ELEMENTS OF A NEW MODEL

2.1. Finance/Banking: 'Traders in Record Bet against the Euro'[4]

There is a Christian critique, widely shared by secular commentators, of the theoretical economic model and its implementation which underpin our present crisis. Put simply, we

---

[2] See Bradstock's Public Lecture citing research by Wilkenson and Pickett, Richard Layard, and Marhsall Sahlins (5 August 2009, 17-27 and passim).

[3] Cf. Frank Turner (2010, pp. 275-285) where the author draws, inter alia, on the classic text of Karl Polanyi (The Great Transformation, 1944) to argue for the relative importance of economic growth and to begin to outline criteria for so-called good growth.

[4] Financial Times, headline, Tues Feb 9, 2010.

have been living under the hegemony of a neo-liberal form of capitalism (also referred to an infinite-growth capitalism/the short-term Shareholder Value model)[5], with proponents such as economists Friedrich von Hayek and Milton Friedman, and leading politicians like Ronald Reagan and Margaret Thatcher. This model favors the workings of unregulated free-markets. It led to a situation where banks were reckless in their lending and markets have been involved in mystifying, labyrinthine transactions whose complexity was opaque even to insiders. Too much of this involved high risk, in pursuit of short-term gain, with egregious inequalities. While there were some good outcomes – one thinks in Ireland and elsewhere, above all, of gains in employment – we know, at least in hindsight, that it was built on sand and is unsustainable. What needs to be done?

We need, in short, to find ways to make banks and financial markets more socially responsible. A disconnect has arisen between their activities and the 'real' economy. Banks, first, need to recognize that they have obligations not just to shareholders but also to all stake-holders – to private customers, businesses, employees and society at large. Several consequences follow: more effective regulation and oversight; probably a separation between retail and so-called 'shadow' or investment banks; perhaps a consideration of having at least some major banking along nationalized or cooperative/credit union lines and not only Public Limited Company (PLC) lines; some kind of cap on salaries and bonuses so as to model greater social equality as well as to encourage prudent, long-term behavior rather than the reckless short-term pursuit of profit; a reform of corporate governance which ensures that Boards of Directors function effectively, that Board membership is no sinecure, that the practice of cross-directorship be examined, and that loans to Directors or CEOs are regulated – and more ordinarily vetoed altogether- in strict observance of any clashes of interest. The remarks of Rowan Williams, Archbishop of Canterbury, with respect to the bonus culture of entitlement enjoyed by bankers are apt – he noted that there is bafflement and anger among the general public that 'people are somehow getting away with a culture in which the connection between the worth of what you do and the reward you get becomes more obscure' (Williams: 2009).

With regard to financial markets, one notes the proliferation of innovative financial instruments over the last 20 years or so (hedge-funds, short-selling, securitization and derivatives, collateralized debt obligations (CDOs), contracts for difference (CDFs), leading to the perception of a giant gambling casino, a spread-betters paradise, which almost constitutes a world unto itself, with scant positive relationship to the 'real' economy, much less any regard for fairness.[6] So, for example, speculators 'betting' against the Euro, while European governments and citizens struggle to return to monetary and fiscal stability with all

---

[5] See the interesting analysis by Roger Martin, Dean of the Rotman School of Management at the University of Toronto. Martin (2010) shows how the emphasis on maximizing share-holder value has little to do with real business performance and is unsustainable in the long-term. He contrasts this approach with the 'credo' of the likes of Johnson and Johnson, P&G (the world's biggest consumer products company) and RIM (maker of the BlackBerry), which all focus more on responsibilities to the customer but also to the wider community, without detriment to business success. In this context he notes the J&J insistence on 'doing the right thing' regardless of the impact on profits and how its CEO James Burke 'didn't put meeting quarterly profit expectations at the top of his list. In fact he put is squarely at the bottom' (op. cit. page 63).

[6] Cf. Hutton (2010), where in reference to investment bankers and traders and the claim by Lloyd Blankfein, CEO of Goldman Sachs, that they are doing 'God's work', Hutton states: 'This is not God's work. It is an old-fashioned rigged market by a bunch of smart insiders who have managed to get away with it for decades because hard questions were never asked about fairness or proportionality...at the heart of the financial crisis – and the criticism of the recovery – lay disregard for fairness' (op. cit. pp. 22-23}.

the accompanying hardships and sacrifices for public and private sectors, for citizens and their families. We need to ensure that markets are more transparent and fair; that high-risk activity is reduced; and that the size and importance of the financial sector is reduced and that it functions in the service of society and the economy. For this to happen in our globalised world, in order to obviate the risk of unfair competition, there needs to be global reform of both banks and financial markets. Institutions like the EU, the UN, the G20, the IMF need to take seriously the notion of a political economy at global level which will ensure fairness and outlaw reckless behavior.

One concrete way of ensuring more responsible behavior by markets and banks is to introduce a so-called Tobin or Robin Hood tax (to be set somewhere between 0.1 and 1per cent) on international financial and currency transactions: it would help to discourage undesirable currency speculation and provide considerable revenues to a body like the IMF to help meet socially desirable ends like the realization of the Millennium Development Goals.

2.2. The Economy

We need to structure our economies both globally and nationally in a way that leads to greater justice, equality, and a care for the poor. Half the world's population, 3 billion people, are living on less that 2$ a day (Wallis, 2010: 5). Estimates vary, but it is said that CEOs in the USA were paid 344 times the average worker's wage in 2007, against 42 times in 1980! (Bunting: 2009). We need more urgency to finalize a fairer world trade agreement (at WTO level), and we need either salary caps or more progressive redistributive tax policies in countries like Ireland. A more equal society is desirable, of course, from a social justice point of view, but also because, 'as Wilkinson and Pickett (2009) demonstrate, less equal societies have poorer outcomes in nearly every social domain' (NEF, 2009: 23).

We need to respect markets and yet not think that they can take care of all the needs of society, as reminded by Pope John Paul II 9/1991: 40) '…there are collective and qualitative needs that cannot be satisfied by market mechanisms'. One thinks of such basic needs as shelter, health-care, education, transport, welfare provision, the penal system and so on: and our sad deficiencies under most of these headings in an Ireland that in the recent past was happy to be seen as closer to 'Boston than Berlin'.

We need to accord priority to labor over capital (CST): a focus on employment, on dignified working conditions, on more stakeholder as opposed to shareholder models of ownership (Co-operatives), a search for a 'race to the top' as opposed to a 'race to the bottom'.

We need to plot a way forward that is environmentally sustainable. This is one area where one can say there does seem to be genuine, if somewhat belated engagement and even change. There is a lot of talk of a 'Green New Deal', harking back to Roosevelt's Great Depression New Deal, and in Ireland we have introduced such as a levy on plastic bags and the December 2009 budget carbon-tax. However the New Economics Foundation (NEF) estimates that 'for everyone to live at current European levels of consumption, we would need more than double the biocapacity actually available – the equivalent of 2.1 planet Earths –to sustain us. If everyone consumed at the US rate, we would require nearly five' (NEF, 2009: 20). Clearly these are not viable options: do we have the political will to change course as radically as the environmental and other considerations alluded to here require?

2.3. Culture/Politics/Religion

We need a change of culture – of values – for all this to happen. In the Western world in particular, we have been inhabiting the cultural space of Modernity and Post-Modernity which has allowed a neo-liberal economic model to flourish, privileging the self-interest of the individual over the good of society as a whole, and relativizing the notion of right and wrong. We need a more humane cultural paradigm, with a focus on integral human development, the common good, and solidarity. We need to show how this change of culture, with its stress on greater sustainability, fairness and equality can heal the broken covenant between different groups in society, mend the anger and resentment, and restore that sense of trust that is in the interest of all actors, including those in business and finance. We delude ourselves if we imagine that more effective regulation on its own will solve our problems. Regulation is a necessary but not sufficient condition for a more humane society: we need as well that kind of foundation of values and virtue which make it second nature for us to do what is good and right 'even when no one is looking', (Bishops of England and Wales, 2010), those 'habits of the heart' which counter the inevitable human tendency to want to circumvent regulation through greater ingenuity.[7]

This change of culture in civil society needs to go hand in hand with a more radical politics, nationally, regionally and globally, so that the well-justified outrage that we experience in so many quarters can be sustained and institutionalized. We in Ireland have shown in the past – think of the European referenda when we really got involved, think of the intelligent determination regarding Northern Ireland – that we are capable of such politics. Why not a national conversation, a New Ireland Forum around our way forward? We need to find ways of including and channeling prophetic voices in our political discourse – whatever about the rights and wrongs of the particular case, the political demise of figures like George Lee only adds to public apathy and cynicism about politics which often seems to be dominated by a local, clientelist ethos that is poorly equipped to deal with issues of national and global significance. Part of this more radical politics will surely involve an enhanced role for civil society.[8]

Robert Putnam has noted that religions remain 'one of the most reliable and impressive sources of social capital' and the chief Rabbi in the UK, Jonathan Sachs, has said that 'religion is an agent of social change, the most powerful there is' (O'Hanlon b, 2009: 44). Ban Ki-moon, Secretary General of the UN, told 200 religious leaders in 2009: 'You can inspire, you can provide, you can challenge your political leaders through your wisdom and through your followers' (McDonagh, 2009: 16). Of course, as we too well know now in Ireland, religion too can be a force for evil, and indeed for mediocrity (arguably in Ireland the Catholic religion in particular, perhaps for very understandable historical reasons, has been in

---

[7] In this context I note the remarks of Andrew Bradstock (2009), that '…while Harvard University has responded to the current concern about the behaviour of certain financiers and bankers by asking students on their MBA programme to sign, on graduation, an oath to behave ethically in their business dealings, fewer than half of the nearly 900 graduates were actually prepared to promise that they wouldn't in effect lie, cheat or steal in their future careers!' (*op cit*, p.6). Of similar importance is one of the findings of a Global Opinion Poll on Values and Ethics carried out by the World Economic Forum (WEF, 2010) - the poll was conducted through Facebook, with over 130,000 respondents in France, Germany, India, Indonesia, Israel, Mexico, Saudi Arabia, South Africa, Turkey and the USA, almost 89 per cent of whom were under 30, and found that over 60 per cent of respondents believe that people do not apply the same values in their private and professional lives.

[8] Cf. Commission of Inquiry into the Future of Civil Society in the UK and Ireland, *Making good society,* Carnegie UK Trust, 2010.

general a force for social conservatism). But at its best, Christianity is not like that: it has an inspirational focus on human dignity, on self-transcendence, on the good of all and in particular the poor, and it has, in the likes of Catholic Social Teaching, a well-developed critique of economic, social and political life (O'Hanlon, 2010). This is a call to religious people, and to Christians in particular to exercise the responsibilities that come with the privileges of baptism in such a way that this is reflected not just in personal life but also in the public domain. Christians can learn from their elder brothers and sisters from the Jewish tradition: Rabbi David Rosen has a beautiful commentary on the Biblical story of the Tower of Babel (Genesis 11), in which he likens the plot to that of an ancient industrial collapse. What was at stake, according to Rosen, was that the enterprise of building a city tower that would reach the heavens 'went to the heads of its developers to the extent that they see it as their supreme value and they were oblivious to anything transcendent, higher than their subjective material interest...if in the course of building a human being fell and even was killed, no one batted an eyelid; but if a brick fell and shattered, they all sat down and cried'. What this commentary reveals is 'a profoundly distorted sense of values in which human life and dignity are subordinated to material achievement'.[9]

So, the task is enormous, and in our fragmented society it will not be easy to develop the kind of common vision and values that would enable a new economic model to emerge. But often the first step on a Long March is the most significant one, in that it shows intent. And maybe a good first step towards more radical cultural and political change would be to tackle the resistance in banking and financial sectors to caps on salaries and bonuses? Might this be the kind of symbolic act that would trigger a more general cultural revolution?[10] Stephen Hester, head of the Royal Bank of Scotland, told a House of Commons Treasury Select Committee that RBS was 'a prisoner of the market' and that they needed to pay competitive salaries and bonuses in order to retain 'good people'.[11] All this begs the question: how much intelligence does it take to take money 'from governments (and others) and lend it out at vast profit, almost risk free? 'What sort of person could be described as "good" who would get out of bed if he could thereby add millions of pounds to his already six-or-seven-figure salary'?[12] Do we not want our smartest people to be artists, researchers, diplomats and so on? Why not take a stance on this issue, and begin defining our society along the lines of integral human development by saying, albeit reluctantly, to those who demand inordinate salaries to do what in effect is quite ordinary work, no, we are sorry, but perhaps you would be happier living elsewhere? Don't we have the confidence to believe that there are enough intelligent, public-spirited people around to do the job- and perhaps do it a good deal better than these excessively remunerated bankers and traders who live in a kind of bubble, with a strong culture of entitlement and yet with a track record of fallibility and failure? Perhaps a strong stance in this area might be a concrete example of the kind of 'cultural agency' which would

---

[9] Rosen (in *WEF*, op cit,, 2010: 43).

[10] For the importance of symbolic acts in cultural transformation, cf. Roger Martin (op cit, 64), in which the decision of the CEO of P&G to remove the screen that tracked the company's stock price from its headquarters as a means of de-emphasizing the importance of share-holder value in contrast to customer satisfaction. Similarly the founders of RIM made a rule that any manager who talked about the share price at work had to buy a doughnut for every person in the company – in a high-profile infringement of the rule in 2001 the chief operating officer was saddled with the task of delivering more than 800 doughnuts to the next weekly meeting of employees and no infraction of the rule has been recorded since!

[11] *The Tablet,* 16 January, 2010, 2.

[12] Op cit, 2.

give impetus to more widespread transformation?[13] And perhaps too we ought to consider the more comprehensive suggestion that the top 20 per cent in Ireland be limited to an income of 10 times, or even 5 times, that of the bottom 20 per cent, and that the Irish Constitution might include some such policy objective?[14]

3. Brief Outline of a New Model

A particular narrative of how things are can become so dominant that it assumes the nature of how things have to be. Oscar Wilde, for one, knew the value of the imagination and alternative ways of thinking, as is evidenced by his famous remark that 'A map of the world that does not include Utopia is not even worth glancing at'. Similarly, it is interesting to recall that Thomas More, a man deeply rooted in the economics and politics of his day, wrote a piece entitled *The Best State of a Commonwealth and the New Island of Utopia*.

There are many contemporary attempts to outline an alternative economic model, with varying degrees of radicalism: one thinks in Ireland of publications by Comhar, NESC, TASC, NESDO, and the Government's own Smart Economy.[15] Here, however, the focus will be on the 2009 publication of *The Great Transition* by the New Economics Foundation (NEF), an independent think-tank based in Britain. The aim is to indicate, at least in sketch form, how the kinds of radical principles outlined above may be imagined in concrete, pragmatic form.

NEF (2009) is involved in an exercise to outline how things could 'turn out right' by 2050, in face of all the challenges we have mentioned to date. The title of their work, *The Great Transition*, suggests the process by which this outcome can happen. It will be of interest to list some of the main features of this process.

The headline figures are that the authors estimate that the measures proposed in the report would create up to 8.65 trillion pounds sterling of environmental and social value in the period up to 2050. This would represent a growth in 'real value', albeit a reduction in consumption (especially by the well-off) and a fall in GDP by up to a third (to 2001 levels). So, for example, rapid decarbonization that moves towards global fair deal limits would avoid between 0.4 and 1.3 trillion pounds sterling in environmental costs, and a progressive redistribution of incomes to reach Danish levels of equality would cut the costs of inequality-related social problems and increase social value by 7.35 trillion pounds sterling (NEF, 2009: 3-8). For all this to happen, market prices need to reflect real social and environmental costs and benefits: 'we need to make "good" things cheap and "bad" things expensive – too often this is the opposite of what we have today' (op. cit. p.5). We can do this by targeted and variable consumption taxes (on junk food, for example) or subsidies/reliefs (on food grown locally), which would replace income tax for the majority of the population. This implies the

---

[13] I note the remarks of Niall Fitzgerald, former CEO of Unilever, along these lines – 'There's too much of 'we can't do this because our competitors will grab our best people away'. Fine, let them grab them away. You mean those terribly valuable people who either didn't understand the risks they were running, or understood them and continued anyway without thought for the consequences? You know what? I could do without those valuable people' - in interview with Fintan O'Toole, Irish Times, Saturday, 6 March, 2010.

[14] See Paula Clancy, Director of TASC (Think Tank for Action on Social Change), at TASC Autumn Conference, Dublin, 2009 – see www.tascnet.ie.

[15] Comhar: Sustainable Development Council; NESC: National Economic and Social Council, and NESDO: National Economic and Social Development Office; these are all based in Dublin.

need to collectively determine - by means perhaps of a national census, helped by increasingly refined measures of well-being, with government making determinations where there are competing interests – what, as a society, we deem to be of social and environmental value. From this, would follow certain restrictions on advertising and a 'race to the top' in terms of prices which reflected social and environmental values.

Since equal societies are happier societies there would occur the *Great Redistribution* of income and wealth through a combination of taxation policies (including an inheritance tax of 67 per cent on all estates to help fund a citizen's endowment of up to 25,000 pounds sterling), a shortening of the working week to four days (thus creating a better balance between paid work and the vital 'core economy' of family, friends and community life), and an encouragement of more mutual, cooperative ownership forms in order to promote a more participatory and democratic form of stakeholder ownership.

This notion of participatory democracy surfaces again in the encouragement of an expansion of the concept of subsidiarity so that decisions are taken at as local a scale as possible. This is needed to ensure food and energy security; for example, a local economy should not be excessively dependent on supermarket chains which may easily move in and out of areas as profits dictate. There is need to be more conscious of the environmental degradation in the so-called boomerang trade by which ships, lorries and planes are all around us still, passing in the night, wastefully carrying often identical goods from city to city across the globe and back again to meet consumer demand (for example, in 2008 the UK exported 4,400 tons of ice cream to Italy, only to re-import 4,200 tons (NEF, 2009: 59). We need, then, at local level to become less passive with regard to production and consumption, and we need to relearn many skills that have been forgotten 'from agriculture to manufacturing and the provision of local finance' (op. cit, p.6). There would be a need for greater local self-sufficiency in some areas, combined with regional, national and international trade in others.

With regard to financial issues, the report recommends a shift from taxing 'goods' such as work to taxing 'bads' such as pollution, consumption and short-term speculation (including the introduction of the Tobin tax). There should be a Green Investment Bank to support green energy and transport infrastructure. Retail banks should be separated from investment banks, 'nor is it apparent that we need many of the complex financial innovations which characterize modern commercial banking' (op. cit, p.60). Financial institutions should function within a stable regulatory framework that also encompasses the capital markets (op. cit, p.83) – in such a way that company profitability should become directly linked to social and environmental value, and share prices for listed companies would reflect this. This would mean that 'the composition of the FTSE 100 would change rapidly in some instances, as ethical and environmentally sustainable companies replaced unsustainable incumbents which were unable or unwilling to change their business practices and so saw their market share and profitability plummet' (op. cit, p.84).

. These few recommendations give a flavor of the attempt to concretize an economic model perhaps best summed up in slogans like 'prosperity without growth', or at least a 'steady-state economy' (op. cit, p.93) that seeks a sustainable way forward and is not entirely geared towards maximizing growth.

4. A THEOLOGICAL REFLECTION

At the time of the so-called Asian financial crisis, a letter was addressed in 1999 from an Ecumenical Council of Asian Churches to Churches of the North. In it, the following interesting question was posed: 'Have you not forgotten the richness that is related to sufficiency?'

The question is evocative, because it raises the specter that, like the people of Israel in the Hebrew Testament, we too 'have gone astray'. We have worshipped idols. Idolatry of course is not limited to believers: provocatively the Brazilian Dominican Frei Betto called Britain pagan, not secular, in that it just so happens that 'we do not call the things we worship "gods"' (O'Hanlon, 2009b: 31-32). In that classic pursuit of Golden Calves, of riches to the detriment of moderation, justice and sustainability, we in Ireland too may agree and understand, in retrospect, that, like the Prodigal Son, we have 'squandered our money' (Lk 15).

But, again like the Prodigal, Christians believe that in Jesus, their brother, they have a way back to God, their Father and Mother, back to 'the good life', understood in the sense of a life of human flourishing. The way of Jesus is not one of signs and wonders, not one which ignores human weakness and evil, the evil that is not just personal sin but also Original Sin and that 'bias of common sense' which the Canadian philosopher/theologian Bernard Lonergan wrote about (O'Hanlon, 2009b: 41-46), the social and structural sin which the Catholic Church in Ireland has learned so much about over the last 20 years or so. Against this dead weight of sin the way of Jesus, while tempted to other means, adheres to the commandments and beatitudes with a love that is costly. Christians are called to no less. This is a way which respects the relative autonomy of the secular (give unto Caesar what belongs to Caesar), and yet knows that this is not an absolute autonomy, as evidenced by the way Jesus turned on the free market idolatry of his day by forcibly expelling the traders and dealers from the Temple. It is a way which has particular care for the poor and marginalized ; we read in the letter of James that the rich are to be grateful that they have been humbled, because 'riches last no longer than the flowers in the grass' (James 1, 9-10). It is a way which calls Christians to the seemingly impossible task envisaged by the social grace of the 'Long March' through structures, cultures and institutions as, in addition to personal conversion and flourishing, they strive with fellow-citizens to transform our public space into one of a shared concern for the common good. And, because of the life, death and resurrection of Jesus, Christians are right to have a sure hope that this way will win out, that love is stronger than evil no matter how pervasive and how radical, that personal, social and structural grace will prevail. In this context the words of John-Paul II are worth noting – he says there is personal sin involved in taking refuge 'in the supposed impossibility of changing the world' (John-Paul II, 1984: 16). This is what is celebrated in the Eucharist, if only we could be more aware of it: as Daniel O'Leary has put it – 'We would strap ourselves to our seats if we understood the full impact of what is happening around us when we attend Mass', to which one might add the remark of Timothy Radcliffe that in church 'the appropriate headgear is not posh hats, but crash helmets' (O'Hanlon, 2009b: 44-45).

It is in this theological context that the decision about what way to go forward arises for Christians. There are no simple answers as to whether modest reform or a more radical approach is required: in theological terms, it is not always clear that the prophetic should always simply trump the sapiential. It will, in any case, always make sense for the prophetic to be presented also in a wise way, attempting, as the NEF document does, to show that ultimately we will all benefit from this new way of doing things, that it is in the interest of bankers, businesses and so on to move in a new direction – 'the combination of the smart argument and the moral argument together is the winning argument' (Wallis, 2010: 4). There are deep methodological issues involved here, already referred to from time to time during this analysis. Bismarck once said that one could not run a State according to the Beatitudes of the Sermon on the Mount. His observation addresses the wider issue of how to integrate principles (whether Christian or not) with pragmatism. An exclusive focus on vision and values is likely to give precedence to a Platonic notion of the ideal which at its heart does not value the material and will not attract the 'buy-in' necessary for communal action. An entirely pragmatic approach, on the other hand, leads to the kind of unbridled and ultimately unsustainable free- for- all that has caused the present crisis. However, Aristotle's approach is principled, and it values the material and experimental. It has prestigious Christian followers in the likes of Aquinas, Rahner, Lonergan and many others. In this approach there is a balance between self-interest and care for others[16], the input of practitioners and innovators is valued in the design of the overall model[17], and the focus on the common good need not be to the detriment of what works.

However, this acknowledgment of the 'relative autonomy of earthly affairs' (Vatican II), which counsels serious engagement between those who espouse religious principles and scientists and practitioners of other disciplines, needs as well to be accompanied by a recognition that it is part of human sin that the poor will want to share much more than the rich, and that there will be a commonsense bias against such sharing. And so there is a particular call to Christian discipleship in this matter on those of us who have money, and the power and influence that go with it.

CONCLUSION

The obstacles to radical reform are immense. And yet it if often said that radical, even utopian-like ideas are at first mocked, then fiercely contested, until finally they become the new common- sense and we wonder what all the fuss was about. There was a time, a long time, when people viewed the N. Ireland problem as uniquely intractable and the idea of a DUP-Sinn Fein coalition would have been laughed at. And Abraham and Sarah laughed when the angel told them that Sara would become pregnant, she being well past the age of child-bearing. Like Abraham we need to 'hope against hope', to use this crisis to make a fresh start that will respect our own need for moderation, the need of the poor for amelioration, the need of the earth for healing. 'The richness of sufficiency' – we need to recover the desire, the delight, the *jouissance*, the joy in living the kind of modest life of 'integral human

[16] See Cronin (2009: 669-676), where the author argues against an exclusively altruistic approach to morality and instead for 'a balance between self-interest and caring for others' (op. cit. pp.670-671). But Cronin makes it clear that this notion of self-interest is not purely pragmatic, but is deeply ethical. See also Mark Vernon (Ethics with a little help from Friends, 11-12), and Aditya Chakrabortty (How Shareholder Value took over, 24-25) in Hutton (2010).

[17] See Rory O'Donnell, Director of NESC and Chief Officer of NESDO, opening presentation at the Futures Ireland Project Ireland at Another Turning Point, July 2009; and Carey Oppenheim, Ethical Policymaking (46-47) for the notion of the compatibility between ethics and evidence-based policymaking, in Hutton (2010).

development', treasuring friends, hobbies, health, nature and not returning headlong like the Gadarene swine to the imprisonment of an exclusively market-driven life-style. And so as we, rightly, seek to stabilize things in Ireland and further afield, we need also to be asking ourselves bigger questions about more long-term goals and means. There is a rich religious heritage to support this kind of questioning, and, in bringing this to bear on public debate, Christians can join with fellow citizens of all beliefs and none so that together we may 'offer this state some service'.

REFERENCES

Bishops of England and Wales (2010). *Choosing the Common Good.*

Bradstock, Andrew (2009). Profits Without Honour? Economics, Spirituality and the Current Global Recession, *University of Auckland School of Theology Public Lecture,* August 5.

Bunting, Madeleine (2009). 'Our speechless outrage demands a new language of the common good', *The Guardian,* Oct, 19th.

CMEPSP (2009). *Commission on the Measurement of Economic Performance and Social Progress,* Paris.

Comhar (2009). *Towards a Green Deal for Ireland,* Dublin: Sustainable Development Council.

Commission of Inquiry into the Future of Civil Society in the UK and Ireland (2010). *Making good society,* Carnegie UK Trust.

Cronin, Kieran (2009). Morality and Self-Interest, *The Furrow,* 60, December, 669-676.

Hutton, Will (2010). Self-Serving Half Truths Trick Us, *Citizen Ethics in a Time of Crisis,* Citizen Ethics Network.

Irish Government (2008). *Building Ireland's Smart Economy – A Framework for Sustainable Economic Renewal 2009-2014,* Dublin.

John-Paul II (1984). *Reconciliatio et Paenitentia,* Rome: Vatican City.

John-Paul II (1991). *Centessimus Annus,* Rome: Vatican City.

Logan, George, M. and R. M. Adams (eds) (1993). *Utopia by Thomas More,* Cambridge: Cambridge University Press.

Martin, Roger (2010), The Age of Customer Capitalism, *Harvard Business Review,* January-February, 58-65.

McDonagh, Sean (2009). Earth's last chance, *The Tablet,* 14 November.

NEF (2009). *The Great Transition: A Tale of How It Turned Out Right,* London: New Economics Foundation.

NEF (2009). *Happy Planet Index,* London: New Economics Foundation.

NESC (2009). *Next Steps in Addressing Ireland's Five-Part Crisis: Combining Retrenchment with Reform,* Dublin: National Economic and Social Council.

NESDO (2009). *Ireland at Another Turning Point, Reviving Development, Reforming Institutions and Liberating Capabilities,* Dublin: National Economic and Social Development Office.

O'Hanlon, Gerry (2009a). A New Economic Paradigm?, *Working Notes,* 63, Dublin: Jesuit Centre for Faith and Justice, 3-10.

O'Hanlon, Gerry (2009b). *The Recession and God,* Dublin: Jesuit Centre for Faith and Justice.

O'Hanlon, Gerry (2010). *Theology in the Irish Public Square,* Dublin: Columba.

Reynolds, Brigid and Healy, Sean (2009). *Beyond GDP: What is Prosperity and How Should it be Measured?,* Dublin: Social Justice Ireland.

Rosen, David Rabbi (2010) .The Tower of Babel: Constructing a Healthy Economy. In WEF (ed), *Faith and the Global Agenda: Values for the Post-Crisis Economy,* p.43, Davos: World Economic Forum.

TASC (2010). *Stimulating Recovery,* Dublin: Think Tank for Action on Social Change.

The Observer (2010). 'Economists start to consider that money can't buy happiness' by Ashley Seager and Heather Stewart, Sunday, 10 January.

Turner, Frank (2010). The Crisis and Poverty: Reflections on the Global Economic and Financial Crisis, *Sozialalmanach: 'L'annuaire Caritas sur la situation sociale du Luxembourg',* Luxembourg: Caritas Luxembourg, 275-285.

UN (1990). *Human Development Report,* New York: United Nations.

Wallis, Jim (2010). When your calendar is a moral document, *McKinsey Quarterly,* January, 1-5.

WEF (2010). *Faith and the Global Agenda: Values for the Post-Crisis Economy,* Davos: World Economic Forum.

Wilde, Oscar (1891). *The soul of man under Socialism,* London: Penguin Classics (modern edition).

Wilkenson, Richard and Pickett, Kate (2009). *The spirit level: why more equal societies always do better,* London: Allen Lane.

Williams, Rowan (2009). *The Guardian,* Thursday, 16 September.

PART 2: RESPONSES TO THE CRISIS BY ASIAN GOVERNMENTS AND OTHER ACTORS

In: The Transformation of Asia ...   ISBN: 978-1-61470-873-5
Editors: B. Andreosso-O'Callaghan and P. Herrmann   © 2012 Nova Science Publishers, Inc.

Chapter 4

CHINA'S OUTWARD INVESTMENT: CRISIS, OPPORTUNITIES AND CHALLENGES

Duncan Freeman

ABSTRACT

Government policy has been important to the growth of China's outward investment. The Chinese government adopted the "go global" policy in 2001, and in the following years China's outward investment increased enormously as a result of the removal of previous restrictions and the provision of positive official support. The advent of the global financial and economic crisis which first emerged in the US in 2007 changed the global investment environment. While the changed environment could have been regarded as an opportunity for Chinese investors to exploit, the reaction in China was ambivalent. Outward investment growth was retarded during the crisis. Furthermore, there was considerable ambivalence in the position adopted in China on whether the crisis represented an opportunity or a risk.

Views offered by officials show that the crisis was seen as creating serious risks as well as opportunities. Official policy documents suggest that the government did not adopt a policy that focused on exploitation of opportunities during the crisis.

1. INTRODUCTION

Prior to the financial and economic crisis which first emerged in the US in 2007, outward investment by Chinese companies had come to be seen as symbolic of a new stage in China's involvement in the international economy. The increase in outward direct investment (ODI) appeared representative of a greater degree of internationalization of Chinese enterprises and the growing power of China in the world economy. Many Western observers appeared to believe that the way in which Chinese enterprises invested abroad during the global financial and economic crisis which became global in 2008 would be a demonstration of this internationalization and strength, and that it would be indicative of a response that was different from other economies that were affected by the crisis. Indeed, there was a widespread belief that China would profit from the crisis by asserting its new strength by acquiring foreign assets at distressed prices on a large scale, thus furthering the aims of its government and enterprises, especially in the energy and resource sectors.[1] While not all Western analysts of China agreed with this view, the popular idea of a Chinese bargain hunting "shopping spree" was born.

The accepted explanations of outward investment offered in the West focus on the behaviour of firms. But it could be argued that the traditional models of internationalization have limited value in relation to China as a result of the role of government in directing and supporting outward investment. Certainly there is a widely held view outside China that government strategy determines business decisions of Chinese companies investing abroad. Ever since Chinese companies began investing overseas, and especially following the inception of the "go global" policy, this has been the case. The degree to which this view is correct may be debatable, but it is clear that the Chinese government does have a policy on ODI. This chapter investigates policy views and measures adopted in China in response to the crisis. The chapter first analyses the amount of China's ODI during the crisis, and argues that there was no dramatic increase, The chapter then provides a discussion of the views of ODI adopted primarily by policymakers during the crisis, and is followed by a review of the policy response adopted in China. The evidence provided by public statements and discussion by policymakers in China, suggest that there was no simple single view of the crisis as a buying opportunity for China. Rather than having a clear strategy of aggressively exploiting the crisis, the evidence suggests a more mixed response based on a cautious assessment of the effects of the crisis.

2. CHINA'S OUTWARD INVESTMENT IN THE GLOBAL CRISIS

The rapid growth in China's ODI in the period prior to the crisis attracted considerable attention among Western media, policy makers and academics. There have been academic studies on outward investment by Chinese firms, although they have been limited in their success in explaining the patterns, motivations and methods of Chinese ODI. The dominant theories of the multinational enterprise (MNE) are the internalization/transaction cost (see Buckley and Casson 1976, Rugman 1981, Hennart 1982) and internationalization theories (Johanson and Vahlne 1977, 1990) and the so-called eclectic model (Dunning 1993). These theories attempt to explain why firms develop into multinational enterprises (MNEs) and engage in FDI. The focus of these theories is on strategies adopted within firms in response to the market, or market failures, that they face. The advent of outward investment in China, at least *prima facie*, appears to challenge these models of the development of MNEs in a number of respects. One of the most important of these is that in China the state has adopted policies that are intended to encourage and direct investments abroad, thus at least in appearance, the firm is not the only locus of decision making. At the same time, the provision of government

---

[1] Crisis Could Mean Bargains for China, Associated Press in USA Today, 18 November 2008, China Starts Investing Globally, New York Times, 20 February, 2009, China, Taking Advantage of Global Recession, Goes on a Buying Spree, Christian Science Monitor, 20 February 2009, China's Shopping Spree, Stratfor, Business Spectator, 21 February 2009, China Goes on a Smart Shopping Spree, Time, 2 March 2009. China's Shopping Spree, The Independent, 18 March 2009.

aid through, for instance, direct financial support and officially sanctioned soft loans for investors as happens in China may significantly change the equation of advantages perceived by the investing firm in ways that traditional approaches do not fully account for. Little detailed research has been done on Chinese outward investment outside of China, and efforts to analyze it and draw broad conclusions suffer from theoretical and empirical limitations (Rugman and Li 2007, Li 2007, Kang and Liu 2007, Deng 2004). The literature on China's MNEs has in recent years been expanded by Chinese scholars. The work of Chinese scholars, while adopting the mainstream Western theories of MNEs, suffers from similar limitations as their Western colleagues (for instance Li and Zheng 2001, Feng and He 2004, Li and Cui 2005, Zhang, Wang and Wang 2007). To some extent, this is the result of limitations in the data available on Chinese ODI even at the macro level. There are considerable question marks surrounding the quality of the macro data from China and even from host countries in the developed world.

Nevertheless, whether measured by the Chinese government or by the United Nations Conference on Trade and Development (UNCTAD), the statistics show a similar pattern of very strong ODI growth prior to the crisis. According to China's Ministry of Commerce (MOFCOM), total ODI flows including financial and non-financial investment increased from US\$21.2 billion in 2006[2] to US\$55.9 billion in 2008. Non-financial investment increased from US\$5.5 billion in 2004 to US\$41.9 billion in 2008.[3]

What might be termed the "wave of money" view of potential Chinese ODI came into existence almost as soon as the increase in investment flows from China became evident in the early years of the "go-global" strategy which was integrated in official policy in 2001. The rapid growth in China's ODI was expected to bring large amounts of investment to host countries throughout the world, including Europe. This of course did not happen in the case of Europe. Despite a few significant investments such as the acquisition of the Thomson colour television business by TCL, Europe saw very little of the investment, which flowed mainly to Asia and Africa. Although some more recent investments such as the acquisition of Volvo by Geely have raised the profile of Chinese investment in Europe, it remains relatively small. Much of the ODI by Chinese enterprises remains focused in the resource and energy sectors, and is directed toward Asia and Africa. Europe does have attractions for Chinese investors, including technology, brands and markets, but for the most part investments have been of a relatively small scale compared to other regions. The reasons for the reluctance of Chinese enterprises to invest in Europe are complex and relate both to the investors themselves (the large state owned enterprises which have dominated ODI have interests elsewhere) and the investment destination (Europe, for all its attractions, is seen as a complex, and even difficult business environment). Nevertheless, if anything, the idea that a wave of money would flood from China became only more widespread after the onset of the crisis. One of the persistent themes of Western media reporting and commenting on China's response to the crisis was that it represented an opportunity for Chinese firms to exploit to their advantage. But the quantitative evidence suggests that following the onset of the

---

[2] 2008 niandu zhongguo duiwai zhijie touzi tongji gongbao [China Outward Direct Investment Statistical Bulletin 2008], MOFCOM, National Statistical Bureau, State Administration of Foreign Exchange, Beijing 2009. MOFCOM only began collecting statistics on ODI in the financial sector in 2006.

[3] The Chinese authorities keep separate statistics on financial and non-financial ODI. As a result of the lack of published data on total ODI in the most recent period, this chapter refers mainly to non-financial ODI.

financial crisis there was no wave of Chinese ODI, although the data is somewhat ambiguous in this regard.

Any impact of the crisis on the amount of ODI appeared to be delayed. In 2008 China's ODI continued to rise sharply, the total figure for that year of US$55.9 billion was an increase of 111.0% over 2007. Of this figure US$41.9 was non-financial investment. In 2009 this pattern of growth changed. In the first half of 2009 there was a decline of 51.7% in China's non-financial ODI,[4] followed by an increase in non-financial ODI in the second half of the year.[5] The total non-financial ODI for 2009 was US$43.3 billion, resulting a relatively small increase of 6.5% over 2008. These figures would suggest that the crisis had a negative rather than positive impact on China's ODI, even if this somewhat lagged behind the development globally of the crisis itself. Compared with global investment flows, however, the picture for China was less negative. Already in 2008 global investment flows fell to US$1.69 trillion from US1.97 trillion in 2007, a decrease of 14.2% (UNCTAD, Foreign Direct Investment Database)'.This was repeated in 2009 when flows fell even more sharply by 38.7% to US$1 trillion.[6] Even within Asia, in contrast to China, FDI outflows from other major economies in the region slowed down considerably in 2008 (UNCTAD 2009).

China would thus appear to have been going against the tide in 2008 when its ODI more than doubled, and also even in 2009 when the rate of growth in its ODI slowed considerably.[7] The recovery in China's ODI that appeared in the second half of 2009 seemed to continue in the first quarter of 2010, when the amount grew by 103.3%. This arguably did not constitute strong real growth, however, as it was in comparison with a very low base in the first quarter of 2009. The official forecast from the Chinese government was that there would be only a small increase in ODI in 2010,[8] although according to UNCTAD global prospects for FDI were negative.[9] Despite a number of high profile overseas investments made by Chinese companies during the crisis, on the evidence of these statistics it is difficult to make the case that they have exploited the crisis on a large scale to increase ODI. While China's ODI did not decrease in the same way as global flows did, neither did it continue the dramatic increases that had been the norm in the years prior to the crisis. It is difficult to discern from the statistics alone any clear policy response from China, nor business reaction from Chinese companies, to the crisis. It is certainly not obvious that the Chinese state or enterprises sought to exploit the crisis on a large scale.

---

[4] Shang bannian woguo duiwai zho touzi tongbi xiajiang liucheng [China's Outward Investment Declined by 60% in First Half of Year Compared to Previous Year], Xinhua News Agency, 16 November 2009. At the time of writing no statistics for financial ODI in this period had been released by the Chinese government.

[5] Sanjidu feijinrong duiwai zhijie touzi tongbi zengzhang 190% [Third Quarter Non-financial Outward Direct Investment Increased 190%] china.com.cn, 27 October 2009.

[6] UNCTAD, Global Investment Trends Monitor, Global and Regional FDI Trends in 2009, No. 2, 19 January 2010, The Outlook for the Development of China's International Investment [Zhongguo guoji touzi fazhan zhanwang], Zhongguo Fazhan Guancha [China Development Observer], 8 April 2010.

[7] It could be argued that these statistics give a false picture of the changes in ODI. The sharp fall in Chinese ODI in the first quarter of 2009 can in large part be attributed to the effect of one deal in the first quarter of 2008, the US$18 billion acquisition of the stake in RTZ by Chinalco. Or, to put it another way, approximately one third of Chinese ODI in 2008 when the amount more than doubled was actually accounted for by one single investment.

[8] Fagaiwei: Jin nian fei jinronglei jingwai touzi you wang da 480 yi mei yuan [NDRC: Non-financial Outward Investment Expected to Reach US$48 Billion], Mei ri jingji xinwen [Daily Economic News], 19 January 2010.

[9] UNCTAD, WIR 2009.

3. OUTWARD INVESTMENT: OPPORTUNITIES AND RISKS

The explanation of the apparent reluctance to exploit the crisis can be found in the analysis within China of the opportunities and risks that investors faced. This can be seen in the analysis offered by government officials and also in policy documents that were issued after the advent of the crisis. In the decade after 2000, China's policy on ODI underwent a complete transformation. Although it was not only intended to refer to outward investment, the "go global" strategy adopted by the Chinese government in 2001 came to symbolize this policy transformation. From one which was highly restrictive of ODI, government policy was reoriented to support and encouragement. Many of the previously existing restrictions on ODI were removed, procedures were simplified and support and even incentives provided by the government. This trend has continued during the crisis, when, for instance, new reforms of the approval procedure for ODI were implemented in 2009. Nevertheless, the stance adopted by the government in the crisis remained ambivalent.

In the view of UNCTAD, the crisis did not have a significant impact on policy worldwide:

> Although numerous countries have adopted FDI-related legislation since the beginning of the crisis, it is difficult to determine whether and to what extent these measures were taken in response to the crisis. Also, while some new legislation is likely to have a positive effect on FDI flows, other regulations might produce the opposite result. (UNCTAD: 2009 p31).

Nevertheless, UNCTAD recognized that China may be something of an exception to the general rule, noting that, "Supportive government policies have also played a role, especially in China" (UNCTAD: 2009 p52).

In China itself the question of whether or not the crisis represented an opportunity for Chinese enterprises was widely discussed in the media and by officials, although scholarly analysis preferred to address broader issues related to China's ODI (see for instance Yang, DX, 2008, Feng, PC, 2009 Guo, B, 2009 Ma, K, 2009 Wang, Y, 2010). In contrast to the perception from outside China, where it was often taken for granted that the answer was positive, within China the judgment was far from being uniform that this was the case. Such ambiguous judgments were key to China's response to the crisis.

A recurrent theme in the Chinese analysis was that the result of the crisis would be a restructuring of the global economy. Yet the results of this restructuring appeared far from certain. In China views of the implications of the crisis for ODI were both negative and positive. Many analyses would include both types of factors. The views offered in China took into account a wide range of both domestic and external factors that could be considered to either support or constrain outward investment. These domestic and external factors included those that were short term and contingent on the crisis itself as well as others that were long term and unrelated to the crisis, but which underlay the capacity of companies to react to it.

For example, the crisis created opportunities for investment reducing asset prices in economies that it affected, but it also raised the level of risk, since the weakening of economies in destination countries increased the possibility that investment would not be successful. To these short-term factors contingent on the crisis could be added long-term effects. As we shall see, some Chinese argued that reform and the development of the

Chinese economy had created conditions that made it possible to exploit the opportunities made available. However, others argued that poorly developed policy in China actually inhibited investment. This *mélange* of factors was used in analyses that even at its most positive, far from giving a unified, clear view of the crisis as an opportunity, often emphasized the complexity of the situation that Chinese companies faced.

In January 2009, no less a voice than the *People's Daily* pronounced that the crisis was an opportunity for outward investment. While the paper may not provide the most authoritative version of the details of economic policy, its pronouncement appeared to give strong support to the view that the crisis was indeed an opportunity that China would exploit to the full. The paper called for the opportunity to be grasped:

> The major adjustment caused by the crisis may form a new global economic structure. The process of reshuffling may also create openings in the industries of some countries. Following the constant deepening and widening of the crisis, the real economy is bordering on collapse, there is a big fall in the price of foreign investment assets, and many countries have relaxed restrictions on investment from outside. We must grasp this juncture, appropriately accelerate foreign investment and raise the level of foreign economic cooperation. [10]

The *Peoples' Daily* called for a more active and thorough implementation of the "go global" strategy. While it emphasised its depth, the paper also noted that many rising countries had not been severely hit by the crisis, and that places such as Brazil, India, Russia, Africa and the Middle East had great potential, and should be major markets for investment. Although it sounded several caveats, the paper proclaimed in conclusion that, "'[g]oing global' is not just an expedient calculation, but is in tune with the trend of the times".

The question of ODI and the crisis was widely discussed in the Chinese media, and some, like the *People's Daily*, have taken a positive view of the opportunities available. The *China Industry and Commerce News*, published by the State Administration for Industry and Commerce, argued in July 2009 in very clear terms:

> The development of Chinese enterprises has reached a certain stage, and "going global" is a necessary trend. Prior to the crisis, the performance of many foreign enterprises was very good, and Chinese enterprises had almost no opportunities for acquisitions., but after the crisis many foreign enterprises are making losses or bankrupt. Only at this time do Chinese enterprises have to go out and acquire, and there really are bottom fishing possibilities. [11]

But other media were not slow to point the very poor record of success for Chinese ODI. The crisis was often portrayed in the media as an opportunity to "bottom fish".[12] However, even bottom fishing was not without its risks.[13] Although the costs of acquisitions are low

---

[10] "Zouchuqu" shi shidong bu mangdong ["Going Global" is the Trend of the Times, Not a Blind Action], People's Daily, 28 January 2009, p 2.

[11] Zouchuqu: guoqi minqi tiaotiao daolu tong haiwai [Going Global: State Owned Enterprises, Privately Owned Enterprises Have Many Roads to Going Overseas], China Industry and Commerce Times, 3 July 2009.

[12] Qiye haiwai binggou yao zhuazhu "shaodi" shiji [Enterprises Must Grasp Opportunities for "Bottom Fishing" in Overseas Acquisitions], Xinhuanet, 11 April 2010.

[13] Yingdui jinrong weiji taozhan gouzhu duiwai touzi baohu xin tixi [Handling the Challenge of the Financial Crisis Constructing a New System for Protecting Outward Investment], Shanghai Securities News, 19 March 2009.

during the crisis, the rate of success was also low. It was widely recognised that globally the rate of success for cross-border acquisitions is about 20-30%.[14] Numerous articles focused on the failures of Chinese investors and figures reflecting the lack of success were cited by many writers.[15] Liu Mingzhong noted the very poor record of Chinese ODI and quoted MOFCOM statistics stating that in 2008 China's foreign mergers and acquisitions totalled US$20.5 billion, but their losses were US$29 billion and also cited figures from McKinsey showing that in the previous 20 years 67% of China acquisitions abroad had failed.[16] Mei Xinyu, a researcher at the MOFCOM research institute, pointed to the high level of non-commercial risk in some outward investment by Chinese companies, such as Chinalco in Rio Tinto and Ping An in Fortis.[17]

The divisions in opinion were by no means limited to media commentators. As the crisis developed officials in positions close to work on ODI offered their views which tended to offer an analysis that reflected a more complex set of considerations, although not always the same ones, and were not always entirely positive in their conclusions.

In April 2009, speaking at a special news conference called to discuss the impact of the crisis on outward investment, Wu Xilin, the head of the Department of Outward Investment and Economic Cooperation[18] of MOFCOM said that the global financial crisis had had a big impact on Chinese enterprises "going global". Wu offered the view that, "[g]enerally speaking opportunities and challenges coexist". He noted two main challenges. The first was that difficulties in fundraising by enterprises had increased, and the second was that market risk had increased. In his view the prospects for outward investment were far from certain: "Because the world economy is not stable, this causes an increase in uncertain factors for us. Therefore, risk is also increasing."[19] Unlike the view offered by the *People's Daily*, in this analysis, the main risk to Chinese ODI derived from the uncertainties created by the crisis itself.

Wu still asserted that opportunities were also very important. The risks inherent in the crisis which were largely external to China were counterbalanced by positive factors derived from the situation of the Chinese economy and enterprises. He argued that foreign investment and cooperation is an "internal requirement of the national economy", and pointed out a number of positive factors, including that China's macroeconomic situation was good, it had plentiful foreign exchange reserves, and that the international competitiveness of Chinese enterprises had been raised. He also argued that foreign investment and cooperation had "a relatively good foundation for development".

---

[14] Zouchuqu: guoqi minqi tiaotiao daolu tong haiwai [Going Global: State Owned Enterprises, Privately Owned Enterprises Have Many Roads to Going Overseas], China Industry and Commerce Times, 3 July 2009.

[15] Why Is Success Rate Not High for Chinese Enterprises in Overseas Acquisitions, China Value Net, 10 July 2009.

[16] Haiwai touzi: jiyu yu fengxian de boyi [Overseas Investment: The Game of Opportunities and Risks], Xinhuanet, 27 October 2009.

[17] Jinrong weiji xia zhongguo qiye haiwai touzi jiyu yu bixian zhi ce [The Opportunity and Risk Avoidance Policies of Chinese Enterprises' Overseas Investment Under the Financial Crisis], Shanghai Securities Daily, 7 August 2009.

[18] Outward investment has been considered a form of foreign economic cooperation, thus it was traditionally placed under the Economic Cooperation Department at MOFCOM. Hence also the frequent conflation of outward investment and international cooperation in discussions by Chinese media and officials.

[19] Shangwubu zhaokai "Yngdui jinrong weiji, tuidong qiye 'zouchuqu'" zhuanye xinwen fabuhui [Ministry of Commerce Holds Special News Conference on "Handling the Financial Crisis, Encouraging Enterprises "Going Global"], MOFCOM News Office, 30 April 2009.

Like the *People's Daily*, Wu also asserted that the international financial crisis had caused a readjustment of the global economic structure. This fact did not mean that the major trend of deepening development of economic globalization would change. This trend was to a large extent dependent on developments external to China itself. At the news conference, Wu argued that Chinese enterprises "going global" were still in a period of major strategic opportunity: "There are increasing opportunities for foreign investment to acquire high-quality enterprises and assets, the cost of investment has been reduced, and conditions for deal-making improved. There are more opportunities for foreign investment and acquisitions, there is a reduction in the cost of investment, at the very least if the RMB has risen, and the cost of transactions has fallen."[20]Thus, while the crisis created risk, in equal measure it creates opportunities.

At another press conference in August 2009, the relatively positive view of the crisis as an opportunity was endorsed by Fu Ziying, vice minister at MOFCOM, who once again reiterated the view that a global restructuring would result from the crisis:

> This financial crisis has accelerated the adjustment of the structure of global industry. At the same time, I believe that it is a major opportunity for our enterprises "going global". The crisis has caused a fall in the price of many assets worldwide, and the cost of our foreign investment or foreign acquisitions has fallen further.

To these external economic factors he also added a policy dimension, noting the fact some countries had removed barriers to investment in their efforts to tackle the crisis. He referred to other positive conditions for outward investment that were domestic. The US$2 trillion in foreign exchange reserves held by China meant there was no lack of capital and 30 years of reform had created enterprises with international experience. [21] The long-term advantages built by the Chinese economy prior to the crisis enabled the exploitation of both the short and long-term effects of the crisis.

At the same time, other colleagues of vice minister Fu were less positive. Wang Zixian, head of the Policy Research Centre at MOFCOM, in August 2009 argued that both risks and opportunities were many. [22] Wang listed seven specific risks to ODI: bad debt, political risk, currency risk, foreign credit and financial risk, protectionism, increasing operating risks resulting from deteriorating business environment, and the challenge of managing in accordance with international practices. The risks that Wang pointed to were mainly related to the effects of the crisis itself, but others were not. The question of political risk is one that has overshadowed much of China's ODI, but is not often given prominence in domestic discussion. When pointing to the rise of protectionism, Wang appeared to directly contradict some of his colleagues who argued that barriers to investment were being removed. By raising the question of the difficulties of Chinese companies in operating in accordance with

---

[20] Ibid.

[21] Shangwubu cheng weiji shi zhongguo qi haiwai touzi jiyu binggou zijin chongyu [Ministry of Commerce Says Crisis is an Opportunity for Chinese Enterprises Investing Overseas: M&A Funds Plentiful], Chinanet, 12 August 2009.

[22] Guoji jinrong weiji xia zhongguo qiye zouquchu de "wei" yu "ji" - fang shangwubu zhengce yanjiushi fuzhuren Wang Zixian [The "Dangers" and "Opportunities" for Chinese Enterprises Going Global in the International Financial Crisis – interview with MOFCOM Research Centre deputy head Wang Zixian], State Council Development Research Centre, 16 December 2009.

international practices, Wang hinted at more fundamental questions about their capacity to exploit the opportunities that might be offered to them.

In the Chinese tradition of balance, Wang also listed seven opportunities or positive conditions for investment abroad. Like others, he noted both that the crisis had created better conditions for investment abroad and that at the same time there were factors in China itself which permitted them to be exploited. According to Wang, the barriers had decreased and space for investment had increased, and secondly the opportunities for strategic investment to obtain technology, human resources, brands and distribution networks and the space for cooperation to develop foreign resources to investment had increased. Furthermore the implementation of stimulus policies had created investment opportunities and there had been an increase in strategic cooperation with neighbouring countries and emerging markets. There were opportunities arising from the internationalisation of the renminbi and finance. Like others he argued that the relative strength of the Chinese economy such as its good macroeconomic performance, financial stability and foreign exchange reserves and the rising *renminbi* had created a comparative advantage. Hence, in this analysis the risks were once again counterbalanced by positive conditions created by a combination of economic and financial factors as well as policy changes resulting from the crisis, and also long-term advantages derived from the position of the Chinese economy.

If vice minister Fu was optimistic in the summer of 2009, some of his colleagues were less so by the end of the year. By then it had become very clear that the crisis had been far from an unalloyed opportunity for Chinese ODI. In December 2009, vice minister Chen Jian of MOFCOM, in a speech on the subject recognised that the negative impacts had been significant:

> In the international financial crisis ODI and foreign cooperation also suffered serious impacts, and met huge challenges. But with strong support from the state and collective efforts by numerous enterprises, this area of foreign economic and trade work soon realised growth.[23]

Chen Jian went on to discuss the state of the world economy. In his view, the crisis which had caused the challenges to China's ODI was far from over. While there were positive signs of recovery, there were also negative factors at work. Chen argued that the contradictions in the world economic system had not been fundamentally resolved, and the underlying causes of the crisis still remained. Furthermore, the strength of increases in consumption and investment were insufficient and high unemployment also affected the recovery of the global economy.

According to Chen, in these circumstances, many outstanding opportunities for outward investment and cooperation existed for Chinese enterprises which were prepared and strong, but at the same time they faced many problems and difficulties. The fact that the opportunities were conditioned on Chinese enterprises being prepared and strong was significant, as he argued that, "Internally, there exist the problems that experience of cross-border management is insufficient, capacity to foresee risk abroad is lacking, and capability to judge and

---

[23] Vice Minister Chen Jian Invited to Attend and Speak at the Europe-US Alumni Association Entrepreneurs Fraternity "Forum on the 8th Anniversary of the Implementation of the 'Go global' Strategy by Chinese Enterprises", MOFCOM Department of Outward Investment and Cooperation, 6 December 2009.

understand the international environment is not strong."[24] Chen went on to point to a number of other factors, including increasing international, but also more strikingly growing regional terrorism, constant social and political instability in some countries and regions, and cultural differences between China and abroad. He concluded that, "How to eliminate these negative factors and to actively use the positive factors, and accelerate 'going global' is a problem that requires the careful consideration of Chinese enterprises."[25] Chen argued it was necessary to continue strongly implementing the "go global" strategy, and at the same time maintain a clear understanding of and correctly handle all the problems and contradictions faced in going global.

4. POLICY RESPONSE

The varying views expressed by government officials, and also politicians, business leaders and in the media in China, reflected the fact that there was no single definitive position adopted either officially or more widely on outward investment in the crisis. This was also reflected in the official policy positions during the crisis, which, rather than adopting an aggressive strategy of expansion, in fact were rather cautious in their approach.

China's policy on ODI underwent a transformation after the inception of the "go global" strategy in 2001. As has usually been the case with regard to reform in China, this was a gradual process, although its result was to create a policy that in the period prior to the onset of the crisis, faced in completely the opposite direction compared to the previous one. Despite talk in China of a restructuring of the world economy as a result of the crisis, and a strategic juncture that must be seized, there was little sign that this signaled any sudden shift in government policy on outward investment.

After the outbreak of the crisis, the most important policy initiative on ODI was the promulgation by MOFCOM of new regulations on approval of investments (Outward Investment Administration Procedures, 2009). These regulations provided for a simplification of the procedures for investment approval. In an interview on the new regulations, one MOFCOM official indicated that the new regulations were at least in part motivated by the crisis.

In recent years, China's investment abroad increased rapidly, and some new circumstances emerged, for example entities investing abroad were increasingly diversified, and sectors were more and more broad, reinvestment by investors abroad increased. At the same time, the Party centre, and the State Council required government departments to accelerate the transformation of government functions, and to establish a service-type government, and to concentrate on public service. In addition, in order for all countries to jointly deal with the current crisis, and promote demand, it is also necessary to encourage accelerated development of investment abroad.[26]

---

[24] Ibid.

[25] Ibid.

[26] Shangwubu youguan fuzeren tan << Jingwai touzi guanli banfa>> [Responsable Person at MOFCOM Discusses "Outward Investment Administration Procedures"], MOFCOM, 4 April 2009.

Other commentators also argued that the regulations would benefit Chinese enterprises investing abroad in the crisis. [27] Nevertheless, the crisis appears to have played only a small part in the promulgation of the regulations which may be considered to be a continuation of the process begun a decade earlier to reform policy on ODI. As such they do not represent a new departure in Chinese policy.

An official assessment of Chinese policy on ODI after the onset of the crisis was offered in early 2010. In March MOFCOM issued a Guiding Opinion on National Work on Outward Investment and Cooperation in 2010 which offered a rather mixed view of the impact of the crisis on ODI and the policy response to it. According to this assessment, China's outward investment and foreign economic cooperation had faced a severe test in the international financial crisis. However, it asserted that under the correct leadership of the Chinese Communist Party Centre and the State Council, MOFCOM had brought together the relevant departments to promptly formulate and implement policies and measures to handle the crisis and support "going global". As a result the deterioration in outward investment and foreign economic cooperation was reversed.[28] If the policy view offered in the Opinion was intended as a response to the crisis then it indicates a rather more sober perspective than much of the rhetoric describing the crisis as an opportunity. The implication is that the efforts of the Chinese government were reactive and focused on reversing a deteriorating situation, rather than proactive and seeking to exploit an opportunity.

Despite the grounds for MOFCOM's self-congratulation on saving the situation, the assessment offered mixed prospects for the following year, "In 2010, the domestic and foreign situation faced by 'going global' is still complex and volatile. From the point of view of the international situation, the momentum of global economic development has improved. But the foundation of the recovery of the global economy is not stable. The influence of the global financial crisis still exists."[29] It argued that revival of the domestic economy was becoming solid, but there were many difficulties and challenges., and structural contradictions continued to exist. The Opinion concluded that, "Overall, it can be forecast that the environment for outward investment and economic cooperation in 2010 will improve on 2009, and the opportunities for 'going global' will be greater than the challenges." But even with this positive note, the document set a target of US$46 billion for non-financial ODI in 2010, indicating that expectations for growth were limited given that in 2009 the figure was US$43.3 billion. Despite official claims of strong support for ODI, the effects of such policy were not apparently expected to be very great.

Also in early 2010 MOFCOM promulgated 10 major tasks to be accomplished for the year. The sixth of these concerned "going global", and if anything gave a less than ringing call for outward investment. The policies prescribed were somewhat anodyne in nature, referring in generalities to deepening reform of the administration system, promulgating administrative regulations on foreign investment and labour cooperation, and encouraging enterprises that have the right conditions to invest or open RandD abroad.[30]

---

[27] Jingrong weiji xia, jingwai touzi guanli banfa chutai [In the Financial Crisis, Outward Investment Administration Procedures are Released], www.yicang.com 18 March 2009.

[28] Shangwubu guanyu 2010 nian quanguo duiwai touzi hezuo gongzuo de zhidao yijian [Guiding Opinion on National Work on Outward Investment and Cooperation in 2010], MOFCOM, Department of Outward Investment and Economic Cooperation, 26 February 2010.

[29] Ibid.

[30] 2010 nian shangwu gongzuo shi da renwu [Ten Major Tasks for Commerce in 2010], International Business Daily online [Guoji shang bao zaixian], 25 December 2009.

At a higher level of authority, a meeting of the State Council in April 2010 discussed the economic situation, and emphasised the continuing problems China faced. The meeting set out key areas of economic work. These included the overall goal of raising the level of opening the economy to the outside world, which included "going global", but again did not set any clear indication that aggressive expansion of outward investment was envisaged. On ODI the meeting merely set the requirement to, "strengthen overall planning coordination, policy support and risk management of outward investment projects." [31] This focus appears to indicate a greater concern with correcting the failings in policy formulation and implementation in China than with exploiting the opportunity afforded by the crisis.

In contrast to some opinions expressed elsewhere in China, official policy documents indicate a cautious response to the crisis with limited expectations for the prospects of ODI. The policy documents indicate that this was based both on an assessment of the situation of the international economy as well as domestic factors such as the capacity for policy implementation and risk control. The views expressed by officials in MOFCOM following in the advent of the crisis, with their ambiguity of positives and negatives, were reflected in official policy formulations that were cautious in their prescriptions.

CONCLUSION

The policy of the Chinese government has been important in the growth of China's ODI. The fact that the state has a policy on outward investment arguably differentiates China from developed economies. Nevertheless, during the financial crisis which emerged with full force in 2008, the Chinese government found difficulty in adopting a clear-cut policy stance. Views in China of outward investment, including those held by officials working in this area, were not uniform. The crisis was commonly seen as marking the restructuring of the global economy, but the consequences of this were not clearly defined. Many of the views of the crisis expressed in China show that it was seen as a dynamic of opportunities and risks, or strengths and weaknesses. But the reading of dangers and opportunities was far from straightforward. The analyses commonly adopted in China saw both elements at play in the crisis and even the most optimistic Chinese advocates of outward investment did not ignore the weaknesses or risks.

While there were investments that seized opportunities that arose during the crisis, it is unclear that there was systematic implementation of a coherent strategy to exploit them. Although there were a number of significant investments after the onset of the crisis, the overall amount of ODI fluctuated and did not increase markedly. Officials close to ODI policy in MOFCOM appear to have held views which, while not necessarily conflicting, did not present a clear-cut strategy. Neither did official policy documents themselves set out a view that marked a dramatic policy shift as a result of the crisis. Hence, the onset of the crisis did not bring about a sharply different policy approach or rapid acceleration of outward investment from China.

The recognition of the coexistence of opposites is of course a hallmark of the Chinese view of the world. It is of course widely believed in the West that the Chinese term for crisis

---

[31] Wen Jiabao zhuchi zhaokai guowuyuan changwu huiyi [Wen Jiabao Leads in Opening State Council Standing Committee Meeting], People's Daily, 15 April 2010.

(危机) is made up of the characters for both danger and opportunity. Thus, in viewing the crisis as entailing both opportunities and risks for outward investment, the Chinese officials would appear to have held beliefs that are true to type. Whether the analysis of problems of policy or business decisions is made different by such a world view may not be entirely clear. Nevertheless, it is evident that in this case the conclusion of the analysis was much less clear-cut than might otherwise have been expected. The result was that China's policy on ODI during the crisis rather than being simply a call for an outward investment shopping spree was actually marked by a significant degree of caution.

REFERENCES

Buckley, P and Casson, M. (1976). *The Future of the Multinational Enterprise.* London. Macmillan.

Deng P. (2004). Outward Investment by Chinese MNCs: Motivations and Implications. *Business Horizons, 47* (3), (May-June), 8-16.

Deng P. (2009). Why do Chinese firms tend to acquire strategic assets in international expansion? *Journal of World Business, 44* (1), 74-88.

Dunning, J H. (1993) Multinational Enterprises and The Global Economy. Reading, Mss. Addison-Wesley.

Feng, P.C. (2009). Zhongguo qiye duiwai zhijie touzi yangjiu [Outward Investment by Chinese Enterprises]. Beijing. Yinzhi gongye chubanshe [Graphic Commuincations Press].

Feng, Z and He Y. (2004). Lun zhongguo qiye duiwai zhijie touzi zhanlue [Strategies for Chinese Companies' FDI]. Shandong Gongshang Xueyuan Xuebao, 3.

Guo, Bo. (2009) Guoji touzi: lilun, zhengce, zhanglue [International Investment: Theory, Policy, Strategy]. Beijing. Zhongguo shehui kexue chubanshe [China Social Sciences Press].

Hennart, J-F. (1982). A Theory of Multinational Enterprise. Ann Arbor. The University of Michigan.

Johanson, J and Vahlne, J-E. (1977). The Internationalisation of the Firm: A Model of Knowledge Development and Increasing Foreign Market Commitments. *Journal of International Business Studies, 8* (1) (Spring-Summer), 23-32.

Johanson, J and Vahlne, J-E. (1990). The Mechanism of Internationalisation. *International Marketing Review, 7* (4), 11-24.

Kang, Y and Liu, W. (2007). Internationalisation Patterns of Chinese Firms: Entry Mode, Location and Government Influence. *International Journal of Business Strategy, 7* (3), 13-31.

Li, J and Cui, Y. (2005). Zhongguo qiye jingwai touzi de dongin [Motivations for Outward Investment by Chinese Enterprises]. Haiwai touzi yu chukou xindai [Overseas Investment and Export Credit], 5.

Li, P. (2007). Toward and Integrated Theory of Multinational Evolution: The Evidence of Chinese Multinational Enterprises as Latecomers. *Journal of International Management, 13* (3), 296-318.

Li, W and Zhang, M. (2001). Fujian fazhan duiwai zhijie touzi de jichu tiaojian fenxi [Analysis of the Basic Conditions for Fujian's Development of Foreign Direct Investment]. Xiamen Daxue Xuebao, 3, 2001.

Ma, K. (2009). Zhongguo duiwai zhijie touzi qianli yanjiu [The Potential for China's Outward Investment]. Beijing. Jingji kexue chubanshe [Economic Science Press].

MOFCOM (2009). China Outward Direct Investment Statistical Bulletin 2008 [2008 niandu zhongguo duiwai zhijie touzi tongji gongbao], Beijing. National Statistical Bureau, State Administration of Foreign Exchange.

Rugman, A M. (1981). *Inside the Multinationals: The Economics of Internal Markets.* London. Croom Helm.

Rugman, A M and Li, J. (2007) Will China's Multinationals Succeed Globally or Regionally. *European Management Journal, 25* (5), 333-343.

State Council. (2009). Outward Investment Administration Procedures [Jingwai touzi guanli banfa],18 March 2009.

UNCTAD (2011). Foreign Direct Investment Database. Geneva: United Nations Conference on Trade and Investment, www.unctad.org.

UNCTAD. (2010). Global and Regional FDI Trends in 2009. *Global Investment Trends Monitor*, No. 2, 19 January.

UNCTAD. (2009). *World Investment Report (WIR).* United Nations.

Wang, Y. (2010). Zhongguo qiye dui fada guojia zhijie touzi yu zizhu chuangxin nengli yanjiu [Investment by Chinese Enterprises in Developed Countries and Their Capacity for Internal Innovation. Beijing. [Zhongguo jingji chubanshe [China Economic Publishing House].

Yang, D.X. (2008). Zhongguo haiwai touzi lun [The Theory of China's Overseas Investment]. Beijing. Zhongguo caizheng jingji chubanshe [China Finance and Economy Publishing House].

Zhang, X, Wang W and Wang Z. (2007) Woguo duiwai zhijie touzi jueding yinsu de shizheng yanjiu [Empirical Study of Determinants of China's Foreign Direct Investment], Guoji Maoyi Wenti [Problems in International Trade], 5.

In: The Transformation of Asia …   ISBN: 978-1-61470-873-5
Editors: B. Andreosso-O'Callaghan and P. Herrmann   © 2012 Nova Science Publishers, Inc.

Chapter 5

CYBER POLITICS IN CHINA

Yantao Bi

ABSTRACT

The political scene in China is evolving rapidly and one of its major driving forces is the rapid development of the Internet. In China, the virtual struggle between the ruling and the ruled is increasingly fierce. On the one hand, the information and communication technologies (ICTs) are empowering the citizens, and on the other hand, the authorities have been censoring and manipulating information available to the public.

INTRODUCTION

The Chinese cyberspace is probably the most revolutionary domain, which both the political elites and grassroots movements have recognized (BBC, 2009; *Singtao Daily*, 2008). Zhou Ruijing, one of the famous political commentators in China, asserts that the 'netizens' who are keen on political issues have formed a new class of opinion makers (*Singtao Daily*, 2008). He believes that this new class is a very important force to advance political reform and social progress in China. For example, a poll shows that 71.9 percent of Chinese 'netizens' deem free expression online as a new route to China's democratisation (*Singtao Daily*, 2008). Evidence shows that certain western countries have been helping China's non-governmental organizations (NGOs) to make better use of the new media.

This chapter will analyze how ICTs have been transforming China's political scene by revealing how the political struggle in China's virtual space is being carried out. It will also try to predict how ICTs will shape China's political landscape in the future.

To achieve these research targets, an integrated qualitative-quantitative approach, case studies, discourse analysis, and a historical method, will be employed. The quantitative approach takes the form of a questionnaire, which enabled the collection of both qualitative and quantitative data, from primary or secondary sources. On the one hand, some established databases and a large number of existing research results were also used, and on the other hand, some surveys, interviews, observations, and independent analysis with the aim to generate reliable first-hand data were also conducted.

To enhance the validity and credibility of this research, a number of measures were taken, such as the use of a 'go-between' strategy to narrow the distance between the interviewee and the author and at the same time to protect participants through rules of confidentiality. In the meantime, adequate evidence from various sources and data types was collected.

Data were analysed as objectively as possible, making judgment and generalizations tentative and careful, based on complete and detailed evidence. In this way, verification and replicability of this research can been enhanced.

1. BACKGROUND

Politically, China is at a crossroads. The political elites are not confident how to maintain the regime. Some officials have realized that the traditional governance models are no longer effective while a few still insist that any concession will lead to political disaster. Pei (2008:47) asserts that "suppressing personal freedom and interfering in the private lives of ordinary citizens is not only a wasteful use of the regime's resources, it is counterproductive". Fortunately, an increasing number of Chinese people, including the Communist Party and governmental officials, have come to this conclusion.

1.1. Channels for Opinion

In China, it is difficult for grassroots movements to voice their complaints. Even today, most of the Communist Party and departmental officials still choose not to report grassroots complaints and other "negative" information to their superiors. In the second half of 2008, I conducted a poll about the channels for petitions and expressing opinions in Hainan Province. The results show that of the 209 interviewees, only 27.8 per cent have channels to express their demands, opinions and suggestions, and that 56.5 per cent of the 209 respondents are in urgent need of reliable channels to express them. Another poll about the current channels for opinion by the *People's Daily* (Ji, 2009), found that of the 7111 respondents, 96.8 percent 'netizens' evaluate the local channels for opinion as not effective, and that 32.6 percent of them opted for new media (Internet and mobile phones).

Compared with other countries, Internet is the most reliable and important source of information for the Chinese people in urban China. On November 24, 2008, the Center for the Digital Future at USC Annenberg along with 13 partner countries released the first World Internet Project Report.

1.2. Political Impact of ICT Development

While Chinese citizens are hungry for channels to voice their opinions, the fast development of the Internet offers great help. To a great extent, to visit social websites is to advance democratization. For example, in the mini blogsphere, to publish, forward and follow-up is efficient in shaping public opinion and therefore exerting pressure on the authorities involved. In this sense, it is critical to popularize ICT in China.

According to the China Internet Network Information Center (CNNIC), China had 457 million netizens by the end of 2010, representing a 5.4 percent growth compared to the previous year. The penetration stood at 34.3 percent by December 31, 2010. China's netizens account for 23.2 percent of the global netizens, and 55.4 percent of Asian netizens. The Chinese netizens go online for searching (81.9 percent), music (79.2 percent) and news (77.2 percent). Meanwhile, the number of bloggers has risen to 294.5 million by the end of 2010, accounting for 64.4 percent of the netizens.

For China, the Internet is a double-edged sword, advancing its modernization while frustrating the authorities with the provision of unprecedented challenges. China has already marched into uncharted waters. There are at least three implications for the political actors.

First, the Internet has provided a platform for expression for people who lacked such channels in the past. In the words of Xie (2007): "The Internet collects these 'micro-powers' into a force that cannot be ignored in today's society". Yu Guoming, a professor of People's University of China, observed that in the cyberspace there are not only "spokespersons" but also "direct speakers". Anxiously, the Chinese netizens use the Internet as a social and political arena to defend their rights.

Second, the credibility of state media has declined as more people turn to alternative channels for information. The traditional models of censoring and suppression of unwanted information have already failed, due to the fact that the Chinese authorities have actually "lost much control over the information and images that now circulate through Chinese society" (Li Xiguang, 2003). Furthermore, as the consciousness of freedom of speech sharpens, a tighter control policy would dramatically undermine the legitimacy of the ruling party and the government. Moreover, as netizen's Internet literacy improves, more people are capable of bypassing China's Great Firewall to access blocked information.

Third, the CPC (Communist Party of China) and governments at all levels must make the necessary adjustments to fit in with the dramatic change in the political environment. The more open and flexible governance model should be adopted, which means the political discourse should be changed from one-way to two-way mode. Chinese President Hu Jintao is reported as urging officials in January 2007, at a lecture attended by members of the CPC Central Committee Political Bureau, to improve their Internet literacy and use it to "improve the art of leadership" (Wang, 2007). To showcase his attention to online opinion, Hu Jintao visited Qiangguo Forum, a virtual forum under *the People's Daily*, on June 20, 2008. For the first time, he chatted with 'netizens' for four minutes and said he got to learn of people's concerns through 'netizens'.

1.3. Virtual Politics

'Internet politics' (also called 'cyberpolitics', and 'virtual politics') has become a buzz term in China, which denotes the interaction between virtual politics and practical politics. When the netizens participate in politics online, their ultimate target is to influence practical politics. Some people are so optimistic about cyber democracy (also "virtual democracy", or "electronic democracy") that they believe cyber democracy will certainly promote practical democracy, while some "cyber-utopians", who think the web can quickly open up once-closed societies, have been disappointed by the considerable amount of control that the Chinese government exerts over its Internet.

In March 2009, when the Chinese People's Political Consultative Conference and the National People's Congress convened in Beijing, the online "e-Two Sessions" was in full swing in cyberspace. Before the two conferences commenced, a number of official websites of the state media and several major Internet news portals created special forums where netizens held their e-Two sessions, by posting their questions or suggestions to state leaders and/or the people's representatives. Chinese Premier Wen Jiabao himself took part in a two-hour online chat on February 28, 2009. The websites received more than 300,000 questions for the Premier ahead of the event, from which the moderator selected some 30 questions. Wen Jiabao said he goes online almost every day to listen to public opinions and suggestions.

1.4. Cyber Power

Politically, the greatest effect that the Internet has brought about is the re-distribution of power: part of the traditional power is transferred from the authorities to the citizens, from the elites to grassroots movements. Therefore, cyber power is characterized by knowledgeability, flattening and decentralization. In our information age, governmental power is dramatically affected by cyber power, prompting the decision-making structure to change from a downward mode to an interactive mode (Liu, 2002:13). Some even wonder whether the Internet will function as a fifth estate, following the judiciary, the legislative, the executive and the traditional news media.

Michel Foucault (cited in Liu Wenfu, 2002:25) suggests that modern power resides in a relational network, and that power and resistance are two forces that work in opposition to one another to fix and dissolve social identities. Resistance is not a force opposed to power but rather an unavoidable consequence of the disjunctive nature of power relations or power mechanisms themselves. Therefore, there are no relations of power without resistance. That is to say, absolute power without resistance does not exist any more in modern times.

Today in China, many CPC and governmental officials are not accustomed to the empowerment of the people. Yi (2009) reported that some party and governmental cardholders are suffering from cyber-related oppression and anxiety, including the awareness of being marginalized, being wronged and being endangered. Yi reports also that the cardholders are afraid of the renewed political environment.

Mr. Lin Jiaxiang, the Party secretary and deputy director of the Shenzhen Maritime Safety Administration of the People's Republic of China was sacked on October 31, 2008 for molesting a young girl while he was drunk. His misbehavior angered 'netizens' who succeeded in tracking him down by "human flesh search", a Chinese model for tracking people by searching for information online. But Mr. Liu Gongchen, deputy director of Maritime Safety Administration of China, defended Mr. Lin Jiaxiang on March 5, 2009. Mr Liu claimed that the Internet is able to murder a person, to make black white and white black, and he proposed that the cyberspace be further regulated. Understandably, his intention is to cut down the cyber power and thus consolidate the traditional power held by the authorities.

1.5. Precautions

It is vital to keep in mind that online opinion does not represent public opinion in China. There are several reasons for this assertion:

- Only 34.3 percent of Chinese citizens are 'netizens', who are not spokespersons for other people (CNNIC, 2011).
- 72.7 percent of the 'netizens' are rural residents, who are not necessarily representative of rural residents (CNNIC, 2011).
- 28.4 percent of the 'netizens' are below 20 years old, are not politically mature, and are not necessarily keen on politics. Meanwhile, only 18.4 percent are over 40 years old, and 76.9 percent of the 'netizens' are high school and primary school students, who are politically immature (CNNIC, 2011).
- Most of the 'netizens' do not "speak" online; only a small portion of them participate in virtual politics. Some observers are worrying whether this highly homogeneous "virtual race" will constitute a new ruling class (Liu, 2002).

It is widely believed that virtual political participation will advance democratization (Liu, 2008). To a great extent, the cyber politics has already changed the political landscape in China. The "new opinion leaders" are actually functioning as members of a virtual parliament, exerting direct influence on practical politics. In fact, the top principle of cyber politics is the power of the minority. Mr. and Mrs. Alvin Toffler have warned that nowadays it is the minority, not the majority that has the final say (quoted in Liu Wenfu, 2002: 303). In this case, how to guide and supervise cyber politics is really a difficult task for the authorities to undertake.

2. GOVERNMENTAL COUNTERMEASURES

This section discusses the measures taken by the Chinese authorities to respond to the challenges of ICT, from the perspective of political communication, censorship, astroturfing, political surveillance and other related struggles of ideas in the virtual space. In each case, the definitions are provided, the people and sectors involved are presented, and the techniques are explored; finally some comments, when necessary, are suggested.

The major benefit of online opinion is that it offers an opinion tank for policy makers, without challenging the authorities' power to make decisions. Considering the internal contradictions of online opinion, the proactive interfering with the online agenda-setting process can function as a buffer mechanism, containing the pressure of online public opinion. This reflects the CPC's policy regulating online public opinion. China's control of information flows is not as effective as before. One reason is that the netizens' ICT has improved so quickly that more people are able to bypass the Great Firewall. Another reason is that some netizens now use coded language to express their complaints. For example, some people use '河蟹' ('river crab') to denote deletion of online articles, meanwhile they use '草泥马' ('grass-mud horse') to express their anger with the authorities. Some 'netizens' use

'翻墙' ('climb over a wall') to indicate bypassing the Great Firewall, and '王道' ("the king's way') is used to refer to 'politically correct ideas'. This coded language is frequently updated to bypass internet censorship. At the same time, the party and the government have taken a lot of measures to take advantage of the Internet and contain its challenge. Party and governmental officials are required to enhance their Internet literacy; all websites are required to respect the laws concerning news communication. One of the major measures that the authorities have taken is to establish a national online TV station. As planned, the online TV station not only broadcasts high-quality video content, but also provides a "video-sharing platform" like YouTube.

2.1. Censorship

2.1.1. What Is Censorship?

Censorship is the suppression or deletion of information unwanted by the authorities. The rationale for censorship varies depending on the data censored. In practice, two or more types of censorship may be interlocked, or one type disguised as another. Censorship is sometimes undertaken under the guise of protecting the family, the church and the state.

Negative propaganda, media manipulation, spin, disinformation or "free speech zones" tend to disseminate preferred information, sometimes by forcing open discourse into marginal forums, or by preventing unfavourable ideas from reaching its target audience. But censorship traditionally refers to banning or crowding out certain information. That is, my own definition of censorship is in its narrow sense. Negative propaganda, media manipulation, spinning, disinformation and "free speech zones" fall under other categories of political communication techniques.

2.1.2. Who Are Censors?

At the national level, there are five primary censoring agencies in China. The CPC's Central Propaganda Department (CPD) is the most powerful monitoring body, which coordinates with other supervisory bodies to make sure media content promotes the party doctrine. The CPD gives media outlets directives restricting coverage of politically sensitive topics. Some other government sectors are also involved in reviewing and enforcing laws related to information flowing within, into, and from China: the General Administration of Press and Publication (GAPP), the State Administration of Radio, Film, and Television (SARFT) and State Council Information Office. GAPP licenses publishers, screens written publications (including those on the Internet), and has the power to ban materials and shut down outlets. SARFT has similar authority over radio, television, film, and Internet broadcasts.

The State Council Information Office is another important actor in regulating information flows. On the whole, it decides what information flows out of China through China's own outlets. In addition, the Fifth and the Ninth Department of the State Council Information Office offers directives on China's Internet operations, whereas the Sixth Department serves reporters from Hong Kong, Macao and Taiwan who work in the mainland China.

On May 4, 2011, China set up the State Internet Information Office, which is at the level of a ministry. Mr. Wang Chen, the current Director of the State Council Information Office of

China, is concurrently Director of the newly established office. It is worth noting that the three deputy directors of the new body are concurrently deputy ministers (or deputy directors) of the State Council Information Office, Ministry of Industry and Information Technology, and Ministry of Public Security. It is still unclear how the new sector works.

The local Propaganda Department works the same way as the Central Propaganda Department. The local administration of the press and publications and the local administration of radio, film, and television, receive directives from both local authorities and the relevant sectors of higher-level government(s) (vertical administration) which are responsible for censorship under their jurisdiction. Some analysts estimate that China employs 30,000 'Internet police' to monitor the internet and popular search engines such as Google and Yahoo, but according to the U.S. State Department, China has between thirty thousand and fifty thousand Internet monitors (Zissis and Bhattacharji, 2008).

The Chinese government has made great efforts to induce self-censorship. Independent analysts have found (www.ocf.berkeley.edu/~johnswu/methodology.html) that all Internet Service Providers (ISPs) and private companies are forced to regulate themselves. All ISPs are required to keep logs of their users' Internet activities, and even email archives are required to be available for government scrutiny. All web vendors, including web giants like Yahoo and Sohu, are required to sign pacts to promise that their Poker websites will not post information that will "jeopardize state security and disrupt social stability".

Rekursive (2008), a Beijing based information technology Internet and software consulting company, concluded that instant messaging services in China, including Skype and SMS, have censoring and surveillance capacities. All news websites in China, including that of Phoenix, a Hong Kong-based television broadcaster, practice very strict self-censorship. In 2006 Google.cn agreed to censor its search engine in China.

2.1.3. How to Censor

On the whole, China's methods and technology for censoring have evolved dramatically these years. It regulates media content not only by forcibly implemented censorship itself, but also by the chilling self-censoring effects the government has on media outlets. It is said that China prefers to practice censorship through intimidation and consensus (gilc.org/speech /osistudy/censorship). Zissis and Bhattacharji (2008) have perfectly summarized the tactics China adopts to control its media, which can be summarised and updated as follows:

- *Criticism.* This is the lightest and most common punishment.
- *Dismissals and demotions.* This is an often used technique for the authorities to punish the editors and journalists who are bold enough to test the red lines.
- *Accusations.* Authorities or government officials occasionally use accusations of libel or taking bribes to punish media outlets and publishing houses.
- *Fines.*
- *Closing news outlets.* News organizations that cover issues the Central Propaganda Department considers classified face closure.
- *Imprisonment.*

2.1.4. Internet Censorship

In October 2007, an investigative report entitled *China: Journey to the heart of Internet censorship* revealed how the Chinese authorities control Internet. According to the report, the supervisory bodies are as follows:

- The Internet Propaganda Administrative Bureau and the Center for the Study of Public Opinion of the State Council Information Office;
- The Internet Bureau and Bureau of Information and Public Opinion of the CPC's Central Publicity Department (the former Central Propaganda Department);
- Center for the Registration of Illegal and Unsuitable Internet Content of the Ministry of Information Industry (MII);
- The Computer Monitoring and Supervision Bureau of the Ministry of Public Security.

In 2007, the orders of the Beijing Internet Information Administrative Bureau were divided into three categories: "a first category order that must be implemented within 5 minutes, a second category order that must be executed within 10 minutes and a third category order that must be executed within 30 minutes". (*China: Journey to the heart of Internet censorship*). In order to comply with these orders, all the online companies based in Beijing have set up a section dedicated solely to the monitoring of orders. The most creative measure that the Beijing Information Office has introduced is a system of "license points" for websites. When being fined, sites can also have points withdrawn. If they loose all their points, they risk the withdrawal of their license. But they also have the chance to regain their lost points, and they are encouraged to do so.

To avoid punishment, websites also practice self-censorship by blocking key-words. There are three kinds of key-word censorship: masked words (words replaced by an asterisk), sensitive words (words that need to be checked by moderators before they can be posted) and taboo words (words that cannot appear in an article). In China, all international information goes through state-owned networks. This implies that all the information coming to China is filtered before it reaches the Chinese public. Some may think this system makes it possible to bypass the firewalls by means of proxy servers. The fact is that today it is increasingly difficult for the Chinese public to access blocked information via proxy servers, because the Chinese authorities are working hard to stop the Chinese 'netizens' from using proxy servers.

2.1.5. Prediction

It goes without saying that in China the demand for diversified information is increasing from all circles of life. On January 12, 2009, an open letter was released online signed by 22 young Chinese scholars and lawyers, calling for a boycott of China Central Television (CCTV) and opposition to its brain-washing. The BBC said the Chinese authorities were alarmed with these developments (Chen, 2009). It is true that where there is oppression, there will be resistance and revolt. It seems that the waking-up of the Chinese audience is accelerating.

To ease criticism of China's media policy and maintain its control of the media, the Chinese government has evolved its controlling tactics. For example, on January 5, 2009, an internet cleansing movement or antismut campaign was launched by the Chinese authorities led by State Council Information Office. But this campaign was officially announced "to combat the vulgar information online", which was wisely designed from the perspective of communication studies: it can not only help reshape public opinion, mobilise public support, but also to a certain extent help avoid international criticism of China's intensified grip on its news media.

2.2. Astroturfing

2.2.1. Definition
Etymologically, Astro Turf refers to the artificial grass used in some sports stadiums which looks bright and green. In political, advertising or public relations campaigns, astroturfing means creating a popular "grassroots" opinion and/or behavior by masking the true instigators and/or operators.

In practice, public relations (PR) firms instigate and manipulate fake opinion and/or behavior to create a positive atmosphere which will benefit their clients. Usually, astroturfers try to give the public an impression that a large number of people share the opinion when only a few support it. Therefore, astroturfing is a technique of propaganda or deception.

To understand astroturfing better, we need to look at disinformation and misinformation. Possibly translated from Russian dezinformatsiya, disinformation means: (1) Deliberately misleading information announced publicly or leaked by a government or especially by an intelligence agency in order to influence the public opinion or the government of the targeted nation; (2) deliberate dissemination of misleading information. Notably, disinformation is often undertaken by an intelligence agency, usually for military ends.

It is conceived to deceive enemies. But misinformation is simply incorrect, misleading information. It is not necessarily connected to an intelligence agency. It may be disseminated intentionally or unintentionally.

One difference between astroturfing and disinformation is that disinformation is mostly used to influence people in a foreign country while astroturfing is basically employed to influence public opinion within a country. A second difference is that the information provided by astroturfers is not necessarily false.

2.2.2. Instigation
Nowadays commercial astroturfing is popular in China[1]. This model is called Internet Word of Mouth (abbreviated as IWOM) in China, and it has already been accepted by the global online PR industry. Because the online information can proliferate much faster than in traditional media, it is necessary to manage the dissemination expeditiously and simultaneously via Bulletin Board System (BBS), blogosphere, search engines, Social Networking Services (SNS), etc.

Online PR is very expensive, but multinationals are willing to pay the bill. For example, in April 2008 when a number of Chinese people boycotted Carrefour, the French company

---

[1] Ms. Tong Zijing, a CEO of an online PR firm based in China, admits (www.stnn.cc/society_focus /200809 /t20080923_868667_2.html), "The major technique of online PR firms is astroturfing, utilizing search engines, portals, blogosphere, BBS, SNS, disguised as normal 'netizens'. At present, the scale for online public relations in China is roughly 50 million to 100 million."

spent RMB 2 million in one month on online public relations to defend it.[2] Generally, these online PR firms charge between $500 and $25,000 per month to dispel negative information (Roberts, 2008).

In fact, online PR firms are also involved in manipulating social and political issues. Understandably, the experiences gained from commercial astroturfing prompted the development of political astroturfing in China. An insider in the PR industry once concluded that it was around 2005 that the CPC leaders started getting more creative about how to influence public opinion on the Internet (Thomascrampton, 2008). My conjecture is that the army of web commentators are all orchestrated by local governments, ministries of the central government or departments of the CPC's central committee to safeguard their positive images.

2.2.3. Techniques

The purpose of astroturfing is to disguise the reactions of a political or commercial entity as an independent, grassroots reaction to a certain entity—a politician, political group, product, service or an event. To create an impression that the advocated product is popular or its competitor is unpopular, astroturfers always attempt to orchestrate responses from different sources.

In politics, astroturfing is usually designed and coordinated by think tanks, political consultants, or PR firms serving a politician or political party. Astroturfers may promote their clients directly and/or attack the competitors of their clients. Sometimes, astroturfers employ deceptive, dirty, even vicious means.

To implement astroturfing, it is critical to figure out the following: 1. Will negative commentary flare up? 2. Who is generating criticism? 3. How fast is the complaint spreading? 4. Will it be picked up by Web portals? 5. How to defend or attack effectively? (Where? Who?). In addition to direct astroturfiing, public relations firms also attempt to manipulate the media by leaking something fresh and juicy, because many journalists like to search for news in certain websites.

2.2.4. Consequences

Many of the public relations firms have BBS writers across the country, who pretend to be users of a client's product and post positive comments online, or publish negative posts against its competitors. It is not simple manipulation. By nature, it is deception. Therefore, astroturfing is forbidden in many other countries.

Recently, astroturfing has been frequently adopted in managing social crises in China. On June 28, 2008, a riot broke out in Weng'an County, Guizhou Province to protest against the alleged police mishandling of the death of a 15-year-old girl student. As part of its crackdown, the local authorities immediately launched a behind-the-scenes Internet campaign. At the same time, the local Internet police were busy deleting anti-governmental posts. "As a result, it looked as if public opinion on the Internet overwhelmingly supported the government" (Wu Zhong, 2008).[3]

---

[2] See www.stnn.cc/society_focus/200809/t20080923_868667_2.html.
[3] An article which compares American astroturfing with Chinese astroturfing concludes that "the Chinese government has used astroturfing in a very clumsy fashion by paying bloggers directly for their blog posts and tweets", because the No. 1 rule of astroturfing is "Don't get caught doing it". See: (www.chinavortex.com /2008/07/american-astroturfing-vs-chinese-astroturfing).

2.3. Political Surveillance

Surveillance is the monitoring of the behavior of people, objects or processes. Systems surveillance is the process of monitoring behavior within systems for conformity to expected or desired norm. There are different types of systems surveillance, some of which are beyond my research area.

What this chapter is interested in is political surveillance, the process of monitoring the behavior of people to help maintain the status quo. Political surveillance may be effected by direct observation or by the use of hi-tech equipment. Closed-circuit television (CCTV) is the device most often used in surveillance operations.

Surveillance is necessary for law-enforcement or maintaining security, but it leads to worries about invasion of privacy. According to the 2007 International Privacy Ranking (McKenna, 2008), published by advocacy groups Privacy International and the Electronic Privacy Information Center, the USA, the UK, China and Russia are the four "endemic surveillance societies".

At the national level, the political surveillance in China is coordinated by the Central Committee for Comprehensive Management of Public Security, the Ministry of Public Security (MPS) and the Ministry of State Security (MSS). All local governments have offices for the comprehensive management of public security. At the level of township, this office is usually affiliated to the Department of People's Armed Forces (in pinyin, renmin wuzhuangbu,人民武装部), which maintains certain armed forces and is responsible for the recruitment of regular troops. In China, the CPC leaders and government officials are responsible for what happens under their jurisdiction, including surveillance activities. The principle of the "people's war" has been applied to surveillance and in May 2004, a system of informants was introduced by the People's Political Consultative Conference of Chengdu city (Luo and Du, 2004). The system has now been adopted across the entire country, and the network of surveillance is powerful in that it has covers every corner of society.

2.4. Containing 'Human Flesh Search'

It is believed that the term 'human flesh search engine', a literal translation of the Chinese *ren rou sou suo* (人肉搜索), was first coined in 2001 when an entertainment website (www.mop.com) asked users to track down some film and music trivia. It shot to prominence in 2006. O'Brien (2008) has provided a classical definition of the Human Flesh Search (Engine): "A human flesh search engine is where thousands of volunteer cyber vigilantes unite to expose the personal details of perceived evil doers and publish them on the Web." Why is the 'human flesh search' popular in China? Cowles (2008) explains that "large-scale human flesh search engines are unique to China [because] of China's ubiquitous manpower and ingrained tradition of 'people's war' tracing back to Mao. On the other hand, because China's laws are imperfect, the Internet is seen as a way to seek justice."

Although the 'human flesh search' has incurred public criticism, it has turned to be a powerful weapon to combat corruption. When the People's Congress of Xuzhou City passed the Computer Information System Security Protection Ordinance, one netizen commented: "They are afraid. But they are not afraid enough. We must make them more afraid. We must make them terror-stricken." It can be inferred that China's 'netizens' enjoy the greatest freedom in the history of the country, but the freedom still lags far behind the netizens' increased demands. The 'human flesh search' displays Chinese netizens' strong desire to participate in political life and fight against corruption. But the elites are afraid of this trend because any one of them is likely to become the next target. If more evil officials are exposed, the ruling party will feel humiliated and challenged. China's 'netizens' do not have effective transmission belts to apply direct pressure on corrupt officials or a governmental sector. If officials turn a deaf ear to online criticism and the disciplinary sector declines to investigate the reported incident, then the 'netizens' can do nothing to rectify the situation.

Many cases have already verified the accuracy of this assertion. It seems that if the citizens have not access to legislative procedures to punish corrupt officials, linguistic articulation alone is not powerful enough to transform the political scene. What grassroots movements urgently need now is to establish some aggregation nodes so that more pressure can be exerted on corrupt officials.

CONCLUSION

As consciousness of rights has been increasing, Chinese citizens are more enthusiastic about politics, and have been trying to make better use of ICTs for political leverage. In this context, the ruling class has been forced to adjust its governance model. One case in point is that the governments at different levels have gradually adopted soft censorship, in trying to actively respond to public opinion. Therefore, it is safe to say that ICTs are dramatically transforming the Chinese political landscape. But it is naive to expect that political reforms will be completed in the near future, let alone the transition of the regime. The reality is that "incremental democracy" has become the consensus in China. In this case, it is vital to help the Chinese grassroots' movements enhance their ICT literacy, as it is a short cut to the desired political reform and to social progress.

REFERENCES

BBC. (2009) "Was a new class of opinion leaders born in China?'. [WWW page] (January 9) URL http://www.stnn.cc/ed_china/200901/t20090109_958430.html

Bristow, M. (2008) "China's internet 'spin doctors'". [WWW page] (December 16) URL http://news.bbc.co.uk/2/hi/asia-pacific/7783640.stm

Chen, Shirong. (2009) "China TV faces propaganda charge". [WWW page] (January 12). URL http://news.bbc.co.uk/2/hi/asia-pacific/7824255.stm

Cowles, I. (2008) "Chinese 'Human Flesh Search Engines' Claim Another Victim". [WWW page](June 27). URL http://www.findingdulcinea.com/news/international/May-June-08/Chinese--Human-Flesh-Search-Engines--Claim-Another-Victim.html

Ji, Yalin. (2009) "96.8 percent netizens think channels for opinion not smooth". [WWW page] (January 5). http://npc.people.com.cn/BIG5/8623331.html

Li, Xiguang. (2003) "ICT and the Demise of Propaganda in China". *Global Media Journal*, Fall. URL http://lass.calumet.purdue.edu/cca/gmj/fa03/gmj-fa03-xiguang.htm

Liu, Kuiru. (2008) "Internet Politics and Democratization in China". *Bridge of Century* (15).

Liu, Suhua. (2009) "Learn to diagnose public opinion in cyberspace". *People's Daily.* February 6, p. 11.

Liu, Wenfu. (2002) *Cyberpolitics.* Beijing: Commercial Press.

Luo, Xiao and Du, Cheng. (2004) "Chengdu's CPPCC establishes special informants system". [WWW page] (May 4) URL http://news.163.com/2004w05/12541/2004w05_1083622828878.html

Ma, Wenluo. (2008) "Human Flesh Search—China-Style Anti-corruption". [WWW page] (December 29). URL http://www.chinastakes.com/story.aspx?id=937.

O'Brien, C. (2008) "The Human Flesh Search Engine". [WWW page] URL http://www.forbes.com/2008/11/21/human-flesh-search-tech-identity08-cx_cb_1121 obrien.html

Pei, Minxin. (2008) "How China is ruled". *The American Interest*, Volume III, Number 4, Spring (March/April), p.p.44-51

Rekursive. (2008) "Electronic surveillance in China: Skype, QQ and SMS". [WWW page] (October 2). URL http://rekursive.com/blog/53/electronic-surveillance-in-china-skype-qq-and-sms/.

Roberts, D. (2008) "Inside the War Against China's Blogs". [WWW page] (June 12) URL http://www.businessweek.com/magazine/content/08_25/b4089060218067.htm?chan=search

Singtao Daily. (2008) "71.9 percent netizens deem free expression WWW page is a new route to China's democracy" . [WWW page](December 30). URL http://www.stnn.cc/china /200812 /t20081230_951748.html

The China Internet Network Information Center. [2011] "The 27th Development Report on China's Internet". [WWW page] (January 18). URL http://research.cnnic.cn /img/h000/h12/attach201101211723380.pdf

Thomascrampton. (2008) "China's 50-cent Army of Internet Astroturfers". [WWW page] (July 13). URL http://www.thomascrampton.com/china/chinas-50-centpercentC2 percent A0army-of-internet-astroturfers/

Wang, Qian. [2007] "Creatively enhance the construction and management of virtual culture". [WWW page] (January 24). URL http://news.cctv.com/china/20070124 /111582.shtml

Wu, Zhong. (2008) "China's Internet awash with state spies". [WWW page] (August 14). URL http://www.atimes.com/atimes/China/JH14Ad01.html

Xie, Li. (2007) "Yu Guoming on Internet politics". [WWW page] (May 17). URL http://www.danwei.org/Internet/yu_guoming_on_Internet_politic.php

Yi, Ran. (2009) "Capability crisis of some carders". *Xinmin Wanbao* (or *Xinmin Evening Daily*). January 20, p. A 4.

Zissis, C. and Bhattacharji, P. (2008) "Media Censorship in China". [WWW page] (March 18). URL http://www.cfr.org/publication/11515/

In: The Transformation of Asia …   ISBN: 978-1-61470-873-5
Editors: B. Andreosso-O'Callaghan and P. Herrmann   © 2012 Nova Science Publishers, Inc.

Chapter 6

ADAPTIVE STRESS:
CHINA AND THE GLOBAL ECONOMIC CRISIS

Jörn-Carsten Gottwald and Niall Duggan

ABSTRACT

The People's Republic of China (PRC) has weathered the storm of the global financial crisis with remarkable success. Preserving a substantial growth rate of its economy, China has become the main global engine of growth. A combination of macro-economic stimulus and Leninist party policies has prevented a major economic crisis which could have triggered a substantial social and political upheaval as the legitimacy of the current political order is heavily depending on development. While Western observers take the crisis performance as an indicator of the growing global influence of the PRC, the Chinese leadership takes a much more careful approach when repositioning itself in the global arena. Thus, the economic crisis of 2008 is not only a reminder of the interdependent nature of economic development and political stability in China but also of the interconnectedness of domestic policies and China's participation in global governance.

INTRODUCTION

The default of the US Investment Bank Lehman triggered one of the worst economic downturns in modern history. National governments in America, Europe and Asia nationalised banks, introduced quantitative easing to keep their economies solvent, and started the project of re-writing the rules of global finance. Anglo-American and European capitalism is suffering from a deep crisis (Gowan 2009; Altman 2009). Heads have turned eastwards looking for redemption. The remarkable swiftness of the economic recovery of East Asia 'highlights China's Ascendance' (Schwartz, 2009); the People's Republic of China (PRC) continued to grow at break-neck speed with GDP growth of 8.7 per cent in 2009 and 10.1 per cent in 2010. China overtook Japan in 2010 to become the second largest economy in the world and challenged Germany's status as the number one export nation. China's Socialist

Market Economy has 'emerged relatively unscathed from the global economic downturn' (Kim 2009: 43) creating a new Chinese saying: while capitalism saved China in the 1980s, China now saves capitalism.

In sharp contrast to these outstanding figures, the leadership of the Communist Party of China (CCP) emphasises major challenges to China's development arising from the global downturn as well as from internal imbalances. Their caution is well justified. Any crisis of global trade tests China's social and economic order as well as their export-led growth strategy. Chinese politicians and the global community of China watchers agree on the need to preserve social and political stability as a prerequisite for economic growth (Shambaugh, 2008; Saich 2005; Yang 2005; Shirk, 2007). China's growth is based on its political stability and thus linked closely with global developments which calls for a careful consideration of China's input in global politics (Gottwald and Duggan 2011; Buzan, 2010; Zhu Liqun 2010), The central leadership in Beijing was caught unprepared and needed several weeks to develop a political reaction to the global crisis. In the end they had to acknowledge that the 'globalization of the crisis requires a globalized response' (Bergsten 2008). This raises the question as to how any changes in the global environment are not only digested by China's domestic policies, but more fundamentally by its evolving domestic order and global role.

Contradicting mainstream speculation about China's new power to define global rules, this chapter assesses the real challenges posed by the global crisis on China's socio-economic order and the resulting conflicts for the leadership as to how to interact in the emerging global regime for crisis-management. Linking research in Chinese domestic politics and economics with approaches from the field of International relations, we first reiterate the specific characteristics of China's evolving order in the light of its integration into the global economy. The fundamental contradictions between a partial promotion of free markets and the sustaining and strengthening of the general control capacities of the Leninist single party State are still the dominant feature of the Socialist Market Economy in spite of its successful record of institutional learning and adaptation. The political reaction to the global crisis, therefore, combines some macro-economic measures with traditional measures of the Chinese single party-state. Navigating their way in unchartered waters, the leadership, therefore, takes a much more hesitant approach towards deeper global cooperation and a more proactive role in international regulation than most observers had expected. China's policies towards global governance in the area of financial markets are still following the incremental path of careful analysis and step-by-step learning by doing rather than seizing the opportunity to establish itself as a new leader of world markets.

1. CHARACTERISTICS OF CHINA'S SOCIALIST MARKET ECONOMY

Thirty years after the 3rd Plenum of the 11th Central Committee of the Communist Party of China met in Beijing to officially proclaim policies of reform and opening up of the economy, the constitution states that 'the state has put into practice a socialist market economy'[1] where the state plays an important role in steering, controlling and regulating the

---

[1] Constitution of the PRC (2004/2008), Article 15: ('中华人民共和国建立社会主义市场经济体制')

economy. However, private ownership enjoys constitutional protection. Whether or not this particular economic order fulfils the criteria of a market economy is a sensitive issue in China's foreign relations. The Chinese leadership's claim that China has established a market economy is incorrect: the Peoples Republic China is not a member of the Organisation for Economic Cooperation and Development (OECD) (OECD 2011). Its membership of the WTO is based on its status of an emerging economy, a status that the PRC leadership sought to ensure certain privileges in adopting WTO standards and regulations, with the provision for generous delays. The EU refuses to grant market economy status to the PRC on the grounds that China does not fulfil the relevant criteria (IERMBN University 2005). Here, however, the Chinese government claims it is unfairly treated, as the EU position supposedly ignores the great progress made in China towards establishing the framework for a market-economy. Accusations of dual standards being applied by the EU seem well founded as Market Economy Status (MES) was granted to the Russian federation in 2002, a move that has weakened the EU's viewpoint of the MES as being a technical matter (Remond 2007). As highlighted by China Daily:

> "Market-economy status would avoid China from all European anti-dumping restrictions because it would mean Brussels could impose penalties on Chinese goods only if export price was below the production cost but not by comparing the price of Chinese exports with those of third countries, which is what currently has been doing" (China Daily 2005).

Many of the reasons given to China for the refusal to grant it the MES such as a poor human rights record, serious internal economic diversity, political and military non-transparency etc can also be found in Russia.

Statistically, the non-state sectors of China's economy have far outgrown the state sector. Most goods and services are traded and priced according to supply and demand in competitive markets. In this regard, the difference between the PRC and most European states is not substantial. Yet China-watchers doubt the accuracy of using the private-state distinction in understanding China's economic activities. As Kelley Tsai (2006) and Bruce Gilley (2006) argue, China's new entrepreneurs are closely linked with the party establishment, while studies of China's stock markets have revealed the remaining strong influence of state-owned and state-controlled organisations on publicly traded companies. While entrepreneurial activity in China offers a substantial amount of freedom,[2] the PRC scores relatively low in major indices on economic freedom and even worse in major indices of political freedom. Traditional norms and behaviours co-exist in China's economy with modern, partly-externally-created informal and formal institutions. In the terminology of evolutionary economics, China is an emerging new economic order bearing different sets of formal and informal rules and modes of behaviour. Endogenous and exogenous sources for institutional change coexist and compete with one another and lead to a dynamic process (Gottwald 2010), Nevertheless, the Chinese economy has been highly attractive for private investors and has led to an astonishing and record-breaking increase of private – and state-coordinated –

---

[2] Both the Doing Business in China project of the World Bank (ranked 79 out of 181) and the Heritage Foundations Index on Economic Freedom (ranked 135 out of 179) have China scoring in the upper and lower middle ranks. World Bank (2010), Doing Business in China..; Heritage Foundation (2010), Index of Economic Freedom. At http://www.heritage.org/index/Ranking [accessed 12 February 2011].

economic activities. Its 'institutional amphibiousness' (Ding 1994), apparently did not hamper the inflow of goods and services in spite of severe constraints on the protection of intellectual property rights (IPRs).

Following integrative approaches, the political and economic order of the PRC exhibits the unusual combination of institutions of a market economic order with a Leninist single-party political order. While nobody would doubt the tremendous degree of change within the Chinese one-party-state towards representing differing interests within society, the implementation of a rule of law[3] guaranteeing individual freedoms and private property rights even cases of confrontation with the CCP, is still absent. Describing the change taking place within the limits of the CCP-dominated and controlled Leviathan, various authors have emphasized the soft (Yang 2005; Cabestan 2004), fragmented (Lieberthal 2003), learning (Naughton, 2009), character of the Chinese form of capitalism (McNalty 2008), with cadre (Heilmann 2001) or red capitalists (Dickson 2003), but without democracy (Tsai 2007).

Summing-up, China's Socialist Market Economy can best be described as a dynamic, diffuse and post-Leninist order with a limited degree of political and social pluralism. Since embarking on the project of reforming and opening up China's economy at the 3rd Plenum of the 11th Central Committee of the Communist Party of China in December 1978, the transformation of China's order has been a haphazard process of trial and error. Letting the economy grow out of the plan, as Barry Naughton famously put it, the leadership partly followed bottom-up examples of spontaneous change by the population and partly initiated, implemented and withdrew reform policies top-down (Dreyer 2004; Lieberthal 1995; Saich, 2004). These processes resulted in a diffuse and incoherent co-existence of traditional norms and modes of behavior stemming from Maoist and centrally-planned traditions with different forms of market oriented institutions. Tensions between formal and informal institutions proved a strong stimulus for continuous change (Douglas 1990). The change, however, was by no means linear. Rather, periods of further opening were followed by periods of reinforced limitations (The Economist 2011). Promoting national champions and declaring substantial parts of the Chinese economy to be of strategic importance and thus not open for foreign investments beyond a minority stake (China Daily 2010). The CCP managed to preserve and even strengthen its grip on power by successfully co-opting new elites. The benefits of high-speed economic growth allowed the building of a strong pro-reform coalition that in a political sense was staunchly pro status quo. Preserving CCP rule meant preserving access to entrepreneurial opportunities and economic rents (Minxin 2009). Today, organization and governance within the CCP still adheres to the basic Leninist principles of democratic centralism, nomenclature and cadre management (Brodsgaard,/Zheng 2006). The party controls the elites in politics administration, law, major enterprises and leading societal organizations. While pursuing ambitious reforms of the legal system and proclaiming the objective of the applicability of the rule of law in China, there are only limited moves to bring the CCP under the control of the judiciary. Thus, the Chinese legal system rather aims at rule by law rather than the rule of law (Clarke, 2005). These changes had a tremendous effect on Chinese society: social differentiation has progressed at a surprising rate. The Gini-coefficient as a standard measurement of income inequality within a society has risen from 0.24 in 1978

---

[3] There is little discussion that the PRC has successfully established a rule by law where most actions taken by the government or the party are based on laws and regulations. Chinese claims to establish a 'rule of law' – with or without Chinese characteristics - need to be carefully examined as the fundamental prerequisite for a rule of law – judicial independence – is explicitly rejected in the Chinese constitution.

to 0.46 in 2008, and thereby passed the threshold of 0.4 considered to be a benchmark for unacceptable and politically-unmanageable inequality. Urban China in particular has experienced a dramatic rise in living standards accompanied by an increase in individual liberties regarding living styles, cultural and social activities, access to information and private consumption. However, the limits of politically accepted individual liberty are moving in both directions. Studies of the spread and use of the Internet in China and analyses of public discourse have shown, that testing the limits of what is accepted by the powers-to-be has not only led to an increase of social freedom but regularly to reinforcement and narrowing of limits, too (Wacker, G. 2003; Tai, Zixue 2006).

The global crisis, therefore, threatens to hit China at its weakest spot: social and political stability resting on a concept of legitimacy based on economic development and national strength. Confronting the global meltdown challenges the very essence of the political and economic order in China (Fan 2008).

2. CHINA'S DEPENDENCE ON A POSITIVE INTERNATIONAL ENVIRONMENT

The economic, social, and political changes usually referred to as globalisation would have been incomplete, if not impossible, without China's reform and opening up. It is hard to imagine any form of 'globalisation' excluding one fifth of the world's population. Similarly, the PRC grounded its economic reforms on the influx of capital and know-how from overseas Chinese and foreign investors. Thus, the success of China's reforms is intrinsically linked with access to global sources of capital and foreign markets for products made in China. In this regard, the emergence of China's Socialist Market economy forms an integral part of globalisation making the Chinese leadership a substantial stakeholder in globalisation.

This dependence on access to global trade and investment, however, has for a long time been downplayed in China's foreign policies and the leadership's attitudes towards global governance and multilateralism. Based on the so-called five principles, the PRC has been a staunch supporter of the principle of national sovereignty and non-interference in national issues. (Guoli Liu 2003). For most of the reform era, 'China remains ambivalent, if not suspicious, of global governance' (Economy Elizabeth 1999).

As part of a process of professionalisation, institutionalisation (Lampton 2008) and integration of an ever broader group of stakeholders including a nascent public sphere promoted by the Internet into foreign-policy making (Yu 2006: 88). China's attitude has become more pragmatic. Gaining access to the WTO in 2001 was considered a major breakthrough in bringing the PRC into a multi-lateral, and considering its conflict resolution-mechanism, even supra-national organisation.

In its 2005 White-Book on foreign affairs, the Chinese government stated that the PRC would 'stick to peace, development and cooperation, and together with all other countries, devoting itself to build a harmonious world' (State Council 2005).

Regarding the World Trade organisation, 'China has exerted itself to push forward multilateral economic and trade relations and regional economic cooperation (…) [and] has been an active supporter of and participant in multilateral trade system (sic)' (State Council 2005). However, these commitments to multilateralism are matched by a strong emphasis on

China relying on its own strength and pursuing bilateral cooperation with partners in the same document. Chinese and foreign observers agree that China has benefited enormously from participation in the WTO and can be expected to play an active part in shaping economic governance (Bergsten et al. 2006: 114-116; Zheng 2008).

In a nutshell, China has actively sought integration into global markets for capital, industrial and agricultural products and certain services. Its integration into global rule-making bodies, however, exhibits a certain degree of reluctance as the leadership generally prioritizes national sovereignty and autonomy of action, to a multi-lateral transfer of competences.

Growing dependence on foreign markets and foreign resources increase pressure on the Chinese leadership's political capacities. Growing national strength and increased earnings from exports raise the expectations of an increasingly well-informed Chinese public that the leadership uses these resources to the maximum benefit of the people. This, again, increases pressure on the policy-making capacities of the Chinese leadership that finds itself trapped in relying on the benefits of globalization, while at the same time globalization erodes the legitimacy of the leadership.

3. THE IMPACT OF THE GLOBAL CRISIS ON CHINA

3.1. The Economic Impact

The economic impact of the global crisis on China has been studied in much detail in China and abroad (Schmidt and Heilmann, 2009). Officially, China's economy recorded an annual growth rate of 9% in 2008, down from 13% in 2007. However, some analysts believe that the Chinese economy experienced a much sharper decline in the last months of 2008 (Morrison 2009).

Chinese growth depends strongly on the influx of foreign investment and the capacity of foreign markets to absorb products made in China. Thus, any downturn in global trade and investment has a strong effect on Chinese growth. The PRC countered the threat by stimulating public and private consumption creating the conditions for a massive investment and property bubble, and threatening the safety of its domestic banking system. Local governments expanded their expenditure through half-legal investment vehicles challenging the central leadership's attempts at reining in public debt (Wu 2010).

China has been a driving force behind the high prices in raw materials such as copper and iron ore (Kynge 2006). If the Chinese economy slows, this may result in the global demand for raw materials dropping. As Chinese outward investment is focused on the raw materials sector (Brown 2008), this may result in the slower than expect development of these Chinese projects in countries such as Guinea (Polgreen 2009). This may cause the growth of Chinese companies to slow reducing their ability to act as source of growth for the economy.

3.2. Social Impact

The first immediate impact of the global downturn on China's Socialist Market Economy has been the rise in unemployment among so-called migrant workers. In late 2008, early 2009, a number of export-oriented companies in China's coastal areas sent their employees into the spring festival holiday without offering them new positions for 2009. Estimates of the Chinese government, based on surveys in the home-counties of migrant workers, suggested that 30 to 40 million migrant workers faced unemployment. In urban China, special measures were taken by the government to provide employment for China's universities' graduates. For the central authorities, discontent among highly-trained youth versed in modern communication technologies poses a serious threat to political stability. Growing unemployment and the dip in economic growth adds pressure on the government to improve the social security security. Following Imperial as well as Communist traditions, leading cadres have started visiting various provinces to raise confidence trust in the macro-economic stimulus package of the government, and to see how the global financial crisis – and in China it is still called the global financial crisis: 世界金融 危机 – is affecting different parts of the country. Finally, leading CCP representatives have stressed the need for party unity and called for preparations against social unrest.

3.3. Effects on the Socio- Economic Order

The potential impact of the crisis on China's socio-economic order should not be underestimated. While it is nearly impossible to collect hard data on the direct effects in China at this stage, the behaviour of the top leadership provides a useful signpost. Hu, Wen, Xi Jinping and Li Keqiang have all emphasized the risks that the economic problems pose for the stability of China's political order. Stability and steady improvement of everyday living conditions for the Chinese population, however, lie at the heart of the Socialist market Economy. The leadership justifies its reluctance to share its control of political power by providing a vision of a better life and a stronger China. When the leadership gets publicly nervous about social stability, the situation must be serious.

But the threat to stability is only one impact. In addition, the current crisis has lessened the attraction of the capitalist role models and best practices. While this has allowed for a certain degree of triumphalism in some Chinese statements (Barber 2009; The Economist 2009), it cuts off the Chinese leadership from one of its preferred channels for policy-learning: the international example. With most of the regulatory agencies and consultational bodies for better governance coming under attack in the established market economies in Europe and the United States, their relevance for bridging the gap between authoritarian rule and individual economic activity gets questioned.

3.4. Threat to the Party-State

Finally, despite huge progress made in the area of economic and social modernisation, China's economic order is still a bizarre co-existence of a strong-state and a burgeoning private and semi-private business sector. Core areas of China's economy – energy, aviation, finance – are kept under strict control of the party or the state which not only sets the rules for business activity but has reserved the right to appoint the leading managers in enterprises, to provide or block credit, and to allow or prevent foreign investments.

The official 'Socialist Market Economy' has not yet found its balance between the two mutually-exclusive principles of freedom of individual choice, and activity, and state-control. While this helps in some regards, such as protecting its financial services during the current economic slowdown, it has, in turn, directly linked the current leadership's legitimacy with economic success.

Economic success has been used by successive Chinese leaders since the 1990s as a second source to legitimize party-rule; the primary source is nationalism. The promise to help China return to a prominent position within global politics has helped raise support for the CPC among the Chinese population.

Finally, the leadership warns continuously against the threats of chaos if political change progresses too fast. But the CPC's ability to preserve stability and raise China's image in the world relies heavily on further economic growth and modernisation. Minxin Pei argues convincingly, that the economic slowdown threatens the fabric that keeps the CPC elite together: joint access to economic benefits as part of cadre capitalist elite (Minxin 2009). Lacking alternative means to generate diffuse support for its rule, the current crisis not only threatens the government in power but also the whole political and economic system as there is no legal alternative to the Communist Party.

4. China's Domestic Crisis Management

In macroeconomic terms, China is in a much better position than most Western economies for a number of reasons. First, its banking and financial services system is still government controlled, partly state owned and comparatively little exposed to global markets. Thus, Chinese banks have in essence escaped the financial crisis with only comparatively minor losses. However, the balance sheets of the main banks are regularly propped up by the state coffers[4] and its securities markets offer only limited access to foreign investors, while Chinese savers still face hurdles if they wish to have their deposits outside the Chinese system. Secondly, China's 'economic miracle' has created a growing middle class and an emergent consumer culture. Even though exports have been the main driver of China's boom, its domestic market has only now just begun to realize its full potential. A government that is decisive in fostering private consumption as part of a domestic demand boost clearly has a powerful tool at hand to fight any economic slowdown. Thirdly, the Chinese government has gained a reputation for its high-quality technocrats running the show in close cooperation with world leading think tanks and organisations. While many voters in Europe turn their heads away from their leaders, shocked by their perceived or real lack of economic competence, the Chinese population has little reason to doubt the expertise of a leadership

---

[4] In February 2009, the government announced plans to transfer 30 billion US$ to the Agricultural Bank of China. See Ftd online, 'China päppelt Bauernbank mit Milliarden', at www.ftd.de/politik/international/:Neues-Konjunkturpaket-China-p%E4ppelt-Bauernbank-mit-Milliarden/468766.html (10 February 2009). According to The Economist, from 1998 to 2005, China has propped up the balance sheets of its major banks by 260 billion US$.

that has an impressive record of policy learning. Finally, the vast foreign exchange reserves managed by the State Authority for Foreign Exchange (SAFE), low public debt and no parliamentary or social opposition to challenge the government policies, offers an excellent basis for boosting domestic demand.

4.1. China's Macro-Economic Stimulus Package

After a lot of speculation, the Chinese leadership announced a 4 trillion *Renminbi Yuan* package to boost domestic demand on Sunday, 9th November 2008. (Xinhua News Agency 2008), The international reaction was euphoric. Only a few observers voiced their concern mainly due to the fact that little information was given as to how the money was going to be spent. The Chinese leadership also kept vague as to how the package would offer additional spending and as to how it consisted of measures which had been planned and budgeted beforehand.

But even then, doubts remain whether China will be able to offset the drastic fall in global demand for its products by boosting its domestic economy. China is extremely dependent on multi-nationals to produce their goods in Chinese enterprises and on American and European consumers to buy them. Figures from export statistics (Mackinnon (2009), indicate a strong decline in intra-Asian trade as having a dramatic impact on China's export-oriented industries. With dozens of millions of Chinese migrant workers loosing their jobs, the Chinese leadership warns of coming social unrest. China's population has learned the hard way that a booming market economy can produce considerable side-effects that may affect areas such as health care, education, and social security. For this reason, Chinese families have ample reason to keep their budgets tight and to save money. As a result, China's savings rates are now among the highest in the world. Consumer caution shows no sign of suddenly turning into a credit-fuelled retail therapy arena dreamt of by CEOs in Western multi-nationals.

4.2. Mobilizing the Party-state

The Chinese leadership might praise macro-economic control, but it does not fully trust it. Reacting to the global crisis, the leadership is complimenting macro-economic policies with traditional measures. On an institutional level, the Chinese leadership announced a rather unusual co-operation policy between the Central Bank and the ministry of technology to concentrate on the technological rebuilding (*chuanxin*) of credit-finance provision and to support technological innovation (Caijing Online 2009). This cooperation should support the implementation of state plans to promote high-technology and develop high-technology zones, but also improve the use of technology in the provision of credits to small and medium size enterprises.

The Chinese media operate in a tight framework of censorship and market orientation (Holbig 2008). While they stretch their limits on investigative journalism and controversial debate on a daily basis, they follow the official party-line on important policy issues. A cursory look at Chinese news reports reveal two distinctive features: the current crisis is described as being a financial crisis (金融危机) and it threatens to spill over into the real economy. This allows for portraying the Chinese leadership as a management team working hard to contain the impact of the global crisis on China and leaving open the possibility that the average Chinese might not be affected by the crisis. Furthermore, articles, statements and reports stress the opportunities arising from the crisis for Chinese structural reform, overseas investment and comparative gain in the global economic and political system. At the same time, the Chinese population is called upon to reduce its high rates of saving and 'consume China out of the recession'.

Underpinning the image of a caring leadership, top representatives of the party-state followed the imperial and Leninist tradition of inspection tours to the Chinese provinces. These tours are officially declared to pursue two objectives: first, to create trust in the policies conducted by the central leadership in containing the crisis and second to gain a better insight into how the crisis affects the lives of the people in different provinces.

4.3. China's Global Crisis Management

These attempts to counter the impact of the global crisis on China's domestic development have been complemented by various steps to deal with the changes in the international environment. Western and Chinese analysts alike have been discussing the global consequences of the economic crisis as a shift in power from the West to the East (Altman 2008). Governments in Asia are considered to be in a much better position to lead the way out of the global crisis by introducing huge spending plans.

5. CHINA'S CHANGING ROLE IN THE NEW G 20

China's foreign policy response to the crisis exhibits its traditional step-by-step approach particularly in the context of the new G 20. This loosely knit forum representing the major established and emerging economic powers was reinvented as the main forum to organise a global response to the financial and economic crisis.

A first summit took place in Washington in 2008, convened by the outgoing Bush administration. Shortly before the meeting, China announced its macro-economic stimulus package hoping that this would also contribute to sustain the global economic growth and thus contain growing international pressure on China for a more active involvement in global governance (Niquet 2009).

During the end of 2008 and the beginning of 2009, China used all its channels of bilateral and multi-lateral cooperation to define its policies. In his speech at the Washington Summit in November 2008, President Hu Jintao stressed the need for close cooperation and a fundamental review of global rules. He called for fast and decisive action by national governments but within and according to their individual circumstances. Hu Jintao emphasised the special responsibility by the more advanced economies and warned against premature moves.

The United States, the EU and emerging countries all expressed clear expectations of the Chinese leadership to become crucially involved and to support the crisis reaction through 'responsible investment' abroad. The Chinese domestic audience, however, discussed the potential new dominance of China and its economic preferences in the new world order.

The Chinese leadership expected the financial crisis to further strengthen China's reform policies and its integration into the world economy including global governance. The preservation of China's economic stability and growth is considered to be the most important Chinese contribution to the global actions supported strongly by the Chinese leadership. In the view of China's leaders, global governance reform was intrinsically linked with ongoing reforms at home.

A deeper integration and more pro-active attitude to the revision of financial regulation on a global scale should support the refinement of the domestic regulatory framework – and open up attractive opportunities for outward investment (Qi Bao 2009). Based on the principle that every country should contribute according to its specific circumstances, China calls for an orderly and systematic reform of the financial system that should strengthen the involvement of emerging and developing countries.

In the ongoing negotiations regarding the reform of the global architecture, China is showing an increased assertiveness in pressuring for a reform of the Bretton-Woods institutions, as well as defining the structure and reach of new organisations like the Financial Stability Board (FSB). Its commitment, however, still fall within the limits of a carefull-designed adaptation to global standards, combined with a long-term strategy to influence future rule-making through early contributions, and a long-term strategy to build up a network of high- and medium-level Chinese experts in global organisations like the IMF and the World Bank (Gottwald 2011).

CONCLUSION

The effects of the global economic crisis on the international order has received enormous attention in media and academia. The PRC is usually portrayed as the main beneficiary of a shift in global power. Obvious as this development might be, it is neither new nor certain. China's economic order is intrinsically-linked to a global economic system dominated by American and European principles of global governance and – theoretically – free access to the most solvent consumer markets. While the immediate macro-economic effects have been successfully cushioned by a massive stimulus package and a policy of cheap credits, the crisis management was marked by a return to party-state mechanisms combining propaganda, direct intervention and a crowding out of private enterprises. As European and American governments raised their voices to call for a more substantial role by the PRC in global reforms, one consequence becomes increasingly clear: the inherent contradictions within China's Socialist Market Economy have become sharper and the government's response relies heavily on non-market means.

The 'Beijing Consensus' praised by some predominantly Western observers (Ramo 2004), highlighting the unique combination of high-speed export led economic growth with authoritarian politics, does not have the full support of the party establishment. Chinese academics prefer the label of a 'Chinese Model" (*zhongguo moshi*) or a 'Chinese way' stressing the uniqueness and the special circumstances of China's development. A country that returns to more authoritarian and hierarchical policies in dealing with economic insecurity seems ill-posed to become a leader in global regulatory reform. The Chinese leadership has carefully avoided claiming such a lead role. Following its able approach to domestic reforms, the government of the PRC has cautiously developed its policy regarding global governance. It has portrayed itself as a responsible stakeholder, and with few exceptions has lived up to its claims. The increased global profile should help with continuing its policies at home.

The decision of the Chinese leadership to rely on a strategy of economic growth and social modernisation leading to enhanced national strength and thus providing some legitimacy to its continued one-party rule, requires access to foreign markets and foreign investment. Therefore, the PRC has little choice but to join the redefinition of global market rules. Attempts to replace this strategy with a stronger role for domestic demand have made little progress. Therefore, the current economic crisis works as a catalyst both for the tensions within the Chinese socio-domestic order, and between the preference given to Leninist policies in crisis-reaction, and China's role in global economic market-based governance. Socialism with Chinese Characteristics seems to have reached the limits of its capacity to adapt.

REFERENCES

Altman, R.C. (2009), 'Globalization in Retreat', in *Foreign Affairs*, 88/4, pp 2-7.

Barber, L, Dyer, G. ;Kynge, J. Lifen Zhang (2009), Interview: Meassage from Wen Financial Times http://www.ft.com/cms/s/0/ae6805b4-f08c-11dd-972c-0000779fd2ac. html#axzz1 M9RW2IyX [access 2/3/2010],

Bergsten C. F., Gill B., Lardy N.R., / Mitchell D. (2006), *China. The Balance Sheet. What the world needs to know about the emerging superpower.* New York: Public Affairs.

Bergsten, C.F. (2008), 'Globalizing the Crisis Response', Op-ed in *The Washington Post*, 8th October 2008 <http://www.iie.com/publications/opeds/oped.cfm?ResearchID=05> [10th November 2008]

Brennan L (ed), *The Rise of Southern Multinationals,* Basingstok: Palgrave Macmillan.

Brodsgaard, K.E. and /Zheng Y (2006) (eds), *The Chinese Communist Party in* Reform, London: Routledge.

Brown, K., (2008), *The Rise of the Dragon: Inward and Outward Investment in China in the Reform Period 1978-2007.* Oxford: Chandos Publishing

Buzan, B. (2010), "China in International Society: Is 'Peaceful Rise' Possible?", *The Chinese Journal of International Politics*, Vol. 3, No. 1, pp. 5–36;

Cabestan, J.-P. (2004), 'Is China Moving Towards "Enlightened but Plutocratic Authoritarianism?', in *China Perspectives* [Online], at http://chinaperspectives.revues.org /412 [accessed 12 November 2010]

Caijing Online, (2009) Zhonghang jiangyu kejibu zai liu lingyu hezuo', *Caijing Online*, in 29 June 2009, at http://www.caijing.com.cn/2009-06-29/110190888.html (3 July 2009)

China Daily, (2005) UK to EU: Grant China Market Economy status, Chinadaily.com.cn http://www.chinadaily.com.cn/english/doc/2005-07/05/content_457312.htm [access 21/04/2008]

China Daily, (2010), China mulls $1.5t Strategic industries boost: sources, China Daily
    http://www.chinadaily.com.cn/bizchina/2010-12/03/content_11647452.htm
    [access 1/2/2011]

Clarke, D.C. (ed) (2005), *China's Legal System: New Developments, New Challenges*, The
    China Quarterly Special Issue. Cambridge MA.: Cambridge University Press.

Dickson B.J. (2003), *Red Capitalists in China: The Party, private Entrepreneurs, and the
    Prospects for Political Change*. New York: Cambridge University Press.

Ding X.L. (1994), "Institutional Amphibiousness and the Transition from Communism: The
    Case of China', in *British Journal of Political Science, Vol. 24*, No. 3, p 293-303.

Douglas N (1990) *Institutions, Institutional Change and Economic Performance*, Cambridge
    University Press,

Dreyer JT (2004). China's Political System: Modernization and Tradition (4th Edition)
    Longman.

Economy E (1999), 'The Impact of International Regimes on Foreign Policy-Making:
    Broadening Perspectives and Policies… but only to a Point', in D Lampton (ed.) (1999),
    The Making of Chinese Foreign and Security Policy in the Era of Reform. Stanford: SUP,
    p230-253,

Fan G (2008), 'China confronts the global meltdown', in *The Daily Times* (Pakistan), 23
    December 2008. At http://www.dailytimes.com.pk/default.asp?page=2008%5C12%5C
    23%5Cstory_23-12-2008_pg5_22

Gilley, B. (2006). 'Elite-Led Democratization in China: Prospects, Perils, and Policy
    Implications,' *International Journal of China* Studies, Vol. 61, No. 2; pp. 341-358.

Gottwald, J.-C. (2010), 'Cadre-Capitalism Goes Global: Financial Market Reforms and the
    New Role for the People's Republic of China in World Market', in Louis Brennan (ed),
    The Rise of Southern Multinationals, Basingstok: Palgrave Macmillan, pp 281-302.

Gottwald, J.C. (2011), 'China, ASEM and G 20: In Search of a New Global Financial
    Architecture', in S Bersick/P van der Velde/B Gaens (eds.), *ASEM 8: Towards a New
    Role in Global Governance*. Amsterdam: Amsterdam University Press (Forthcoming
    June 2011).

Gottwald, J.C. / and Duggan, N. (2011), *Hesitant Multi-Lateralist*, in S. Harnisch, C. Frank,
    H.W. Maull, (eds.), *Role Theory in International Relations,* London: Routledge pp 234-
    251

Gowan, P. (2009) 'Crisis in the Heartland. Consequences of the New Wall Street System', in
    New Left Review, No 55, January-February 2009, p.5-29.

Guoli L (2003), *Leadership Transition and Chinese Foreign Policy*, in *The Journal of
    Chinese Political Science*, Vol. 8, No 1 and 2, pp 101-117.

Halper, S. (2010), *The Beijing Consensus*, New York: Basic Books.

Heilmann J (2001) "Regulating China's Equity Market" [in German], *Asien*, No.80, July
    2001, pp.25-41.

Holbig, H. (2008). 'Ideological Reform and Political Legitimacy: Challenges in the Post-
    Jiang Era,' in Heberer, T. and Schubert, G. (eds). *Legitimacy in Contemporary China:
    Institutional Change and Stability*, London / New York: Routledge.

Institute of Economic and Resources Management Beijing Normal University (2005),
    'Review of the EU's Preliminary Assessment of China's Market Economy Status', in
    China and World Economy , Vol 13 No 2; pp 54-63.

Kim, S.S. (2009), 'China and Globalization: Confronting Myriad Opportunities and Challenges', in *Asian Perspective*, Vol. 33, No. 3, pp41-80.

Kynge, J. (2006), *China Shakes the World, The Rise of a Hungry Nation*, London: Orion books.

Lampton D (ed.) (1999), *The Making of Chinese Foreign and Security Policy in the Era of Reform*. Stanford: SUP, pp. 230-253.

Lampton, D.M. (2008), *The Three Faces of Chinese Power: Might, Money, and Minds*, Berkeley: University of California Press.

Lieberthal K, 2003, *Governing China: From Revolution to Reform 2nd Edition*, London:W.W. Northon and Company.

Lieberthal, K (1995), Governing China: from revolution through reform, W. W. Norton and Company, Inc. New York.

Mackinnon M (2009), As Japan"s exports, cave, all eyes turn to China', at http://business.theglobeandmail.com/servlet/story/RTGAM.20090226.wibtrade26/BNSto ry/Business/?page=rssandid=RTGAM.20090226.wibtrade26 (2 March 2009)

McNalty C (Ed) (2008), *China's Emergent Political Economy Capitalism in the Dragon's Lair* New York: Routledge.

Minxin P (2009), 'Will the Chinese Communist Party Survive the Crisis?" in *Foreign Affairs*, No.1, January / February 2009, at http://www.foreignaffairs.com/articles/64862/minxin-pei/will-the-chinese-communist-party-survive-the-crisis

Morrison, W.D. (2009), 'China and the Global Financial Crisis: Implications for the United States'. *Congressional Research Service*, February 9, 2009, at http://www.fas.org/sgp/crs /row/RS22984.pdf http://www.fas.org/sgp/crs/row/RS22984.pdf (21 February 2009).

Naughton, B. (2009), "Singularity and Replicability in China's Developmental Experience", China Analysis, No. 68, January <http://www.chinapolitik.de> [10th December 2010]

Niquet, V. (2009), "L'action politique en Chine: de la prise de dècision à la rèalisation", *Asie Vision*, No 14, Paris: ifri, pp5-8

OECD (2011), List of OECD Member countries - Ratification of the Convention on the OECD, OECD.org http://www.oecd.org/document/1/0,2340,en_2649_201185_1889402 _1_1_1_1,00.html [access 10/5/2011]

Polgreen, L. (2009), As Chinese Investment in Africa Drops, Hope Sinks, The New York Times http://www.nytimes.com/2009/03/26/world/africa/26chinaafrica.html?page wanted =1and_r=2andthandemc=th [access 2/10/2010]

Qi B (2009), *Quanqiu jinrong weiji xia de Zhongguo jihui*. In CNET, 17 September 2008.

Ramo, J.C. (2004), *The Beijing Consensus*, London: The Foreign Policy Center.

Remond, M. (2007), 'The EU's Refusal to Grant China 'Market Economy Status' (MES)', in *Asia Europe Journal* , Vol 5, No 3; pp 345-356.

Saich, T. (2005), *Governance and Politics of China*, Basingstoke: Palgrave Macmillan.

Schmidt, D. / Heilmann, S. (2009), *Dealing with Economic Crisis in 208 and 2009. The Chinese Government's Crisis Reaction in Comparative Perspective*. China Analysis No 77 (January 2010) At http://www.chinapolitik.de/studien/index.htm [accessed 12 January 2011]

Schwartz, N.D. (2009), 'Asia's recovery Highlights China's Ascendance', in *New York Times*, 24 August 2009 at http://www.nytimes.com/2009/08/24/business/global/24 global.html [access 21/2/2010]

Shambaugh, D. (2008), *China's Communist Party: Atrophy and Attrition*, Berkeley: University of California Press.

Shirk, S. (2007), *China Fragile Superpower: How China's Internal Policies Could Derail Its Peaceful Rise*, Oxford/New York: Oxford University Press.

State Council (2005), *China's Peaceful Development Road* www.china.org.cn/ennglish/2005 /Dec/152669.htm (10 January 2008).

Tai, Z (2006), *The Internet in China: Cyberspace and Civil Society*, New York: Routledge.

The Economist (2009) 'China and the West, A Time for muscle-flexing As Western economies flounder, China sees a chance to assert itself carefully.' At http://www.economist.com/node/13326082 [access 20/4/2010]

The Economist (2011), 'China's Crackdown. Repression and the New Ruling Class', in *The Economist*, 16th-22nd April 2011, p11 and pp51-52.

Tsai K.S. (2007), *Capitalism without Democracy. The Private Sector in Contemporary China.* Ithaca/London:Cornell University Press.

Tsai, K.S. (2007), *Capitalism without Democracy. The Private Sector in Contemporary China.* Ithaca/London:Cornell University Press.

Wacker, G. (2003) (ed) *China and the Internet: Policy of the Digital Leap Forward*, London: RoutledgeCurzon.

Wu G (2010), "China in 2009: Muddling through Crises?", in *Asian Survey*, Vol. 50, No. 1, pp. 25-3928.

Xinhua News Agency (2008), 'China's 4 trillion yuan stimulus to boost economy, domestic demand', at http://english.gov.cn/2008-11/09/content_1143763.htm (10 November 2008)

Yang D (2005), T*he Chinese Leviathan: Market Transition and the Politics of Governance in China*, Stanford: Stanford University Press.

Yang D (2005), *The Chinese Leviathan: Market Transition and the Politics of Governance in China*, Stanford: Stanford University Press.

Yu Y (2006),'The Role of the Media: A case Study of China's Media Coverage of the U.S. War in Iraq', in Yufan H and Lin S (eds) (2006), *China's Foreign Policy Making: Societal Force And Chinese American Policy*, Ashgate Publishing.

Zheng X (2008), 中共中央政策研究室副主任郑新立演讲, at http://www.sina.com.cn (16 Feb 2009).

Zhu L (2010); *China's Foreign Policy Debates* , Chaillot Papers No 121; Paris: EU Institute for Security Studies.

In: The Transformation of Asia …   ISBN: 978-1-61470-873-5
Editors: B. Andreosso-O'Callaghan and P. Herrmann   © 2012 Nova Science Publishers, Inc.

Chapter 7

THE CRISIS AND SOUTH KOREA

Órlaith Borthwick

ABSTRACT

This chapter examines the impact of the 2008 global economic crisis on the South Korean economy (hereafter referred to as the 'Korean economy'), an economy that avoided a prolonged recession despite the global turmoil. It shall present an overview of some key economic indicators and government policies pursued to highlight the classic V-shaped recovery that has occurred in the economy. The chapter shall also examine the Korean response to the 2008 crisis and investigate if the lessons learned from the 1997 Asian currency crisis furnished Korea with the necessary tools to bounce back from the 2008 crisis more quickly.

INTRODUCTION

Korea is perceived as being a rather successful international economy. The Organisation of Economic Cooperation and Development (OECD, 2008) found that this small[1] country on the periphery of East-Asia has the world's highest ranking IQ, with students excelling in subjects such as mathematics, science, problem solving and reading. The country also has the most sophisticated IT infrastructure in the world, and was the first country to boast having Digital Multimedia Broadcasting,[2] Wireless Broadband (WiBro) and 100Mbit/s broadband. Indeed, the world's first cloned dog '*Snuppy*' was created at the country's most esteemed third level institute, Seoul National University (SNU). The 'knowledge economy' tag that other countries are so desperately trying to clutch at and promote is a historical reality for

---

[1] The population of Korea is much smaller than other countries in Asia. With a population of 48,747,000 Korea is just over one-third the size of Japan (with a population of 127,560,000) while India and China operate on a different plateau with populations of 1,155,347,678 and 1,331,460,000 respectively (The World Bank, 2010a).

[2] DMB is Digital Multimedia Broadcasting and was developed in South Korea. European countries such as Norway, Germany and France have introduced DMB broadcasting, while trials are occurring in other countries such as Canada, Ghana and the Vatican City.

Koreans. Korea is the 11th largest exporting country in the world, led by exports of cars, electronics and semiconductors and by international brand names such as Hyundai, Kia, Daewoo, LG, Samsung and Hynix. Korea is the largest shipbuilder in the world, is the third largest economy in Asia and the 13th largest in the world.

So how did this former Asian Tiger survive the recent collapse in world financial markets instigated by the collapse of Lehman Brothers on the 20th September 2008 and the subsequent ripples that rocked some of the most advanced and developed economies of the world? The answer is very simple: Korea bounced as quickly out of negative growth as it bounced into it, based on aggressive and timely government policies, - having entered into the turmoil with healthy corporate and bank balance sheets that facilitated a swift rebound -, and a flexible exchange rate system.

The Korean economy was hit hard by the crisis. The tightening of global financial flows and the sharp decline in international demand had a serious and sudden effect on the economy. With a high reliance on wholesale funding, bank credit default swaps (CDS) spreads spiked and capital left the country at an unprecedented rate, resulting in the collapse of asset prices (International Monetary Fund, 2009). Coupled with a slump in exports,[3] a hit to the domestic market was inevitable and by March 2009 consumer goods sales had fallen by 5.2 percent when compared with the previous year (Lall, 2010). Indeed the Korean economy experienced one of "the sharpest contractions worldwide" (International Monetary Fund, 2009, p.3) when growth fell by 5.1 percent quarter-on-quarter in the last quarter of 2008. However this decline did not last and by the first quarter of 2009 Korea had recorded a positive 0.2 percent GDP growth rate quarter-on-quarter, as illustrated in figure 7.1.

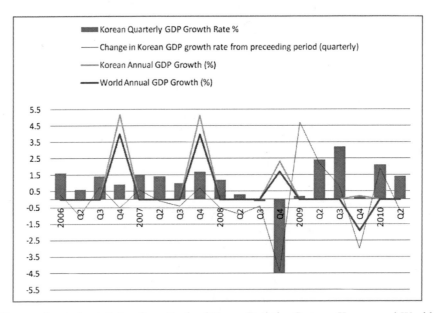

Source: Korean Quarterly statistics from Bank of Korea Statistics System. Korean and World Annual growth rates from World Bank World Development Indicators. October 2010.

Figure 7.1. Korean and World GDP growth rates. Quarterly, Q1 2006 – Q2 2010.

---

[3] In January 2009 Korean exports were down 35 percent year-on-year.

The stabilisation of the economy by the first quarter of 2009 paved the way for the recovery that followed, and while output in advanced economies contracted continuously throughout 2009[4], the Korean economy posted positive growth rates. One year on from the initial shock that led to global financial turmoil, by the third quarter of 2009 Korea had recorded the fastest pace of growth in the country for seven years backed by rising exports, industrial output and investment. Indeed Korea recorded an annual growth rate of 2.3 percent for 2008, ahead of world growth which fell to 1.7 percent for the same period. By the end of 2009, the divergence between the performance of the Korean economy and the rest of the world had really emerged, because while the Korean economy posted an annual growth rate of 0.2 percent, the world GDP rate had contracted by 1.9 percent[5] and advanced economies as a whole posted a 3.1 percent decline (Lall, 2010). The International Monetary Fund (IMF), which had to bailout Korea with a loan of $60 billion to stabilise the economy in the aftermath of the 1997 crisis, estimate that the Korean economy would expand by 6.1 percent in 2010 easing to 4.5 percent in 2011 (International Monetary Fund, 2010).

How has Korea, a relatively small country on the periphery of Asia, a country that is extremely exposed to external shocks as it relies heavily on exports,[6] managed, and from this point of departure, how did it avoid the severe shocks caused by the global depression which affected more advanced economies so harshly? The answer is the successful culmination of decisive front-loaded[7] fiscal and monetary policies enacted by the government which stimulated domestic demand.

These policies were coupled with functioning banking and corporate sectors which reaped the benefits of reform measures that were introduced after the 1997 Asian financial crisis. By providing various funding mechanisms the government eased access to bank credit pressures thereby enabling firms to expand and grow their previously impressive diversified export portfolio of products and markets.

The undervalued won allowed Korea to compete more aggressively on global markets and take full advantage of the demand growth in developing countries. All these culminated in a healthy macroeconomic recovery with industrial output and sales growth increasing, unemployment remaining low and inflationary pressures eased.

This chapter is laid out as follows: Section 1 gives an overview of the Korean economy, before detailing various government fiscal and monetary policy measures adopted to deal with the international banking crisis in 2008 and contrasting this to the country's response to the Asian financial crisis in 1997; Section 2 examines the underlying stability and diversity of certain Korean financial and economic indicators, namely the banking and corporate sector as well as export growth and diversity; Section 3 outlines some of the main differences between the Korean economy entering into the 2008 crisis and the Korean economy before the Asian currency crisis in 1997, showing how the lessons learned from 1997 allowed a more constructive response to 2008. Finally, an overview of the future direction and challenges facing Korea are explored.

---

[4] The International Monetary Fund estimate that "world GDP in 2009 was less than in the year before for the first time in more than 60 years" Shafer, J.R., 2010, p.14.

[5] Annual GDP Growth Rates are sourced from the World Development Bank, Indicators Database (The World Bank, 2010b) The United States had a negative growth rate of 2.4 percent, while the Japanese and United Kingdom economies reported a negative GDP rate of -5 percent and Ireland a staggering -6 percent.

[6] Exports accounted for 60 percent of Gross National Income (GNI) in Korea in Q4 of 2008.

[7] The government spent 68 percent of their economic recovery stimulus budget in the first seven months of 2009.

1. GOVERNMENT POLICY

To sustain the real economy, the government introduced major fiscal and monetary *stimuli*, and established a toxic asset fund to avoid major deleveraging as well as a bank recapitalisation fund of 20 trillion won. This fund was used to replenish banks capital and encourage them to lend. It was funded by the Bank of Korea which pumped in 10 trillion won, public and institutional investors who provided 8 trillion won *via* the purchase of securities with varying maturities, and the state owned Korea Development Bank which funded the remaining 2 trillion won (Reuters, 2008).

The government's supplementary budget introduced in 2009, and the 2010 budget, focused on short-term policies (which are detailed below) aimed at achieving economic growth and recovery; while medium-term policies pursing fiscal soundness are being rolled out between 2009 and 2013.

The government's priorities in the 2010 budget were to improve the standard of living, create jobs, and enhance growth potential while raising Korea's status in the international community.

1.1. Fiscal Policy

As the collapse of the subprime mortgage market wiped out Wall Street and the ripples started to have global consequences, the Korean government, with the acute pain of the 1997 crisis still fresh in their minds, acted swiftly with a large fiscal stimulus package ranging from expenditure expansion on infrastructural projects and support measures for SMEs, to reductions in tax rates to corporations and individuals. The government stimulus packages, introduced between 2008 and 2010, amounted to 70.5 trillion Korean won, a ratio of 6.9 percent of GDP[8] (Jun-kyu, 2010).

The government allocated as much as 67 trillion won as a stimulus package that focused on infrastructural projects, cash handouts for households as well as providing cheap loans and creating job opportunities. Support for businesses included tax benefits, improved financing opportunities and business friendly regulations for both larger and smaller companies. A corporate investment stimulus package introduced tax reductions and deductions: corporation tax was cut from 25 percent to 20 percent for the tax base of 200 million won and from 13 percent to 10 percent for 100 million won or less; and in order to promote R&D investment in core technologies, the government introduced up to a 25 percent tax deduction to larger corporations and 35 percent for SMEs. In addition, 17 new growth areas were identified, and RandD investment in these areas availed of up to a 20 percent tax deduction for large corporations and 30 percent for SMEs; a tax credit for investment in energy saving facilities was expanded from 10 percent to 20 percent. In addition to providing tax breaks for business the government, through The Bank of Korea, offered subsidized loans to SMEs via commercial banks. Loan guarantees of up to 100 percent were offered and banks were instructed to roll over all SME loans falling due in 2009.

---

[8] This compares with a ratio of "5.6 percent in the United States, 4.7 percent in Japan and 1.9 percent in the United Kingdom" Jun-kyu, 2010, p.11.

The private sector was supported through income transfers introduced to lower-income households and various supports for the construction industry also helped boost domestic demand. Income tax rates were cut by 2 percentage points in each tax bracket for 2010, from 8 percent to 6 percent and 35 percent to 33 percent. Capital gains tax was decreased from 36 percent to 33 percent, and tax refunds for the self-employed and workers of up to 240,000 won per year were made available to ease the pressure of increasing oil prices.

Of course the government's ability to introduce such immediate measures without the risk of sovereign debt which threatened other countries was aided by the healthy budget surplus of the Korean government.[9] As illustrated in figures 7.2 and 7.16, the Korean government has maintained a surplus on the current account with current revenues continuously exceeding current expenditure.[10] Overall, the country has run a budget deficit, but this is being driven primarily by expenditure on capital projects which has soared to 45,134 billion won in the year to December 2009 and to a lesser extent by net lending and acquisitions which increased from 5,480 billion won in 2008 to 18,049 billion won during 2009. However, if a country is to run a deficit in its government finances this is the most healthy way to do it; other countries, such as Ireland have struggled to meet current expenditure demands, highly inflated by the recapitalisation of non-performing banks, and have been forced to borrow on the international markets spiralling the economy into long-term debt and recession.

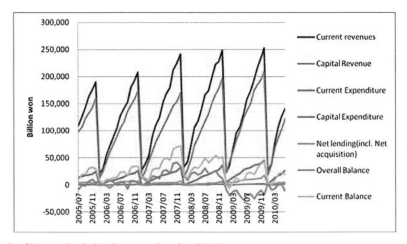

Source: Bank of Korea Statistics System, October 2010.

Figure 7.2. Korean Government Financial Statistics: Annual Current and Capital Revenue and Expenditure, annual cumulative. Monthly, 01/ 2007 – 09/2010.

The medium-term focus and long-term fiscal policies of the Korean government are on increased spending in social welfare to support the working classes, decreasing temporary support offered to weather the crisis, and cutting subsidies given to projects which yield low

[9] The Korean Central government overall balance was 33.8 trillion won in 2007 or 3.5 percent of GDP. This fell to 11.9 trillion won in 2008, 1.2 percent of GDP. By 2009 the government ran a deficit of 17.6 trillion won, or -1.7 percent of GDP. However it is projected that the government will return to surplus this year equivalent to an estimated 0.9 percent of GDP (IMF, 2010, p.26).

[10] The annual current account surplus was 34,403 billion won in 2006; 72,035 billion won in 2007; 51,930 billion won in 2008 and up to September 2010 was running at 19,439 billion won.

returns on investment or deliver poor performance. Other measures such as broadening the tax base and lowering income tax rates are to be introduced, while a decrease in the level of tax breaks available to the high income earners and larger corporations in tandem with increases in tax breaks for SMEs and the self-employed are to be rolled-out.

It is projected that most of the fiscal stimulus introduced in the original and supplementary budgets in 2009 will not be renewed in the next budget. This will allow a more natural adjustment of the economy to the changed global economy. This reduction in economic stimulus has been estimated by the IMF to decrease the government deficit to 1.5 percent of GDP, following a deficit of 4.1 percent in 2009 (International Monetary Fund, 2010, p.9).

1.2. Monetary Policy

As illustrated in figure 7.3 the Korean won depreciated *vis-à-vis* the US dollar from 1,089 won per dollar in August 2008 to peak at 1,534 won per dollar by February 2009. From August 2008 to March 2009 the Korean won/US dollar exchange rate depreciated by 33 percent; or in nominal effective terms by 25 percent taking into account the overall composition of Korea's trading partners (Lall, 2010). Despite a 22 percent appreciation of the won between March 2009 and June 2010 the real effective exchange rate still remains about 8 percent below pre-crisis levels (International Monetary Fund, 2010). The weak won redirected domestic demand away from imports, and coupled with falling oil prices the current account deficit of 3.75 percent of GDP in the third quarter of 2008 changed to a 4.5 percent surplus in the first quarter of 2009. Although reserves fell to $200 billion by the end of 2008, they have since returned to growth and are now higher than pre-crisis levels at $290 billion.[11] The weak won also stabilised inflation, which having peaked in December 2008 at 5.6 percent, however consistently fell throughout 2009 and is at 1.9 percent as of September 2010, which lies well within the Bank of Korea's 3 percent ±1 percent range (figure 7.4). By not intervening and allowing the currency to float, the government pursued a completely different policy than in 1997 when it directly intervened in the market to defend the value of the won resulting in the decimation of the official reserves[12], as illustrated in figure 7.5.

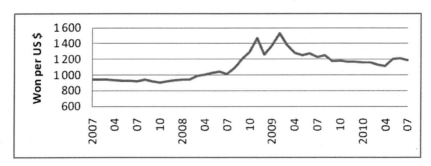

Source: The Bank of Korea, 2010.

Figure 7.3. Korean won US $ exchange rate. Monthly, 01/2007 – 07/2010.

---

[11] Before the on-set of the crisis Korean International Reserves were valued at $262 billion (as at January 2007).
[12] As illustrated in figure 5 Korean holdings of foreign currency fell to $19 billion in December 1997.

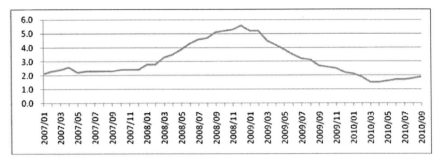

Source: The Bank of Korea, 2010

Figure 7.4. Korean Core inflation, percentage change. Monthly, 01/2007 – 09/2010.

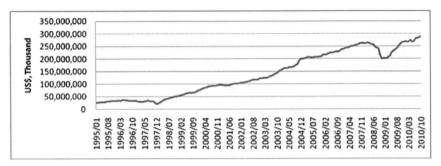

Source: Bank of Korea Statistics System, November 2010. *note over 90% of Korean total international reserves are held in foreign currency reserves; as at October 2010 98.41% of Korea's international reserves are held in international currency. Therefore other sources of international reserves are not analysed.

Figure 7.5. Korean Foreign Currency Reserves. Monthly, 01/1995 – 10/2010.

This change in policy is one of the most striking differences between the two crises; in 1997, the Korean government had no choice but to intervene to defend the won given the speculative attacks on East-Asian currencies at the time. In 2008, despite volatility in the exchange rate, a floating currency "contributed to saving official reserves as well as helping (or forcing) the private sector to quickly adjust to a new currency value and generate a current account surplus" (Dongchul Cho, August 2009, p.14). In addition, by not intervening and allowing market conditions to dictate the exchange rate, the government were free to pursue a more flexible monetary policy than had been available to them in 1997, specifically targeting interest rates.

The Bank of Korea (BOK) reduced its base rate six times from 5.25 percent in October 2008 to an all-time low of 2 percent by early 2009. This rapidly eased monetary conditions and allowed SMEs, larger corporations and households improved borrowing conditions. The rate was increased for the first time since February 2009 when the BOK raised it by 25 basis points in July 2010. The pursuit of a monetary policy aimed at increasing the demand for money is in stark contrast to the policy pursued in 1997 when the interest rate target was increased by the Bank of Korea (BOK) to 30 percent. It is evident that the improved circular flow of money and resulting demand impetus that have been encouraged by the reduction of interest rate during this global recession has had a much more positive effect on the Korean economy, than the dampening of consumption and expenditure in the economy that occurred when there was strangulation of access to credit in 1997.

By not using their foreign reserves to defend the currency, the government was free to support the banking system. In the wake of the crisis, with the striking contraction in the economy and the perceived risk of default by Korean banks, the government set aside $55 billion in foreign exchange reserves to substitute for loans that had up to this crisis been provided by foreign creditors. Indeed the greatest vulnerability to the 2008 crisis of Korean banks was their over- reliance on wholesale funding. It is not surprising that at the onset of the panic in the wake of the reversal of wholesale bank lending owing to liquidity pressures, from September to December 2008, there was an outflow of $50 billion from Korean banks. However the government intervened and took the necessary measures to provide foreign exchange liquidity not only by assuring international markets of the safety of Korean banks, but concluding swap agreements to the value of $90 billion[13] with the central banks of Japan China and the United States (International Monetary Fund, 2009; Jun-kyu, 2010; Shafer, 2010). In addition, the Bank of Korea also maintained a 10 billion US dollar credit line with the Bank of Japan as part of a separate emergency agreement within the Chiang Mai Initiative framework. Korean banks have since tightened up having "raised their average capital adequacy ratio to 14.6 percent, 2 percentage points above pre-crisis levels" (International Monetary Fund, 2010, p.2).

2. UNDERLYING STABILITY AND DIVERSITY

One of the major differences between the Korean economy entering the global economic crisis in 2008 and the Korean economy when the currency crisis hit Asian countries in 1997 was the banking and corporate sector. Under the guidance of the IMF the Korean economy completely transformed its previously corrupt, over-indebted and non-transparent banking and corporate sectors. Indeed, what were the stumbling blocks to recovery in 1997 became the tools facilitating such a speedy upturn following 2008.

2.1. Banking and Corporate Sector

The avalanche of sub-prime mortgage defaults that caused the collapse of Lehman Brothers resulted from the fact that financial authorities were not able to discern the scale of credit or liquidity risk from asset securitisation. Following the reorganisation of the Korean banking system post-1997, Korea, however, had maintained a highly regulated bank-orientated financial system and was therefore far less exposed to the market-orientated policies that had been pursed in the USA and other countries. For example, Korean securities companies' share of investment banking business was only 5 percent in 2005; this figure was 45 percent for US securities companies (Dong-Irwan, 2009). Entering the turmoil of the 2008 global crisis, Korea had a foreign currency reserve of more than $200 billion, 10 times higher than their reserve before their 1997 crisis. In addition, following the improved banking and financial structures introduced after the 1997 crisis, Korean banks entered the 2008 crisis with

---

[13]Some $16.35 billion of this was drawn at the peak of the crisis (IMF, 2009).

healthy balance sheets and a capital adequacy ratio of 12.3 percent at the end of September 2008 (International Monetary Fund, 2010, p.28); this is in contrast to 7 percent in 1997. The ratios of non-performing loans (NPLs) have remained low[14] although savings banks have a much higher rate of NPLs due to their exposure in the construction industry. However, in effect, the Korean government and banking sector had created a financial buffer having learned the lessons from the 1997 crisis to ensure they had the necessary liquidity to bail themselves out of any financial and economic turmoil.

Having gone through a complete corporate governance and transparency overhaul following the 1997 crisis, the larger Korean corporations and *chaebol* also had healthy balance sheets entering the 2008 crisis with low debt to equity ratios of 131 percent in comparison to a rate of 426 percent in 1997. Indeed, their cash rich status coupled with an undervalued won allowed them to expand and capitalise their market share, while other global players struggled to secure finance, thereby facilitating export growth and securing future markets.

As a response to banks exposure to non-performing loans and impaired assets in the wake of the 1997 crisis, the government established the Korean Asset Management Corporation (KAMCO). To date KAMCO has recovered 110 percent on the assets it then bought (International Monetary Fund, 2009). On these returns, it is safe to say that KAMCO has the necessary experience and expertise to handle the valuation process of purchasing toxic and nonperforming assets from banks arising from the current crisis. However, of the 40 trillion won restructuring fund facility made available, only 1.2 trillion won has been utilised, although it was estimated that an additional 2.5 trillion won worth of construction-related nonperforming loans would be purchased during 2010.

2.2. Export Growth

The flexible exchange rate system, coupled with the various government measures introduced to improve the flow of credit in support of the growth and expansion of indigenous industries enabled Korean firms to expand into foreign markets. Korean's traditional dependency on a few export markets had been completely transformed since the 1997 crisis.

In 2000, there was almost a 50/50 split between Korean exports to developed and developing countries; by 2008, less than one-third of Korean exports were destined for developed countries, while 69 percent were to developing countries. Korea's traditional dependency on the United States and Europe as main export destinations had been reduced in recent years,[15] which diminished the potential exposure for Korea to the 2008 crisis. As illustrated in figure 7.6, the value of exports change from month to month increased from a negative 34.5 percent in January 2009 to a positive 33.7 percent growth by the end of the year (Jun-kyu, 2010). Korea's remarkable export growth from the start of 2009[16] was driven

---

[14] Although this is partly due to write-offs.

[15] The USA accounted for 22 percent of the value of total Koean exports in 2000. By 2009 this had more than halved to less than 11 percent (Korean International Trade Association, 2010)

[16] Korea's current account surplus stood about $21.7 billion for the first six months of 2009 and was approximately $21 billion for the second half of the year (Jun-kyu, 2010). The surplus for the first nine months of 2010 is in excess of $29 billion.

primarily by export growth to China, as seen in figure 7.7, which now accounts for one-quarter of all Korean exports.

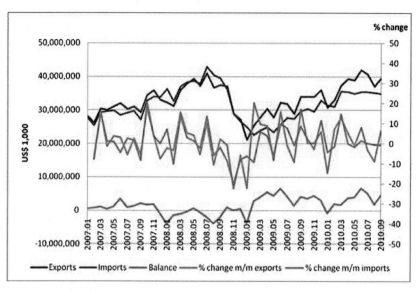

Source: Korean International Trade Association, 2010.

Figure 7.6. Value of Korean exports, imports and trade balance (US$1000). Monthly % change in exports and imports, 01/2007 – 09/ 2010.

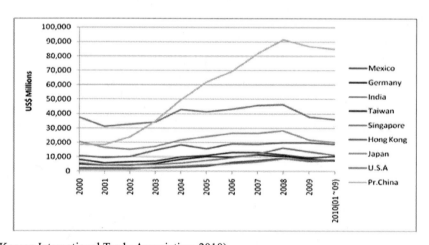

Source: Korean International Trade Association, 2010).

Figure 7.7. Korean Exports by destination country (selected). Yearly, 2000 – 09/2010.

In addition, Korea has always maintained a strong surplus on its trade account with China (figure 7.8), and while Korean exports to China fell year-on-year by 5 percent in 2009, Korean imports of Chinese goods fell by almost 30 percent during the same period. Despite an overall trade deficit of $13 billion in 2008, Korea had a $41 billion trade surplus in 2009 and up to September 2010 had amassed a $29 billion surplus.

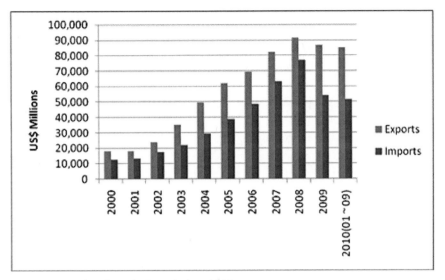

Source: Korean International Trade Association, 2010.

Figure 7.8. Korean trade balance with the People's Republic of China. Yearly, 2000 – 09/2010.

Indeed, the country has consistently maintained a surplus on its balance of goods account since the start of 2009, while at the same time consistently running a deficit in the balance of services account. The overall surplus of goods and services enjoyed by the country is not only driven by trade in goods, but it has been helped by the drastic decline in demand for imported goods. Throughout 2011, it will be interesting to see how the recovery in domestic demand will impact on import recovery and narrow the trade surplus which Korea has accumulated.

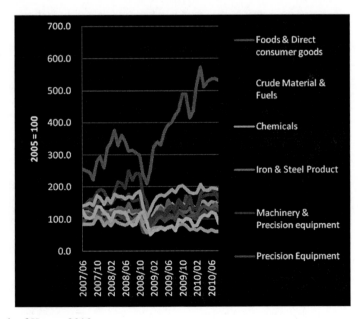

Source: The Bank of Korea, 2010.

Figure 7.9. Volume index of Korean exports by sector. Monthly, 06/2007 – 08/2010.

Export growth, as illustrated in figure 7.9, has been driven by Korea's strong presence in the semi-conductor sector.

Although the volume of exports in this sector slumped in December 2008, the volume had by August 2010 increased more than two-fold from pre-crisis levels[19]; indeed the volume of exports in the sector increased by 97 percent from December 2008 to December 2009, with a further 28 percent increase in the first eight months of 2010. The other strong export growth market for Korea has been Liquid Crystal Display Devices (LCDs), as depicted in figure 7.9 as part of the 'electric machine for domestic purposes' sector. The August 2010 volume of exports in this sector also exceeded pre-crisis levels[20]; having increased by 79 percent from November 2008 to November 2009 with a further growth of 17 percent in the first eight months of 2010.

3. DIFFERENCES BETWEEN 1997 AND 2008

One of the primary differences between the currency crisis that swept through Asia in 1997 and the global financial collapse that sent the world in recession in 2008, on the Korean economy has been domestic demand and export growth. In 1997, the external shock of the currency run on the Thai Bhat had a knock on effect in Korea and domestic demand slumped, and although exports continued to grow modestly, their growth was not enough to offset a huge decline in GDP. In 2008, the external shock of the collapse of the subprime market in the US and the global turmoil that followed sharply affected Korean exports, particularly to developed economies. However, in 2008, domestic demand remained strong and drove growth while exporters focused on new opportunities for growth in new markets.

The recovery was supported by both public and private expenditure on consumption and investment. As illustrated in figure 7.10, private consumption and investment in facilities and construction all recorded negative growth rates in the fourth quarter of 2008. However, by the start of 2009 both private consumption and construction investment had recorded positive growth with facilities investment following this positive trend by the second quarter. Although government spending did decline by 0.8 percent at the start of 2009, it was government stimulus packages that were pushing the expansion in facilities investment with a total of 10 trillion won being made available, with a subsequent increase to 20 trillion won in line with fiscal expansion in 2010.

The unemployment rate peaked at 5 percent in January 2010 but receded back to 3.3 percent by August 2010 (figure 7.11). This was also a welcome change from the previous external shock that shook the Korean economy in the aftermath of the 1997 currency crisis when the unemployment rate peaked at 7.2 percent. The number of people remaining in work has stabilised and remained high due to two factors; firstly, domestic demand remained strong and secondly, restructuring of employment patterns were introduced with people opting to work less hours and accepting a decrease in wages to maintain greater numbers in the work place, as illustrated in figure 7.12. This supply side adjustment to the economy has allowed the demand and supply of labour remain at equilibrium.

---

[19] The index of export volume in semi-conductors was 256.1 in June 2007. By August 2010 it had increased to 532.2.

[20] The volume of exports index in this sector was 89.9 in June 2007. It slumped to 58.2 in November 2008 but has since recovered to 129.0 by August 2010.

Growth indicators for the Korean economy are strong, GDP growth is positive (figure 7.1) and export volumes are increasing, particularly in the semi-conductor sector (figure 7.9). In addition business and consumer sentiment indices are showing signs of improvement[21].

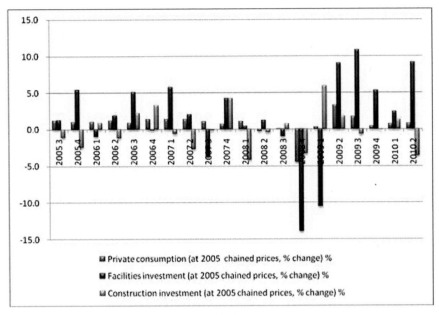

Source: Bank of Korea Statistics System, October 2010.

Figure 7.10. Korean Private Consumption, Facilities Investment and Construction Investment. Quarterly, Q3 2006 – Q2 2010.

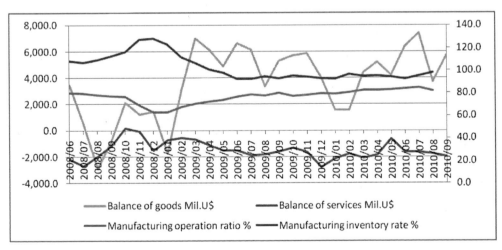

Source: The Bank of Korea, 2010.

Figure 7.11. Korea's unemployment rate. Monthly, 01/ 2006 –08/ 2010.

---

[21] As illustrated in figure 13 the Korean consumer sentiment index has increased from a low of 81 in December 2008 to 108 by October 2010.

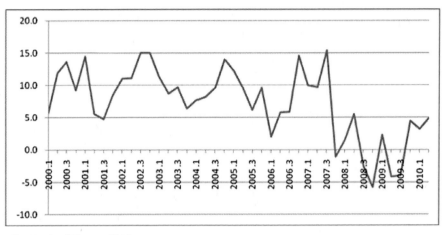

Source: The Bank of Korea, 2010.

Figure 7.12. Korean per hour wages at current prices (% change). Quarterly, Q1 2000 – Q2 2010.

Financial market conditions have also stabilised, with the stock market having gained more than 70 percent in value in the first half of 2010 (International Monetary Fund, 2010). The inflation rate is likely to remain well within the target range and a surplus is expected on the current account. As illustrated in figure 7.14, the manufacturing production index has increased substantially[25] since its trough in January 2009 as has the service industry activities.

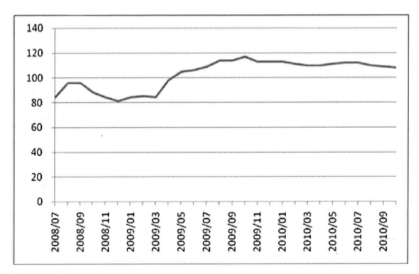

Source: Bank of Korea Statistics System, November 2010.

Figure 7.13. Korean Consumer Survey Index, National. Composite Consumer Sentiment Index. Monthly. 07/2008 – 10/2010.

---

[25] The manufacturing production index has increased from 91.7 in January 2009 to 139.2 by September 2010; the manufacturing shipment index has increased from 91.3 in January 2009 to 133.8 by October 2010 (The Bank of Korea, 2010).

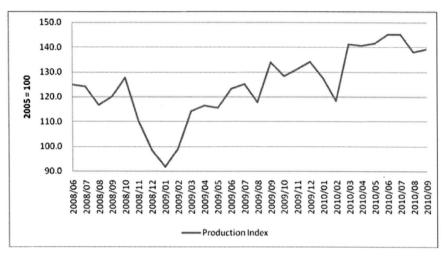

Source: The Bank of Korea, 2010.

Figure 7.14. Manufacturing Industry Production Index. Monthly, 06/2008 – 09/2010.

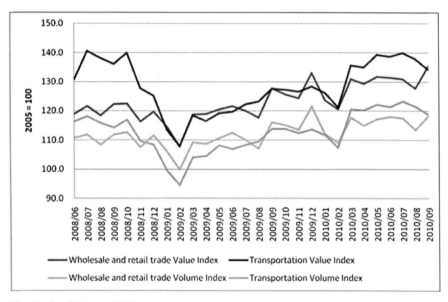

Source: The Bank of Korea, 2010.

Figure 7.15. Korean selected Service industry activities indices. Monthly, 06/2008 – 09/2010.

The service sector, which has a greater impact on domestic demand, has also staged an impressive recovery since the impact of the crisis in late 2008 and early 2009 (figure 7.15). The manufacturing operations ratio has increased consistently since the crisis and the manufacturing inventory rate decreased from a peak of 128.3 percent in December 2008 to 98 percent by August 2010 (figure 7.16).

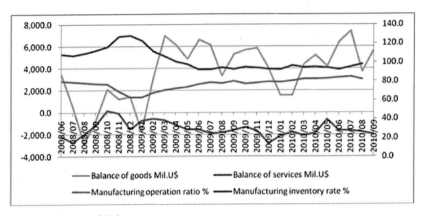

Source: The Bank of Korea, 2010.

Figure 7.16. Korean Manufacturing operations and inventory (%) and balance of goods and services (US$ million). Monthly.

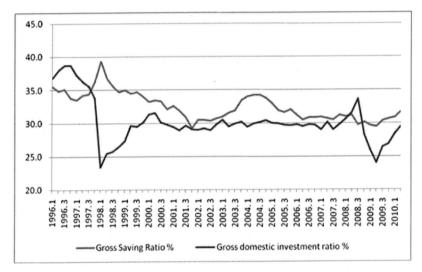

Source: Bank of Korea Statistics System, November 2010.
Note: The Bank of Korea define Gross savings ratio as gross saving/gross national disposable income and Gross domestic investment ratio as gross capital formation/GNDI.

Figure 7.17. Korean domestic investment and savings ratios. Quarterly, Q1 1996 – Q2 2010.

However a worrying trend, as mentioned above and illustrated in figure 7.16, is Korea's consistent deficit on its balance of services account. Although the balance of goods account has improved considerably since the crisis, the services balance remains in deficit. Another trend which policy makers must address is the decreasing domestic savings and investment ratio of households.

As illustrated in figure 7.17, when the currency crisis hit in 1997 the gross domestic savings ratio was circa 40 percent; by the start of 2008, this had fallen to 31 percent. It since reached a historic low of 24 percent by mid-2009. Similarly, the 1997 currency crisis severely dented gross domestic investment, with a slump in early 1998 to 23.4 percent. This slump was mirrored when the global crisis affected the country in early 2009, with domestic investment once again falling to 24 percent.

Coupled with successful government policy, domestic investment has since increased; however, investment must continue if this trend is to be maintained. In addition, household debt, although mainly applicable to high-income households with access to financial assets, still remains above the OECD average and is something that needs to be monitored (International Monetary Fund, 2010).

CONCLUSION

What does – sketched against this background – the future hold for the Korean economy? Macroeconomically, the vital signs for the economy are of envy of many countries which, in the backdrop of the 2008 global crisis, continue to struggle, to regain confidence in their currencies and government policies. Korea's GDP growth is positive and accelerating, export growth is strong, inflation remains within the Bank of Korea target range and employment levels are enviable. How have the Koreans managed this? The lessons learned by the country following the 1997 crisis have been paramount in allowing the Korean government design and implement the right policies at the right time. Following the IMF bailout in 1997, the country tightened and adhered to strict financial practices, forced strict reorganisations of banks and corporations ensuring greater transparency while building up healthy balance sheets and reserves. One can only hope that other economies and countries that are in turmoil will now learn, like the Koreans, from their mistakes and in doing so, ensure that when turbulent times hit international markets in the future, as will inevitably happen, that they have the necessary resolve and reserves to cope.

However, despite the healthy macroeconomic variables some worrying underlying problems exist in the economy. Firstly, the withdrawal of government stimulus packages which saw the economy weather the international crisis will allow a more natural adjustment to a changed global environment and it will be interesting to see how these adjustments will affect domestic demand both for indigenous and imported goods, and the impact that this will have on both the current account and the exchange rate. The economy relies heavily on the export of manufactured goods; the ability of the country to bullishly exploit potential growth markets and diversify their product mix in the midst of a global crisis is admirable. However, much of the growth in the manufacturing sector, through demand side expansionary fiscal policies, has been at the expense of developing the services sector which contributes 55 percent to GDP (Dongchul Cho, August 2009). More policies which improve the supply and demand side of the economy, such as policy measures to boost the services sectors to enhance their productivity, need to be pursed (Dongchul Cho, August 2009). Other potential risks to the continued recovery are tensions on the peninsula between South and North Korea and the threat that these may pose for South Korean international relations with key trade partners; as well as the potential for the problems in Europe to adversely spillover on Korea. However, one of the key and increasing challenges for Korea is its ageing population. It has the lowest fertility rate among OECD countries[26] and "its population over the age of 65 is projected to increase from 11 percent in 2010 to 38.5 percent by 2050" (International Monetary Fund,

---

[26] Which stands at 1.15 children per woman in 2009 (International Monetary Fund, 2010, p.5).

2010, p.5). Government have begun to address the challenges this will create with the launch of Korea's *Master Plan preparing for Ageing Society (2011-2015)* but many challenges still lie ahead.

REFERENCES

Dong-Irwan, K. (2009). The Wall Street Panic and the Korean Economy. In *Korea's Economy 2009* (Vol. 25). Washington: Korea Economic Institute and the Korea Institute for International Economic Policy.

Dongchul Cho. (August 2009). *The Republic of Korea's Economy in the Swirl of Global Crisis*. Tokyo: Asian Development Bank Instituteo. Document Number).

International Monetary Fund. (2009). *Republic of Korea: Staff Report for the 2009 Article IV Consultation* (Vol. 09/262). Washington D.C.: International Monetary Fund.

International Monetary Fund. (2010). *Republic of Korea: Staff Report for the 2010 Article IV Consultation* (Vol. 10/270). Washington D.C.: International Monetary Fund.

Jun-kyu, L. (2010). Korea's Economic Stability and Resilience in Times of Crisis. In *Korea's Economy 2010* (Vol. 26). Washington: Korea Economic Institute and the Korea Institute for International Economic Policy.

Korean International Trade Association. (2010). Trade Statistics Database. Retrieved various dates October and November 2010, from http://www.kita.org/

Lall, S. (2010). Korea's Economic Prospects and Challenges. In *Korea's Economy 2010* (Vol. 26). Washington: Korea Economic Institute and the Korea Institute for International Economic Policy.

OECD. (2008). *PISA 2006: Volume 2: Data*. Paris: OECD Publishing.

Reuters. (2008). FACTBOX: A look at South Korea's bank recapitalisation fund. Retrieved 23.12.2010, from http://in.reuters.com/article/idINSEO22076220081218

Shafer, J. R. (2010). The Republic of Korea and the North Pacific Economy: After the Great Panic of 2008. In *Korea's Economy 2010* (Vol. 26). Washington: Korea Economic Institute and the Korea Institute for International Policy.

The Bank of Korea. (2010). Economics Statistics System. Retrieved various dates October and November, 2010, from http://ecos.bok.or.kr/EIndex_en.jsp

The World Bank. (2010a). World Development Indicators. *Population, total* Retrieved 13.10.2010, from http://data.worldbank.org/indicator/SP.POP.TOTL

The World Bank. (2010b). World Development Indicators. *GDP growth, annual %* Retrieved 20.12.2010, from http://data.worldbank.org/indicator/NY.GDP.MKTP.KD.ZG

In: The Transformation of Asia …
ISBN: 978-1-61470-873-5
Editors: B. Andreosso-O'Callaghan and P. Herrmann © 2012 Nova Science Publishers, Inc.

Chapter 8

BUSINESS GROUPS IN THE GLOBAL RECESSION: THE CASE OF THE JAPANESE KEIRETSU

Tomoko Oikawa

ABSTRACT

In this chapter, we focus on the Japanese business groups – *keiretsu* – in the background of the current global recession, and examine how they are managing through this crisis. *Keiretsu* has been the basic strategy of successful business performance in Japan.

Conventional views on *keiretsu* may have highlighted the changing relationships and diminishing influence of *keiretsu*, faced with the disastrous global crisis. In fact, *keiretsu* transaction relationships are developing closer information exchanges between participating enterprises, as an aid for business survival and sales increase, which has led to increased numbers of enterprises in the *keiretsu* networks. *Keiretsu* is changing and branching off into more complex relationships. However, the principles of *keiretsu* have not changed. These are essentially the core values in Japanese society.

We have attempted to demonsrate that the *keiretsu* is essential to survive this unprecended economic crisis with these principles intact.

INTRODUCTION

The global recession has had a serious impact on the Japanese economy. This has added to the difficulties that Japan had been struggling with for economic recovery from stagnation since the early 2000s. The Japanese economy is in a deeper crisis than the one in the 1990s. The global financial crisis has, however, less affected Japan compared with its western counterparts. This is partly because Japan had learnt a lesson from the 1990's economic crisis (Sato, 2009). The 1990's financial crisis in Japan was caused internally, and started with the collapse of the asset price bubble.

At present, in the real economy, the Japanese machinery manufacturing industry is suffering a decline in domestic and export demand, the latter having been caused by the current global recession. This is different from some of its western counterparts, where financial problems have been central. Declining exports are a serious problem, particularly in the case of the car industry, which has become the pivot of the Japanese economy. In this context, it would be of importance to examine the process about how the *keiretsu* for the Japanese car industry has evolved to survive, and how the *keiretsu* relationships between car makers and parts suppliers have been of fundamental importance to business performance.

In this chapter, we examine the relationships between car makers and parts suppliers, i.e. *keiretsu*, in the background of the global recession. Both car makers and parts suppliers are examining the conventional *keiretsu* relationships and trying to modify them to increase sales and competitiveness in different ways. Under current circumstances, there are two main viewpoints on *keiretsu*; one sees *keiretsu* dismantling and the other sees it developing. We will try to review these perspectives by examining the change in the *keiretsu* relationships in both car makers and parts suppliers. In doing this, we expect that the global recession could be exposing a very important asset, *i.e.* the principles inherent to *keiretsu* relationships in Japanese business.

The chapter is divided in two parts. First, car makers and parts suppliers are examined to see how the global recession has impacted on them in terms of *keiretsu* relationships. Then, we will explore the challenges they pose in terms of management relating to *keiretsu*. In the second part, we will discuss the concept of *keiretsu*. The conceptualisation of keiretsu has not been attempted so far, but it is essential to understand the *keiretsu* relationships as an organic whole. This aspect will help to clarify, to a certain degree, the way they struggle in the face of the current recession while maintaining the conventional *keiretsu* relationships.

1. THE CURRENT STATE OF *KEIRETSU*

Keiretsu has been widely acknowledged as being a symbol of Japanese business strategy allowing to attain high economic performance. After the downturn of the Japanese economy in the 1990s and the Asian economic crisis which followed the collapse of Japan's own asset bubble in 1990, the so-called 'dismantlement of Nissan *keiretsu*' (in 1999) was particularly prominent in the press. In fact, there was disagreement among economists and the press in relation to the nature of the *keiretsu* relationships (Miwa and Ramseyer, 2002; The Economist, 2000; Hosono, Tomiyama and Miyagawa, 2004; McGuire and Dow, 2003; Lai, 1999; Morita and Nakahara, 2004).

The 2008 global recession has had a disastrous impact, in partcular, on the real economy of Japan, and both principal companies and small and medium-sized enterprises have been struggling for survival in different ways. Accordingly the *keiretsu* relationships are changing, a process which started a decade or so ago. As a matter of fact, the problem is how this change can be understood in terms of the concept of *keiretsu*. In the absence of a proper understanding of the concept, it could easily be suggested that *keiretsu* is dismantling, just based on the conventional understanding of *keiretsu*. It should be pointed out that this change of *keiretsu* may not imply the diminishing of, or the maintaining of, the existing *keiretsu* structures either. There is a suggestion that *keiretsu* transaction relationships are developing with closer information exchanges between enterprises, resulting in increased sales among enterprises by meshing and closer information exchanges (Japan Small Business Research Institute, 2007b).

In the following sections we will look at the problems they are facing in the car industry, and how they are trying to cope with them in relation to their *keiretsu* relationships.

1.1. Car Industry

The car industry is the core of the Japanese economy. The ratio of the car industry in the total labour force in Japan is about 8 per cent, and with regard to the shipment of output in Japan, the car industry represents more than 17 per cent. If related materials are taken into consideration, it is almost impossible to find a Japanese industry not related to car making. In contrast to their western countertrparts where around 70 per cent of parts are sourced in house, the Japanese car industry outsources around 70 per cent of parts, bearing in mind that a car consists of in exess of 20,000 parts. In other words, for one car maker there are 3,600 part suppliers involved in the different transactions (Japan Small Business Research Institute, 2007b). These suppliers are normally involved in *keiretsu* relationships. Parts suppliers and related industries have spread out almost all over Japan. Therefore, the global recession has hit the heart of the Japanese economy, the small and medium sized suppliers and also related producers, *i.e.* the vast majority of labour force in Japan. The Japanese car industry has had a structural problem and the global recession has contributed greatly to exposing and to deepening this problem. This problem is broadly the gap between demand and supply: 1. Domestic demand is diminishing; 2. Many parts supplier connected with the car industry failed to properly deploy overseas. This surfaced in 2007 as net operating profit started to decline in the car industry (Nakagami and Yamaura, 2009).

1.2. Nissan and Toyota[1]

During the early1990s, the CEO of Nissan dismantled *keiretsu* and got rid of most of Nissan's *keiretsu* suppliers. Some 40 per cent of the parts suppliers were cut and the share of the rest were mostly sold. Cost reduction was the prime objective for the CEO of Nissan. In the short time span, this was successful in reducing costs of parts, and sales increased. However, Nissan recently changed track, and reconsidered the importance of *keiretsu* transaction relationships with suppliers for reasons of quality and innovation (Nikkan Kogyo Shinbun, 2009). It is said that Nissan focused too much on cost reduction which paricularly hurt Research and Development (RandD), and also that the dismantlement of the Nissan *keiretsu* resulted in the loss of suppliers who themselves nurtured quality improvement and innovation of parts. The extent to which Nissan will restructure its *keiretsu* relationships remains to be seen.

Toyota is in contrast to Nissan in terms of its *keiretsu* transaction relationships. In the same year - 1999 - when Nissan declared the dismantlement of the Nissan *keiretsu*, Toyota declared that they would maintain the Toyota *keiretsu*. Further, the president of Toyota remarked that the Toyota *keiretsu* might be strengthened (Nikkei bijinesu, 2001). This was

---

[1] The following discussion is to a large extent based on the study by Okuto Hajime (2007).

based on the perception that technology for parts production may be lost if *keiretsu* transaction relationships were dismantled, and that the identity of Toyota in terms of technology and differentiation would be lost as well.

1.3. Suppliers

Parts suppliers suffered an unprecendented serious impact resulting directly from the recession in the car industry. They have been most influenced by the hovering car market in the United States. In relation to this, further selection or cuts of suppliers could be happening. Otherwise, supplying parts is indispensable for assemblers; therefore principal assemblers may move to rescue them (Fuji Sankei Business, 2008).

In fact, major manufacturing capacities have been strategically based in Japan since, - in spite of hollowing out -,[2] half of the total output is still produced in Japan, a half of which is exported overseas. This fact may reflect the reason why parts suppliers are relying on domestic demand. Under such circumstances, the suppliers themselves have been trying to expand their relationships with new customers. While still guarding their traditional exclusive *keiretsu* relationshps with existing customers, they have been seeking and creating new patterns of transactions (Tomita, 2001; Shōkōchūkin chōsabu, 2006).

Car assemblers are examining again their manufacturing system and transferring some production bases overseas. This could force structural change in parts suppliers in Japan. Large-sized suppliers of parts are to transfer their production following their customer's development overseas in order to maintain business transactions. In doing this, they require financial power, or they could go bankrupt losing customers.

Two opposing ways have existed among suppliers in terms of developing overseas (Mochizuki, 2005; Japan Small Business Research Institute, 2006). Some 58.4 per cent of suppliers have no transacting business relationships overseas and the rest, around 40 per cent of them, do. Some 72.0 per cent of the former group have a policy consisting in not fulfilling overseas production, whereas the latter group plans further production expansion overseas. However, it is important to suggest that the consistency of the *keiretsu* relationships between suppliers and principal car makers in both domestic and overseas transaction business may be common.

1.4. Prospect

As a general trend, *keiretsu* are expanding their networks and 'meshing' for survival and development (Japan Small Business Research Institute, 2006). This is shown in figure 8.1 below.

The figure shows a change, from a transaction relationship dependent on a small number of business partners to a multifaceted transaction relationship.

It is noted that 57.1 per cent of small and medium-sized enterprises are still under traditional *keiretsu* relationships, *i.e,* the belong exclusively to their long-term customers. This pattern is increasing (Japan Small Business Research Institute, 2006).

---

[2] Globalisation and structural problems have also propelled suppliers to develop overseas.

There are four aspects underlying as to how the *keiretsu* relationships can be reorganised (Nakagami and Yamaura, 2009). Each aspect is dependent on which sector will play the leading role in it; these are: 1. Principal assemblers 2. First tier suppliers 3. External sponsors like funds 4. Bank or municipality.

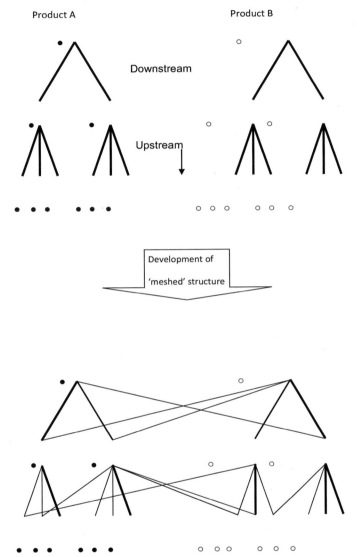

Source: Japan Small Business Research Institute (2007b) compiled by the SME Agency based on Hironobu Oda, Machinery Industry Clustering in Modern Japan (2005).

Notes: 1. The solid lines indicate vertical links 2. The thickness of the lines indicates the strength of the business and marketing ties and level of dependence between enterprises.

Figure 8.1. "Meshing" of transaction relationship.

From the viewpoint of assemblers, e.g. Toyota, it is expected that assemblers will rearrange *keiretsu* transaction relationships (Nakagami and Yamaura, 2009). The 2009 White Paper on SMEs expects that small and medium-sized enterprises (SMEs) will get over the crisis by creating and developing markets through innovation, and the study claims that these SMEs should discern potential needs and provide the products and services that society demands accurately in areas such as food safety and security, environmentally safe products and services. In fact, SMEs are trying to explore new products in pararell to expanding their network, and about 80 per cent of these firms think that keeping up with the current or increasing the level of development is within the capabilities of their current business (Japan Small Business Research Institute, 2006). All in all, the *keiretsu* relationship, although propeled to be reorganised, does look like a *de facto* ruler in management. It is needed to clarify what the nature of *keiretsu* is in order to get a clearer picture of the *keiretsu* relationship.

2. WHAT IS *KEIRETSU*?[3]

Keiretsu has been understood as a Japanese peculiarity in business on the one hand, and yet as an exportable asset in management on the other. We also intend to clarify this contradictory aspect on *keiretsu*.

From the 1990s to the beginning of the 2000s, it was argued that the *keiretsu* model would fade away, either disppearing or changing, in particular by following the dissolution of the Nissan *Keiretsu* (Miwa and Ramseyer, 2002; Chew, 2001; The Economist, 2000; Dore, 1998). However, there were also views that *keiretsu* is still substantial (McGuire and Dow, 2002, 2003), and in the case of the vertical *keiretsu* it had even been strengthened (Morita and Nakahara, 2004).

While *keiretsu* consists of horizontal and vertical organisations, we focus on the vertical *keiretsu*, which is of more significance to performance, for this study. Economists tend to see *keiretsu* essentially as an economic organisation treating the component institutions as independent variables, and sociologists (e.g.Granovetter, 1994, 2001) see cultural values of institutions as the crucial factor for *keiretsu* in their relationships. Granovetter (1992: 4-5) argues that it is important to recognise how economic action is constrained and shaped by the structures of social solidarity in which all real economic actors are embedded, while other scholars such as Emile Durkheim and Max Weber regarded economic action as a subordinate and special case of social action.

From Granovetter's perspective above, the concept of *business groups* comes into focus. Granovetter (1994: 454-465) clarifies *business groups* (original emphasis). They have three main features: (1) they are bound in formal and/or informal ways; (2) they are tied up personally and operationally with all the firms; (3) they are distinguished from those, which are united by common financial origins as in American conglomerates, in the existence of social solidarity and social structure among component firms. In his discussion of the *business groups*, Granovetter (1994) referred to the *keiretsu* in Japan, and to the *chaebol* in Korea. It is important to note that Granovetter distinguished *business groups* through the existence of the principles of social solidarity and social structure among them from other

---

[3] This section is based on Oikawa (2010).

business groups. These principles can be based on region, political party, ethnicity, kinship or religion. Granovetter (1992) stressed the contingencies associated with historical background, and of social structure and collective action and their corresponding constraints, and claimed that his aim was to find general principles that are valid for all times and places.

A key issue arises: what are the principles of social solidarity and social structure in the case of *keiretsu*? In order to explore the principles of *keiretsu*, a linguistic approach is used.

2.1. Principles of Keiretsu: A Linguistic Approach

The object is not given in advance of the viewpoint: far from it. Rather, one might say that it is the viewpoint adopted which creates the object (Saussure, 1983, p.8). Structural linguistics originaged from Saussure's *Cours de linguistique générale* published in 1916. The work of Sapir (1949) and of Whorf (1952) falls into structural linguists. Granovetter (1992) pointed out the contingencies associated with historical background of social structure and collective actions, and their corresponding constraints. This aspect leads to the structural linguistics view.

Importantly, the word '*keiretsu*' has its own particular explanation as a common noun of the Japanese language, as Nakane (1973) described that each group is known informally as 'of the line of A' or 'descended from A', and the word *kei*, signifying descent or genealogical relationship, symbolises the Japanese social system. This indicates that *keiretsu* is an institution at the national level.

The principle of *keiretsu*, therefore, should be considered at a national level. We conjecture that the principles of *keiretsu* represent the core values of social solidarity in Japanese society. Based on these viewpoints, we will explore how the principles of *keiretsu* are expressed and explained in the Japanese language.

First, we briefly discuss how language is linked to thoughts and values; then, the Japanese language will be explored in relation to the principles of *keiretsu*. 'The self ' in terms of language will be the central point in this context.

2.2. Language and Thoughts

Categories and thought patterns built from experience govern much of our day to day thinking. Sapir (1949, pp.68-90) states that language conditions our observation and thinking, which build up the 'real world'.

We live in the 'real world' very much at the mercy of the particular language. This position was extended by Whorf (1952, pp.167-88) who declared 'This study (of language) shows that the forms of a person's thoughts are controlled by inexorable laws of pattern of which he is unconscious [His] thinking itself is in a language – in English, in Sanskrit, in Chinese. And every language is a vast pattern-system, different from others [it] channels his reasoning, and builds the house of his consciousness'.

We will compare and contrast the Japanese language with English, following Whorf's suggestion, in order to clarify the distinction between the two languages in tems of thought and values, and to demonstrate Saussure's axiom that it is the viewpoint adopted which creates object.

Keiretsu

The word 'keiretsu' is a noun in Japanese and commonly used in Japanese society. *Kei* in Japanese means 'a line, lineage, blood to connect or to be connected' such as a group of interrelated elements and *retsu* means a line or a row, or an array of people or things lined up organically (Japanese dictionaries).

Thus we suggest that the predominant meaning of the word 'keiretsu' may be an organic relationship between a group of interrelated elements or of an array of people. This aspect could even imply that all members of such a *keiretsu* group would collapse without trust and dependence upon one another. Such argument refers to individualism and collectivism. As a historical fact, the word 'individualism' was imported; there is no root of this word as a concept in Japanese culture. There is also no concept or word for privacy (Kin'daichi, 2002) – a point that confirms the Sassure/Whorf approach to language. Therefore how the self is viewed in the Japanese language will be the focus in evaluating *keiretsu* as the principles in social solidarity.

Self

Doi (1981) discussed how psychological *dependence* is structured in both personal and social solidarity in Japan. Anthropologists (Cole, 1979; Rohlen, 1974; Vogel, 1975) have remarked on the *dependence* peculiar to Japan, seen in the family, couples and in the workplace.

With regard to the relation between culture and the self, Markus and Kitayama (1991) contrast America and Asia. In their study, two construals of the self are distinguished: the *independent construals of the self* in the west and the *interdependent* in the non-west. These studies suggest that the relation to the self – which distinguishes Japan from America – indicates distinctive core values of social solidarity. In the following we focus on the self in the Japanese language to examine the principles of *keiretsu*.

The Japanese Language and Self

The study of Suzuki (1984) demonstrates the contrastive distinction of first and second personal pronouns between the Japanese and English languages, and shows a striking contrast in core values between two languages. The basic difference is seen in the use of self-reference and address. The Japanese language has no first- and second- person pronouns equivalent to those found in English. Japanese terms of self-reference and address serve to specify and confirm the concrete roles of the speaker and the addressee within a given social context. In English, the speaker designates himself/herself by means of a first-person pronoun and then calls the addressee by a second-person pronoun – *I* and *you*. Thus, the function of first-person pronouns is to designate the user explicitly as the speaker. The meanings of the act of using *I* in English is to express verbally that the one who is speaking at this moment is nobody else but me. In contrast, *self-designation* in Japanese is relative and other-orientated. Other-orientated self-designation is the assimilation of the self, who is the observer, with the other, who is observed, with no clear distinction made between the positions of the two. It can be called 'empathetic identification'. They are accustomed to identifying with, and depending on one another. As Whorf (1952) comments, every language is a vast pattern-system, differenct from others.

English is quite structured compared with the Japanese language, in the way of thinking and expressing logic, concepts and abstraction. In this context, *I* is the axis in the centre of the speaker's own world, restructured through his/her own perception. His/her perceived world should be logical and distinctive from the others because of the fixed and stable dimension of *I*. Such an *I* can be described as independent – individualist, egocentric and autonomous. In this way there should be no room for ambiguity or blurring. By contrast, the Japanese language indicates that Japanese people have no concept of an individual in a western sense, and what is more they view the self as being immersed with the other, and thus regard an empathetic identification in order to overcome the distinction between the self and the other. Such values of the self symbolise the social solidarity in Japanese society. This may be connected with the essential implication of the term *keiretsu* – trust and dependence – in terms of social solidarity. For Saussure, what counts as 'object' is always dependent on the linguistic framework that creates a 'view'of that which constitutes the world. 'Viewpoint' and 'object' for Saussure are interdependent.

CONCLUSION

In this chapter, we have focused on the Japanese business groups – *keiretsu* – in the current global recession, and examined how they are managing through this crisis. *Keiretsu* has been a basic strategy to fulfil successful business performance in Japan. Conventional views on *keiretsu* may have seen that *keiretsu* relationships are changing or diminishing faced with the disastrous global crisis. In fact, *keiretsu* transaction relationships are developing closer information exchanges between participating enterprises as an aid for business survival and sales increase, which has led to increased numbers of enterprises in the *keiretsu* networks. *Keiretsu* is changing and branching off into more complex relationships. However, the principles of *keiretsu* - the core values of trust and dependence – have not changed. These are essentially the core values in Japanese society. We have attempted to demonstrate that the *keiretsu* is essentially intact and is well able to survive this unprecended economic crisis thanks to these inherent and core principles.

REFERENCES

Chew, E. (2001). '*Keiretsu* are fading away,' *Automotive News Europe*, Nov 6 (19), 14.

Cole, R. E. (1979). *Work, Mobility and Participation: A Comparative study of American and Japanese Industry*. Berkeley: University of California Press.

Doi, Takeo (1981). *The Anatomy of Dependence*, Tokyo: Kodansha International.

Dore, R. (1998). 'Asian Crisis and the Future of the Japanese Model,' *Cambridge Journal of Economics*, *22*(6), 773-787.

FujiSankei Business (2008). 'Jidōsha buhin kon'nendo ōhaba gen'eki – Bei hushin tyokugeki touta no namimo (parts supplying industry decreasing profits greatly this year hit by the United State's hovering market; wave of selection),' *FujiSankei Business*, 5 December.

Granovetter, Mark (1992). 'Economic Institutions as Social Constructions: A Framework for Analysis,' *Acta Sociologica*, *35*(1), 3 – 11.

Granovetter, Mark (1994). 'Business Groups,' *The Handbook of Economic Sociology*, N. J. 453–75. Princeton, NJ: Princeton University Press.

Granovetter, Mark (2001) 'Coase revisited: Business Groups in the Modern Economy'. In M.Granovetter and R. Swedberg (Eds), *The Sociology of Economic Life* (2nd ed., 327-356). Oxford: Westview Press.

Hosono, Tomiyama and Miyagawa (2004) 'Corporate governance and research and development: evidence from Japan', *Economics of Innovation and New Technology*, 13 (2), 141-165, March.

Japan Small Business Research Institute (2006). *The actural survey on structural change of small and medium machinery and metal industry*, Japan Small Business Research Institute.

Japan Small Business Research Institute (2007a). *White Paper on Small and Medium Enterprises in Japan* (Ministry of Economy, Trade and Industry).

Japan Small Business Research Institute (2007b). '*Machinery Industry Clustering in Modern Japan* (2005),' pp.107-111.

Lai, G. M. (1999). 'Keiretsu and Keiretsu Business Groups', *Journal of World Business*, *34* (4), 423-448.

McGuire, J. and Dow, S. (2002) 'The Japanese keiretsu system: an empirical analysis', *Journal of Business Research*, *55*(1), 33-40.

McGuire, J. and Dow, S. (2003). 'The persistence and implications of Japanese *keiretsu* organisation,' *Journal of International Business Studies*, 34(4), 374-388.

Markus, H. R., and Kitayama, S. (1991). 'Culture and the Self: Implications for Cognition, Emotion, and Motivation,' *Psychological Review*, *98* (2), 224-253.

Miwa,Y., and Ramseyer, J.M. (2002). 'The Fable of the *Keiretsu*,' *Journal of Economics and Management Strategy*, *11* (2), 169-224.

Mochizuki, K. (2005). 'Keizai no gulōbaru ka no chūshōkigyō heno eikyō jittaichōsa (The actual survey on the influence of economic globalisation upon small and medium enterprises' management).' *Shōkōkin'yū*, 25-44, April.

Morita, Hodaka and Nakahara, Hirohiko (2004). 'Impacts of the information-technology revolution on Japanese manufacturer-supplier relationships,' *Journal of the Japanese and International Economies*, *18*(3), 390 – 415.

Nakagami, T., and Yamaura, K. (2009). 'Car part supply industry facing reorganisation,' *Chiteki shisan sōzō* (Journal of intellectual asset creation, July).

Nakane, Chie (1973). *Japanese Society*. London: Penguin Books.

Nikkei bijinesu (28 June 2001). 'Keiei (management) – Toyota shachō nikiku (interview with the president of Toyota).' *Nikkei bijines*, 82-84.

Nikkan Kōgyō Shinbun (20 April 2009). 'Kigyōken'kyū: Nissan jidōsha (Case study: Nissan)'.

Oikawa, Tomoko (2010). *Economic Organisation and Social Relations – Keiretsu: Concept and Model for the Kanagata (Die and Mould) Industry.* Saarbrücken: Verlag Dr Müller.

Okuto, Hajime (March 2007). Toyota keiretsu to Nissan keiretsu – keiretsu sapuraiya-keisei no chigai ni yoru meiann (Toyota keiretsu and Nissan keiretsu – different destination by different formation of suppliers).

Rohlen, Thomas P. (1974). *For Harmony and Strength: Japanese White-collar Organization in Anthropological Perspective*. Berkeley: University of California Press.

Sapir, E. (1949). *Culture, Language and Personality*. Berkeley and Los Angeles: University of California Press.

Sato, T. (2009). *The global financial crisis and Japan's experience in the 1990s*, Lecture given at the meeting organised by the Association of the Japan security investment advisory committee, 28 January held in the Association of the Japan security investment advisory committee in Tokyo, Japan.

Saussure, F. de (1916). *Cours de linguistique générale*, edited and published by C. Bally and A. Sechehaye, with the collaboration of A. Riedlinger, Lausanne and Paris.

Saussure, F. de (1983). *Course in general linguistics*, translated and annotated by Roy Harris. London: Duckworth.

Shōkōchūkin chōsabu (2006). 'Chūshōkikai kin'zokukōgyō no kōzōhen'ka ni kan'suru jittaichōsa (The actual survey on structural change of small and medium machinery and metal industry),' Tokyo: Shōkō sōgōken'kyūjo.

Suzuki, T. (1984). *Words in Context: a Japanese perspective on language and culture*, Tokyo. New York: Kodansha International.

The Economist (2000). 'Regrouping', *The Economist*, pp. 74-74, 25 November.

Tomita, Kiichiro (2001). Investigation into the actual conditions of shitauke: small and medium sized enterprises in Fukushima Prefecture, Unpublished thesis (M.A.), Fukushima University, Sept.

Vogel, E. F. (1975). *Modern Japanese Organization and Decision-Making*. Berkeley: University of California Press.

Whorf, B. L. (1952). 'Language, mind, and reality,' *Technology Review 9*(3), 167-188.

In: The Transformation of Asia …   ISBN: 978-1-61470-873-5
Editors: B. Andreosso-O'Callaghan and P. Herrmann   © 2012 Nova Science Publishers, Inc.

Chapter 9

ASSESSING THE IMPACT OF 'THE CRISIS' ON SINO-IRISH FLOWS

Louis Brennan and Nicholas McIlroy

ABSTRACT

In light of the sizable shifts in trade, FDI and human flows between Ireland and China in the last decade, this chapter considers the impact of the global crisis on these Sino-Irish flows. The chapter reviews the main theories of international trade, including the Gravity Model of trade and the concept of cultural distance as a barrier to trade. Recent studies that examine the impact of migrants and diaspora cultural and business networks on bilateral trade and investment levels are also reviewed. Sino-Irish trade, FDI and human flows are presented using data from a variety of statistical sources at both national and international levels and the major trends in these flows over recent years are highlighted. An analysis of the data pertaining to these bilateral flows, supported by country-level macroeconomic data from the mid-2000s onwards, highlights the similar pre-crisis trajectories of both countries and their subsequent divergence in the wake of the crisis. The differing responses of China and Ireland to the crisis are also examined from an individual, network and government level perspective. A description of active Irish and Chinese migrant networks in China and Ireland respectively is also provided, outlining their relevant spheres of activity within the community.

The chapter concludes that in light of the contrasting fortunes of Ireland and China since the advent of the crisis, further study into the impact of the Immigrant Effect in the Sino-Irish context and into the role of migrants and migrant networks in promoting trade and investment between China and Ireland is warranted.

INTRODUCTION

This chapter examines the impact of the recent global crisis on bilateral flows of trade, foreign direct investment (FDI) and migrants between the Republic of Ireland and the People's Republic of China. The context of the study is dynamic, with both China and Ireland having undergone massive changes in the levels of imports and exports of goods and services, particularly in the last decade; and with both countries having become large source countries for global investment flows in a move away from their traditional role as destination countries for FDI during the same period. Much empirical work on the role of migrants has demonstrated a positive 'Immigrant Effect' on trade and FDI levels between home and host country.

The aim of this chapter is to assess how these various flows have been affected by the global crisis in the Sino-Irish context.

The content of the chapter is as follows: In the next section, the chapter provides a review of the existing literature relevant to trade theory, with a focus on the Gravity Model of trade and the concept of 'Cultural Distance'. It also examines the growing body of work which addresses the impact of the Immigrant Effect and migrant networks on international trade and FDI. The third section of the chapter examines the Chinese and Irish macroeconomic fundamentals relative to the case at hand, presenting the relevant data for the years leading up to, and after the onset of the crisis.

This section also offers an overview of the current state of Sino-Irish trade, investment and human flows to provide a grounded context for analysis, highlighting any notable shifts in these flows since the onset of the global economic crisis. The data presented here all derive from existing statistics published by a variety of state agencies and other international sources. Where appropriate, a brief evaluation of the reliability of the datasets and sources is offered. Key migrant networks and organisations currently active in both Ireland and China are also considered in this section.

An analysis of the differing approaches to addressing the impact of the crisis by the Chinese and Irish people and governments is presented in the fourth section of the chapter. The final section of the chapter offers some conclusions and recommendations for further study.

1. LITERATURE REVIEW

Firstly, a brief overview of the literature on Trade Theory will be offered, followed by a review of the relevant literature dealing with developments in trade theory vis-à-vis the Gravity Equation and the impact of distance, both geographic and cultural, on trade.

In light of the greatly increased migrant flows between Ireland and China over the years of the 'Celtic Tiger' period[1], the literature review will focus specifically on those studies addressing the impact of the 'Immigrant Effect' and the role of business and social networks on bilateral trade and investment levels. The literature on the Immigrant Effect on trade and investment will then be examined, concluding with an outline of the relevant works dealing with migrant and diaspora business and social networks.

---

[1] The period of strong Irish economic growth and low unemployment from the mid-1990s to 2007 has been colloquially referred to as the 'Celtic Tiger' economy.

1.1. Theories of International Trade

Theories of international trade can be traced back to Mercantilism, which was the dominant theory in Western Europe from the 16th to the mid 18th century.

It espoused a positive balance of trade through protectionism, assuming fixed levels of global capital. Adam Smith (1776) introduced the idea of Absolute Advantage, which David Ricardo (1817) developed for his theory of Comparative Advantage in which he outlined the benefits of trade to both countries through specialisation in production. These theories however have limited application in the 'real world' as they are heavily constrained by assumptions and relate only to a 'two countries, two goods' system. In the early 1900s, the Factor Proportions Theory was developed by the Swedish economists, Heckscher and Ohlin.

In essence, it suggests that a country should produce and export goods which utilise the factors it has in abundance, and import those in which it is lacking (Hecksher et al., 1991). Staffan Linder (1961) proposed the Country Similarity Theory which suggests trade between countries sharing similar tastes, demand and development levels will be greater. Vernon's Product Life-cycle Model (1966) identifies stages of international production, initially beginning in the home market, and eventually moving overseas as the product's life cycle matures. All of these theories have proved useful in some measure in explaining the nature of international trade flows; however, they are bounded by assumptions and are often limited in 'real world' scenarios.

The most commonly used theory of trade in addressing the role of migrants and cultural distance is the Gravity Model, which has stood up to empirical testing in a number of studies. The model predicts bilateral trade flows based on the size of the economies and their geographical distance from each other. There have been many modifications of the model to include a number of variables in the econometric analysis of cross-border trade, notably by Anderson (1979) and Bergstrand (1985).

Many of the studies on the Immigrant Effect discussed below have further modified the model to include the impact of culture, border and network effects among others.

1.2. Cultural Distance

In recent years the debate on the 'death of distance' (Cairncross, 1997) has attracted the attention of many commentators, with proponents arguing that improvements in transport, communications and information technologies have reduced distance as a barrier to trade. However, many studies have shown that cultural distances between trading partners can still act as a sizable barrier to trade.

Frankel and Rose (2000) examine the impact of commonalities on increased trade levels between countries, with an absence of shared culture leading to an increase in cultural distance. Ghemawat's (2001) CAGE Distance Framework identifies four components of distance; cultural, administrative, geographic and economic, with cultural distance being increased by differences in language, ethnicities, religion and social norms. Rauch and Trindade (2002) and Huang (2007), among others, argue that migrants can play an important role in narrowing the cultural distance between home and host countries.

Hofstede's (1980; 2001) work on cross-cultural differences in work-related attitudes, and the GLOBE study (House et al., 2006) which developed his work, also highlight the diversity of cultural differences which may stifle international trade creation.

1.3. The Immigrant Effect

Examining the growing body of literature on the Immigrant Effect[2], Chung (2004) usefully identifies three broad strands of investigation in the existing literature. The first approach examines immigrant links to the trade and investment flows of a country, the second focuses on the nature of businesses established by immigrants within the host country; the final perspective more specifically addresses issues such as a firm's choice of entry mode in a home-host country scenario, such as Chung and Enderwick's (2001) study of the factors influencing New Zealand firms' market entry mode in Taiwan. It is the first area of research identified above that has the most relevance to the study at hand and will be discussed here.

The relevant Immigrant Effect literature may be further sub-divided into studies dealing primarily with goods exports and imports, which to date has received the most attention, and a nascent but rapidly expanding body of work on immigrant links to FDI levels between home and host country which has emerged from the trade-based studies. There is however a gap in the literature addressing the Immigrant Effect and service imports and exports. Table 9.1 below outlines the most important studies to date dealing with migrant impact on trade and investment, presented in chronological order.

In terms of the Immigrant Effect on bilateral trade, many studies have built on the work pioneered by Gould (1994) addressing a variety of different variables -including migrant skill levels, home country income levels, nature of goods traded and the role of networks- for many different countries. Notable subsequent studies have been undertaken by Head and Reis (1998), Rauch and Trindade (2002), and White (2007b), which also examined the role of migrant networks. Combes et al (2005) also noted the positive effect of migrants on intra-regional trade within France.

It should be noted that all studies have found a positive correlation between migrants and increased trade levels, and almost all have employed modified gravity equations in the empirical specification.

More recently, the immigrant impact on FDI has been examined along similar lines of enquiry (Gao, 2003, Murat and Flisi, 2007, Tong, 2005), with similar findings demonstrating the positive effect of migrants and overseas networks on investment levels between home and host country.

1.4. Diaspora and Immigrant Business and Social Networks

Both Ireland and China have long histories of emigration and well established Diasporas worldwide. The role of immigrant networks and organisations is examined by Schrover and

---

[2] The Immigrant Effect relates to the key role that "Immigrants' ties to their home countries can play in fostering bilateral trade linkages" (Gould, 1994: 302)

Vermeulen (2005) in organisational terms as a governance structure for migrant communities. An overview of studies specific to the Irish and Chinese case follows.

Table 9.1. Summary of key works addressing migrant impact on trade and/or FDI

Author	Year	Home country	Model	Trade/FDI	Focus/variable	Findings/Effect
Gould	1994	U.S.A.	Gravity	Trade	Immigrant Links	Positive
Helliwell	1997	Canada	Gravity	Trade	Border Effect	Positive
Head and Reis	1998	Canada	Gravity	Trade	Market Knowledge	Positive
Rauch	2001	U.S.A.	Descriptive	Trade	Ethnic Networks	Positive
Rauch and Trindade	2002	O/seas Chinese	Gravity	Trade	Chinese Networks	Positive
Girma and Yu	2002	U.K.	Gravity	Trade	Commonwealth ties	Positive
Wagner et al.	2002	Canada	Gravity	Trade	Market Intelligence	Positive
Blanes	2003	Spain	Gravity	Trade	Colonial Ties	Positive
Gao	2003	P.R.C.	Gravity	FDI	Inward FDI China	Positive
Combes et al.	2005	France	D-S-K	Trade	Network Effect	Positive
Tong	2005	S.E. Asia	Gravity	FDI	Bilateral FDI	Positive
Kugler and Rapoport	2005	U.S.A.	FDI eqn.	FDI	Skills/Networks	Positive
Javorcik et al.	2006	U.S.A.	FDI eqn.	FDI	Contract Enforcing	Positive
Dunlevy	2006	U.S.A.	Gravity	Trade	Mkt. System/Skills	Positive
Buch et al.	2006	Germany	FDI eqn.	FDI	Agglomeration effect	Positive
White	2007b	U.S.A.	Gravity	Trade	Home Income levels	Positive
White	2007a	Denmark	Gravity	Trade	Pop. Homogeneity	Positive
Murat and Flisi	2007	De, It, Fr, UK	FDI eqn.	FDI	Skills/Development	Positive
White and Tadesse	2007	Australia	Gravity	Trade	Cultural Diversity	Positive
Tadesse and White	2008	U.S.A.	Gravity	Trade	Cultural Distance	Positive

Again, a number of other variables such as skill levels, stage of development of the home country and agglomeration effects have been included in the studies.

Throughout Southeast Asia, ethnic Chinese have established communities and put down roots in host countries, coming to dominate commercial activities despite their relatively small numbers. This 'Bamboo Network' (Weidenbaum and Hughes, 1996; Jacobsen, 2007) of ethnic business linkages has been examined from many perspectives- identity, culture and so on- and has more recently come under scrutiny in terms of its role in the immigrant effect notably by Rauch and Trindade examining its impact on trade (2002), and Gao (2003) and Tong (2005) addressing ethnic Chinese network-FDI linkages. Rauch (2001) has also found that Chinese business and social networks also play a role in trust and contract enforcement thus deterring opportunistic behaviour in markets with weak contract mechanisms. In terms of returned migrants, there has also been a recent focus on the impact of returning Chinese students, the so called Sea Turtles[1], on reverse brain-drain and spill-over effects (Zweig, 2006).

Compared with the overseas Chinese business and social networks and their global commercial footprint, the literature on contemporary Irish Diaspora business links is less well

---

[1] The Mandarin Chinese term for 'overseas returnee' is a homonym for the word for 'sea turtle'.

developed, perhaps due to the level of integration into largely English speaking, euro-centric cultures. Walker (2007) provides a useful overview of numbers and location of Irish communities overseas. Boyle and Kitchin (2007) argue that the Irish Diaspora should be seen as a resource, a call heralded by the popular media of late as an antidote to Ireland's current economic woes. With a growing number of Irish nationals engaging in China, and Chinese in Ireland, there is value in gaining an understanding of the role of migrant business and social networks in the Sino-Irish context, and particularly in the case of trade and investment flows. In light of the contrasting fortunes of Ireland and China since the advent of the crisis (as elaborated in the next section), the literature suggests that there are potential benefits to be derived via the 'Immigrant Effect' for the Irish economy.

2. SINO-IRISH FLOWS

This section of the chapter addresses the volume of trade, investment and human flows between Ireland and China from the mid-2000s, through the crisis period, to-date, using data from a variety of sources ranging from national level, to regional and supra-national agencies. It also focuses on shifts in the trends of these flows arising from the onset of the global economic crisis and offers some explanation for the patterns which emerge from the data. For each of the three areas under scrutiny, there will be a brief discussion of the relevant data sources, and any gaps or shortcomings in the current data sources will also be identified. However, it is useful to first highlight some of the broader macro-economic trends for both China and Ireland for the years preceding the global crisis until the present to provide an appropriate contextual foundation for further discussion of bilateral flows.

2.1. Macroeconomic Context: Ireland and China 2004-2010

Whilst a thorough discussion of Chinese and Irish macroeconomic conditions leading up to and following the onset of the global economic crisis is beyond the scope of this chapter, a brief examination of those indicators most relevant to the trade, investment and human flows under scrutiny here is a worthwhile point of departure, as they underlie the shifts in the trends identified herein. Both countries have experienced unprecedented levels of economic growth over the last two decades, with each rising from relative 'economic backwater' status to regional prominence through different means. An element common to the economic emergence of Ireland and China has been the sizable inward FDI flows experienced by both countries. The role of inward FDI and the emergence of outward FDI is discussed in greater depth later in the chapter.

In addressing the impact of the economic crisis on Ireland and China, Figure 9.1 below highlights the growth rates for gross domestic product (at constant prices) for each country over the last six years.

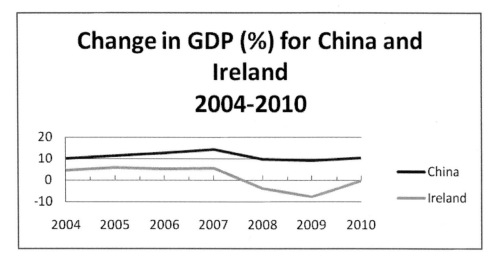

Figure 9.1. Source: International Monetary Fund.

Despite a slight slowing in the annual growth rate for China after the onset of the crisis in late 2007, growth remained strongly positive with the most recent data for 2010 indicating a return to double-digit growth of 10.3 per cent last year[2]. It should be noted however that some commentators have long questioned the magnitude of official economic growth rates pertaining to China due to differences in the national accounting system, among other reasons (Hu and Khan, 1997). In contrast, Irish GDP slumped from the steady trend of around 5 per cent into deep recession between 2007 and 2008, deepening further in 2009.

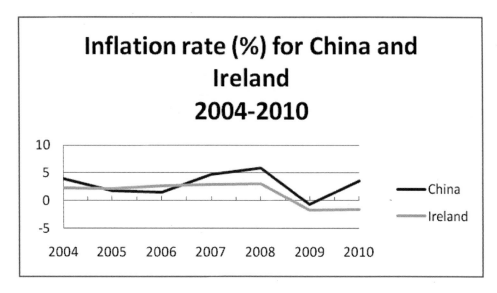

Figure 9.2. Source: International Monetary Fund.

An analysis of the inflation rate in Ireland and China for the same period in Figure 9.2 below illustrates a similar economic picture. Both countries experienced fairly steady

---

[2] Source: Xinhuanet (Online English edition) China's Economy Expands in 2010, tightening fears grow.

increases in their relative consumer price indices (CPI) up until the crisis hit, leading the Irish economy into a deflationary state through decreased demand.

The Chinese economy also experienced deflation in 2009, though at a lower rate of 0.7 per cent. This is attributed to lower fuel demand and increased inventory in line with reduced global demand for Chinese manufactured goods. However, a sharp upturn in inflation has returned to China as a result of income growth and a resultant increase in consumer spending[4].

Considering the two principle macroeconomic indicators above, it is clear that the economic crisis has affected Ireland and China quite differently despite their similar pre-crisis growth trajectories. Bearing this in mind, the chapter shall now examine the impact of the crisis on bilateral trade, investment and migrant flows.

2.2. Trade in Goods and Services

While there are many sources offering data on imports and exports of goods and services between Ireland and China, the primary sources are the Irish Central Statistics Office (CSO) and the Chinese Ministry of Commerce (MoFCOM). Many other sources use the statistics prepared by these two agencies for their own publications however, including the major international organisations dealing with trade and economic issues, such as the WTO, UNCTAD, EUROSTAT and others citing the national statistical bureaus as their sources.

In terms of trade in goods, to put the figures offered on Sino-Irish trade below in some context, the total value of Irish imports and exports for 2009 (the last full year available) was €128,286m, with imports valued at €44,809m and exports valued at €83,477m, giving a trade surplus of €38,667m. In 2009, the impact of reduced trade caused by the crisis was reflected in exports decreasing by 3 per cent and imports by 22 per cent. In the same period, Ireland's trade surplus increased by 34 per cent compared with the 2008 figures[5]. The total value of trade between Ireland and its biggest trading partner in Asia, China, was €5.275 billion, accounting for just over 4 per cent of total Irish trade, with imports down by 33 per cent and export figures up by 4 per cent on the previous year. Longer term growth trends in terms of both imports from and exports to China for the pre-crisis period and its aftermath are clearly visible in Figure 9.3 below which shows the annual value of the merchandise trade between Ireland and China.

Comparing the total value of merchandise exports to China for the period from 2004 and 2009, the figures increase almost fourfold, with an immense jump from €639.2m in 2004 to €2,407m in 2009. The observed decline in imports from China since 2007 reflects the contraction in demand for imports in consumer non-durables, such as children's toys, clothing and footwear, in line with the general recession which emerged in Q3 2007. Another pattern of note, clearly visible from the month-by-month analysis of the data in Figure 9.4 below, is that Irish imports from China are seasonal, with a sharp rise in imports beginning in Q3 each year, building steadily up until it peaks around October, before dropping off substantially at the end of each year until the end of Q1.

---

[4] Source: UNCTAD Trade and Development Report Overview, 2010.
[5]Source: CSO External Trade report. http://www.cso.ie/releasespublications/documents/external_trade /2009 /extrade_dec2009.pdf

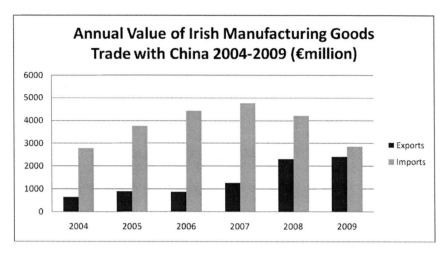

Figure 9.3. Source: Central Statistics Office, Ireland.

This can be explained by the build up in retailer purchasing of consumer non-durables in the run up to the Christmas buying season, with demand falling off sharply in the ensuing months. This is further corroborated by an analysis of the type of goods being imported by SITC code.[6] Taking October as the buying season's peak month, the observed decrease in imports from China from a high of €563.6m in October 2007 down to €269.2m in October 2009 represents a reduction of 52 per cent in import value for the same month over a two year period.

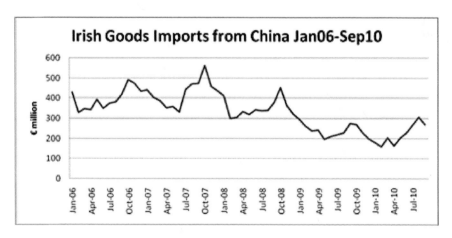

Figure 9.4. Source: Central Statistics Office, Ireland.

In contrast to this decrease, Chinese imports from Ireland for the same period do not however show any reduction in demand, but rather continue to exhibit the same steady growth witnessed in the pre-crisis period. Figure 9.5 below highlights this growth trend which

[6] The vast majority of imports from China fall within SITC section levels 6, 7 and 8, which represent 'manufactured goods classified chiefly by material', 'machinery and transport equipment' and 'miscellaneous manufactured articles' respectively.

may be explained by the increased levels of demand for imports as Chinese household and commercial consumption rises.[8]

In terms of trade in services, the principal source of data on service exports and imports in Ireland is provided by the CSO. The Organisation for Economic Development and Co-operation (OECD) also provides a wide range of statistics on trade in services. China's MOFCOM also offers statistics on international trade in services, denominated in USD and sourced from OECD data.

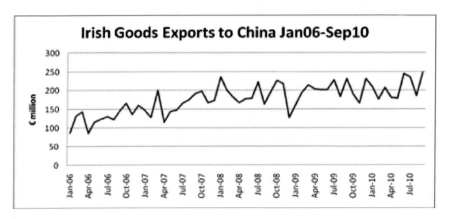

Figure 9.5. Source: Central Statistics Office, Ireland.

Since the CSO began publishing a dedicated report for service exports and imports in 2003, Ireland has been a net consumer of services, with the most recent figures available for 2009 showing that the difference between service imports and exports has narrowed considerably. In the context of Ireland's total service trade for 2009, exports were valued at €66,634m with imports valued at €75,049m, leaving a deficit of €8,415m. According to statistics provided by MOFCOM and published in the People's Daily, China ran a service trade deficit of US$29.6 billion in 2009, representing an increase on 160 per cent on the 2008 figure[9].

In the Sino-Irish context, Ireland enjoys a massive trade surplus in services which has grown enormously over the period for which data is available, to €1,512m in exports, as against €237m in service imports in 2009, leaving a surplus of €1,275 million. This surplus mirrors the growth in goods exports from Ireland to satisfy increased Chinese demand despite the global recession. Figure 9.6 below illustrates the magnitude of growth in services exports and imports with China over the period from 2003 to 2009.

An analysis of the nature of services traded between Ireland and China shows consistency among the CSO's eight broad classifications of service over the time period, with a large share of the trade being generally confined to a few categories. In terms of Irish exports, operational leasing is the largest single traded service, notably with aircraft leasing in the growing Chinese aviation sector which has continued to boom, particularly in the domestic airline sector, despite the global economic crisis.

---

[8] Source: UNCTAD Trade and Development Report Overview 2010.
[9] Source: People's Daily Online 'China's services trade deficit surged 160% in 2009'.

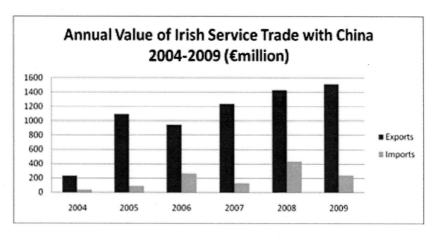

Figure 9.6. Source: Central Statistics Office, Ireland.

For imports from China, insurance services are the sole item transparently listed in the report, with other services making up the balance of services traded. While 2008 witnessed some year-on-year growth in Chinese service exports to Ireland they have on the whole lagged considerably behind the Irish growth in exports.

In conclusion, although many sources offer statistical data on the Sino-Irish goods and services trade, it is prudent to be aware of the inadequacies which are characteristic of any reported data. It should be noted, for example, that currency fluctuations may not be considered in the data, as much Sino-Irish trade is denominated in US dollars, which may mask trade growth or shrinkage due to EUR/USD exchange rate fluctuations. It should also be borne in mind that indigenous Irish firms only account for a relatively small portion of exports to China[10], with the majority of exports being made by foreign enterprises in Ireland. Despite these caveats, clear trends are visible in the data indicating growth in terms of Irish exports in goods and services to China.

2.3. Investment Flows

Sino-Irish bilateral investment flows have also emerged in recent years. Both Ireland and China have traditionally been net recipients of foreign direct investment (FDI) holding large stocks of FDI with large inward flows. However, the levels of outward flows of FDI from both countries have risen particularly in the last decade.

In terms of sources of data on investment flows, China's MOFCOM and its Economic and Commercial Counsellor attached to the Embassy in Dublin offer statistics and reports on bilateral investment activity. Since 2005, the State Administration of Foreign Exchange (SAFE) has collaborated with MOFCOM in publishing FDI statistics. Ireland's CSO also provides statistical reports on FDI levels relevant to the Irish case; however it is only since 2004 that China has been listed in its own right as a source and destination of FDI in its annual FDI report. Internationally, UNCTAD's World Investment Report provides detailed

---

[10] Source: Finfacts Website 'Cowen heads for China; Irish-owned firms' share of Ireland's exports to China in 2007 was as low as 6.7%' http://www.finfacts.ie/irishfinancenews/article_1015020.shtml

FDI statistics for many countries over time including Ireland and China, with the OECD providing useful data in their annual OECD Factbook.

According to UNCTAD's World Investment Report 2010, China became the second largest recipient of FDI worldwide in 2009. It also entered the top 20 in terms of outward investment.[11] Figure 9.7 below illustrates the growth in levels of both inward and outward FDI flows for China for the years preceding the crisis and up to 2009. While inward investment flows still far outweigh outward flows in value, there has been a marked increase in outward FDI from China in recent years. In assessing the impact of the crisis on Chinese FDI flows, it is clear that the year following the 2008 crisis broke the pre-crisis upward trend for both inward and outward investment flows.

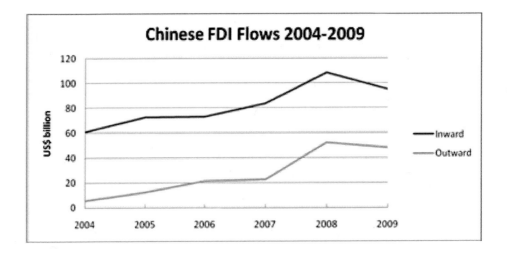

Figure 9.7. Source: UNCTAD World Investment Report 2010.

Figure 9.8 below illustrates the state of FDI flows in and out of Ireland for the period from 2004 to 2009.

In terms of outward flows, a reasonably stable trend is observed over the period with only a minor dip in outward flows in the year following the onset of the crisis and rising again in 2009, although further longitudinal data is required to make any reasonable post-crisis assertions at this point.

The sharp downward spikes in inward investment to Ireland between 2004 and 2006 and again between 2007 and 2009 are explained by the CSO FDI reports for the respective time periods[12], suggesting that high levels of disinvestment by foreign enterprises in the form of non-equity loans and sizeable dividend repatriations to affiliates overseas took place in each case.

In terms of Sino-Irish bilateral flows, data only exists from 2005 onwards. Figure 9.9 below outlines the flows of FDI between Ireland and China from 2005 to 2008 demonstrating

---

[11]Source: UNCTAD World Investment Report 2010 Overview (online edition) http://www.unctad.org/en /docs/wir2010overview_en.pdf
[12]Source: CSO Foreign Direct Investment Report 2004 and 2009
http://www.cso.ie/releasespublications/documents/economy/2004/fdi_2004.pdf;
http://www.cso.ie/releasespublications/documents/economy/2008/fdi_2008.pdf (accessed 9/10/2010)

that for each year reported the investment flows have a positive value, although they exhibit a high degree of volatility.

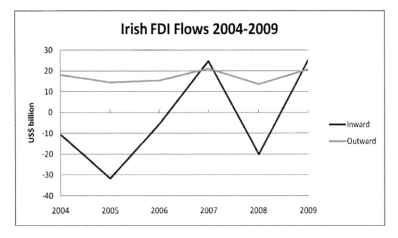

Figure 9.8. Source: UNCTAD World Investment Report 2010.

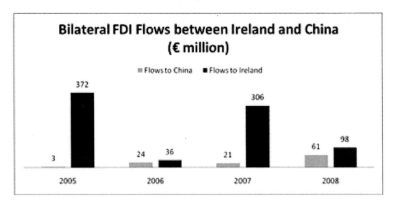

Figure 9.9. Source CSO.

2.4. Human Flows

Of the three sets of bilateral flows considered in this chapter, accurate data on migratory flows between Ireland and China is the most difficult to secure. The data sources for determining the number of Chinese in Ireland can be generally divided into official sources and other less formal sources. The primary source of population statistics for those ordinarily resident in the Republic of Ireland is the National Census, which is carried out typically every four years by the CSO. However, information dealing with respondents' nationality and ethnic background has only been available since the 2002 census.

The CSO figures show a substantial rise of 91 per cent in the number of Chinese between the 2002 census and the 2006 census, rising from 5,766 to 11,161. It is however acknowledged by many commentators that these figures are a gross underestimation of the real figures. In an interview with the Irish Times newspaper in 2004, Chinese premier Wen

Jiabao suggested that at that time some 60,000 Chinese were residing in Ireland[13]. Another official source which records non-Irish citizens in Ireland is the Garda National Immigration Bureau (GNIB); compulsory registration upon arrival in Ireland is required to secure an identity card for those staying longer than 90 days[14]. At the time of writing, the most recent statistics available for student visas were from 2004, in which the GNIB issued a total of 31,338 student visas, 15,933 of which were to students from China.[15] In addition, the Irish Department of Justice keeps records of visas issued to foreign citizens entering Ireland. However, these figures were unavailable at the time of writing.

Despite the increases reflected in the official figures, it is likely that total numbers of Chinese nationals have peaked, with many having already left Ireland. According to Dr Katherine Chan Mullan of the Irish Council for Chinese Social Services[16] one of the main reasons is the difficulty for Chinese people in obtaining student visas following recently introduced restrictions.[17] Importantly in the context of this chapter, she also cited the recent economic downturn and the associated lack of employment opportunities for those who can obtain visas or are currently studying in Ireland. Dr Chan Mullan estimates that at its peak around 2007 the number of Chinese in Ireland may have been as high as 130,000, but that figure has recently reduced to 70,000. Other informal sources on the number of Chinese in Ireland provide similar figures. The most popular internet forum for Chinese in Ireland, known as IrelandBBS[18], has a membership subscription of over 70,000 users, although the site may be accessed from anywhere, and it is not certain that those leaving Ireland will de-register. The Sun Emerald, a newschapter aimed at members of the Chinese community in Ireland, suggests a readership of its weekly publication of up to 80,000 based on its circulation of 20,000 to 24,000 copies[19].

In terms of Irish citizens in China, it is the Chinese Ministry of Statistics (MOFSTAT) which is responsible for national census information; however this does not contain information on Irish nationals in China. Those residing permanently in China must apply for permanent residence status at the city or county-level Public Security Bureau[20]. However central statistics on numbers registered, or nationalities of those registered with the bureaus are not available. One of the more accessible official data sources available is the registry of Irish nationals at the Embassy of Ireland in Beijing, and at the consulates in Shanghai and Hong Kong, where registration with the Embassy is encouraged but not compulsory. Anecdotally, the Vice-Consul of the Irish Consulate in Shanghai estimates the number of Irish in the city at around 350 people. Another less formal estimate of the size of the Irish community in China may be made by an examination of the memberships of Irish business, social and even sports networks, such as the Irish Network China, 'Le Chéile' in Shanghai and the Chinese chapter of the Gaelic Athletic Association (GAA). Unlike the Chinese community in Ireland which is centred largely around students based in urban areas, the Irish community in China is less homogenous, being more geographically dispersed, and includes

---

[13]Source: Xinhua News Agency http://news.xinhuanet.com/english/2004-04/29/content_1448487.htm

[14]Source: Irish Naturalisation and Immigration Service web http://www.inis.gov.ie/en/INIS/Pages/WP07000018

[15] In an interview with GNIB official 7 October 2005, Burgh Quay   http://eprints.nuim.ie/502/1/06_ Chinese_Report.pdf

[16] In a telephone interview conducted 3rd February 2009.

[17]http://www.citizensinformation.ie/categories/travel-and-recreation/travel-to-ireland/student_visas

[18] www.irelandbbs.com

[19] www.sunemerald.com

[20] Source: ChinaOrg website http://www.china.org.cn/english/LivinginChina/185004.htm

people doing business, people working in the non-profit sector, those who are teaching English, and students. These factors combine to make estimating the number of Irish who are resident in China rather difficult. This issue is not unique to the Sino-Irish context however as Zlotnik points out that global figures for international migration are less easy to obtain because of poor data quality and lack of international harmonization in the definition of a migrant (1998).

Bearing in mind the issues surrounding accurate measurement of the numbers of Irish and Chinese bilateral migrant stocks and flows, assessing changes in these flows can be speculative and relies largely on anecdotal evidence.

Figure 9.10 below is useful in terms of aggregate numbers of Irish migrants. There has been a marked rise in outward migration from Ireland since the onset of the crisis. However, as many of those leaving are non-Irish citizens returning to their home country or to a third country for economic reasons, it can be surmised that at least some of these are Chinese migrants. Ireland's Economic and Social Research Institute has forecast a net outward migration of 100,000 from April 2010 to April 2012 (Barrett et al., 2011) and with continued growth and opportunity in China it may become increasingly attractive as a destination for Irish economic migrants. This view is corroborated by Eibhlis Thornton of the Shanghai-based Irish community organisation 'Le Chéile'. She states that 'more people are coming here as they don't have jobs at home.'[21]

In attempting to outline the current state of Sino-Irish flows and observe recent developments in trade, investment and migration, it is clear that problems and gaps in the data exist. Despite these deficiencies, it is clear that the last decade has witnessed tremendous growth in business and human flows between Ireland and China.

It is also apparent from reviewing the relevant macroeconomic, trade and investment data that Ireland and China have both been affected by the economic crisis, although to differing degrees. In terms of the impact of the crisis on human flows, as the stock of Chinese migrants in Ireland has decreased, the stock of Irish migrants in China has increased. In light of the contrasting trends in Sino-Irish trade and migrant flows, it is instructive to consider the business and social networks formed by the new migrant communities in both countries.

The consequence of these heightened Sino-Irish human flows has been the emergence of a growing number of migrant networks. The remainder of this section of the chapter provides an overview of the Chinese migrant networks in Ireland, and the Irish networks in China. It also includes Irish groups in other Asian countries such as Singapore as they have a sizable ethnic Chinese population. To facilitate this overview, it will utilise the system of ethnic network classification outlined by Wang (2009) in her chapter on the Chinese Earthquake Appeal network, which is the most recent and complete survey of Chinese networks and their roles within greater Irish society. In reviewing Chinese networks in Ireland, it also draws on the 'Mapping of Migrant Organisations' document prepared by the Trinity Immigration Initiative (De Tona et al, 2009).

---

[21] In correspondence with the Authors (30th January 2011).

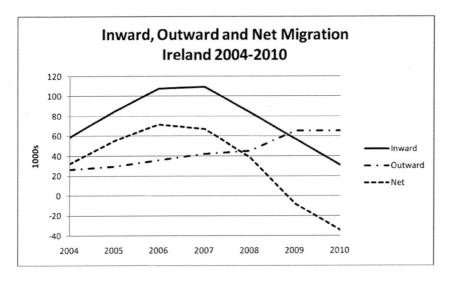

Figure 9.10. Source: Central Statistics Office, Ireland.

Wang (2009) identifies four classifications of Chinese-led associations; commercial organisations, advocacy organisations, professional organisations and cultural/social organisations. The first group includes the Chinese Society of Ireland, the Association of Chinese Business in Ireland and the Irish Fujian Business Association. Advocacy groups include the Overseas Chinese Organisation, the Irish-Chinese Information Centre and the Southside Chinese Residents Association. The professional classification includes the Association of Chinese Professionals in Ireland, and also includes the Chinese Students and Scholars' Association in Ireland which, as the name implies, is student based. The final classification includes cultural/social organisations such as the Chinese Irish Cultural Academy and the Irish Fujian Association. Wang (2009:4) goes on to point out that while each entity has its own particular constituency and set of objectives, the classification is not 'clear cut', as some may have more than one function, for example in providing advocacy services and also organising social events. The Ireland China Association, which is based in Dublin, is a trade-focused organisation comprising both Irish and Chinese members. The association aims to promote Sino-Irish economic ties, promote trade, commerce and greater understanding of both countries, and promote educational and cultural links between Ireland and China by means of regular networking events and through its website.[22]

In line with the recent growth in numbers of Irish people in China, there has been an increase in formal and informal Irish networks and organisations there. Perhaps the most obvious point of departure in any discussion of commercially oriented networks is the role played by the various Irish Chambers of Commerce in China and Asia. The Chambers in Shanghai, Hong Kong and Singapore all provide networking opportunities for Irish business people in Chinese markets[23]. Similarly, the Asia Pacific Irish Business Forum (APIBF) aims to foster links within the Irish business community in Asia holding an annual meeting with speakers on themes relating to Irish business in Asia.[24]

---

[22] Source: http://www.irelandchina.org/section/about (accessed 20/10/2010).
[23] Source: http://www.irishchamber.hk (accessed 20/10/2010).
[24] Source: http://www.apibf.com/ (accessed 20/10/2010).

At city level, the Irish Business Forum Shanghai serves as a network in what is mainland China's largest centre of commerce. In terms of social and cultural networks, both the Irish Network China based in Beijing and Le Chéile in Shanghai are active in supporting Irish nationals in China and, more recently, in organising events such as the annual St Patricks Day festivities. Another active focal point for social activities in the Irish community in China is the Asian County Board of the Gaelic Athletic Association (GAA) which fields seven teams in China and Hong Kong, along with others throughout Asia[25]. Shanghai also hosts the Irish Alumni Shanghai which is a network of Chinese alumni of Irish universities.

Both in Ireland and China, many of these networks, regardless of the level of formality, have sprung up in the last decade due to the increasing bilateral flows of Chinese and Irish nationals living in host communities. Given the historical commercial success overseas of both migrant groups, further investigation into the role they play in strengthening trade and investment links may prove worthwhile.

3. DIFFERING RESPONSES

This section of the chapter examines the responses to the impact of the crisis from three perspectives, namely: the reaction of individual migrants; the reaction of business and social networks in Ireland and China; and finally the differing responses of the Chinese and Irish governments. Firstly, following from the discussion above, many Irish citizens have responded to the downturn by emigrating in search of better opportunities abroad. In terms of Chinese migrants in Ireland, the anecdotal evidence suggests the outward direction of migration is clear. While no official data on Chinese migrants exists (Ducanes and Abella, 2008) the tide of Chinese migration to Ireland has turned.

Perhaps as a corollary to this, there has been a strengthening of Irish social networks in China in recent years. One might speculate that this is due to the increased number of economic migrants seeking a support network and job opportunities within the migrant community. There would appear to be no reduction in the number of active Chinese business and social networks in Ireland, although this may simply represent a maturing of existing networks which were already established in the decade prior to the onset of the crisis, and a shift in focus from offering support services to new migrants to community lobbying and integration initiatives.

In terms of the Chinese and Irish governments' responses to the crisis, the macroeconomic analysis presented earlier in the chapter usefully highlights the different approaches taken. Broadly speaking, Ireland's response to the crisis has been one of fiscal austerity, whereas China's US$500 billion stimulus strategy has been credited with stimulating growth and offsetting a potential reduction in GDP (UNCTAD, 2010).

Conversely, the Irish Government's austerity measures have not brought about the growth in demand witnessed in the Chinese case. Ireland is however constrained by its membership of the Eurozone and thus does not have the monetary or currency flexibility that is available to China, and has been obliged to spend heavily on bailing out its crippled banking sector. It should be recalled from Figure 9.1 above that in 2008 and 2009 the Irish economy was contracting.

---

[25] Source: http://www.asiancountyboard.com/ (accessed 20/10/2010)

Despite the austerity programme to cut spending implemented by the Irish Government, Figure 9.11 below shows the relative increase in expenditure as a result of economic contraction from 2007 onwards. Other than a minor increase in expenditure in 2009 which reflects the slower growth that year (see Figure 9.2) Chinese expenditure has remained relatively stable.

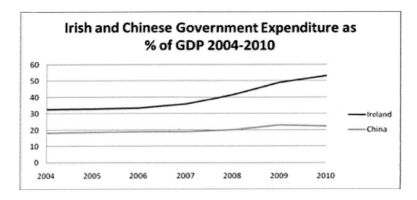

Figure 9.11. Source: International Monetary Fund.

Another Irish response to the crisis was to institute wholesale reforms of the banking sector, including the nationalisation -wholly or in part- of the major financial institutions. China's large-scale reform, regulation and heavy state investment in its banking sector in the 1990s effectively put its financial house in order in the same period that the poorly regulated, privately owned Irish banks were beginning to make rash lending decisions.

In summary, the responses to the crisis from the individual to government level have been very different in Ireland and China despite their similar pre-crisis positive trajectories.

CONCLUSION

This chapter has presented data on Sino-Irish bilateral flows of trade in goods and services, investment and migrants for the period from the mid-2000s up to the present. The flows presented have been analysed in the context of the recent global crisis, with macroeconomic indicators highlighting the similarity in the pre-crisis trajectories of Ireland and China. It has also pointed out the subsequent divergence and contrasting fortunes of the two countries in the wake of the crisis, not only in a macroeconomic context, but also in terms of notable changes in Sino-Irish bilateral flows.

Taking into consideration the different underlying structural elements and macroeconomic conditions at play in Ireland and China, it is clear that China has felt far less impact than Ireland in the wake of the global crisis. The responses of the countries have largely been dictated by environmental constraints, each acting according to the differing sets of resources at their disposal to different effect in each case. Flows of Irish goods and services to China continue to increase serving growing Chinese demand, while reduced Irish imports from China reflect the reduced domestic demand conditions. Migrant flows out of Ireland have risen with China becoming a destination country at least anecdotally, while Chinese migrant numbers in Ireland have also diminished.

Acknowledging that the 'cultural distance' between Ireland and China as defined by Ghemawat is great, many of the studies examined in the literature review have demonstrated that the presence of migrants and migrant networks serve as a mitigating factor in reducing cultural distance as a barrier to trade and have a positive effect on trade and investment flows. Despite huge changes in recent years in the volume of Chinese and Irish migrants in Ireland and China respectively, to date there has been no study of the Immigrant Effect in the Sino-Irish context. However, as the figures discussed above clearly demonstrate, this gap does not reflect an absence of migrant numbers or active migrant business and social networks. Where studies for other countries do exist, there is a dearth of literature addressing the Immigrant Effect specifically on trade in services, which is important in Sino-Irish bilateral exchanges. Furthermore, almost all studies on Immigrant Effects have been quantitative in nature, with no qualitative work offering perspective and 'triangulation' of the empirical results. Given the paucity of reliable migrant statistics for both China and Ireland, a qualitative study which is less reliant on 'hard data' may be of particular import. Furthermore, considering the importance of 'Guanxi' as a cornerstone element in conducting Chinese business, it is worthwhile investigating the role of migrant networks as a starting point for developing and leveraging an international 'Guanxi' network.

Finally, in terms of policy implications, an understanding of the potential of the migrant groups discussed earlier in elevating trade and investment levels may prove useful in driving the export-led growth that is necessary if Ireland is to overcome its present difficulties. This may be achieved by leveraging migrants' home-country knowledge to overcome cultural barriers to trade and identifying opportunities both at home and abroad through stronger engagement with migrants and migrant networks. Furthermore, a positive correlation between migrants and growth in trade and investment may go some way to mitigating the normative tendencies often observed in the formulation of immigration policy.

References

Anderson, J. E. (1979). A Theoretical Foundation for the Gravity Equation. *American Economic Review, 69* (1), 106-16.

Barratt, A., Kearney, I., Conefrey, T., and O'Sullivan, C. (2011). *Quarterly Economic Commentary, Winter 2010,* Dublin: Economic and Social Research Institute.

Bergstrand, J. H. (1985). The Gravity Equation in International Trade: Some Microeconomic Foundations and Empirical Evidence. *Review of Economics and Statistics, 67* (3), 474-81.

Blanes Cristóbal, J. V. (2006). Immigrant's Characteristics and Their Different Effects on Bilateral Trade: Evidence from Spain, *Working Papers 06.08*, Universidad Pablo de Olavide, Departamento de Economía.

Boyle, M., and Kitchin, R. (2008). Towards an Irish Diaspora Strategy: A Position Paper. *NIRSA Working Papers*: NUI Maynooth.

Buch, C. M., Kleinerta, J., and Toubal, F. (2006). Where enterprises lead, people follow? Links between migration and FDI in Germany. *European Economic Review, 50* (8), 2017-36.

Cairncross, F. (1997). *The Death of Distance: how the communications revolution will change our lives.* London: Orion Business Books.

Central Statistics Office, Ireland (1996-2010). *External Trade Report* (Various Editions). http://www.cso.ie/releasespublications/documents/external_trade/2009/extrade_dec2009. pdf (accessed 12/10/2010).

Central Statistics Office, Ireland (1999-2010). *Foreign Direct Investment Report* (Various Editions). http://www.cso.ie/releasespublications/documents/economy/current/fdi.pdf (accessed 9/10/2010).

Central Statistics Office, Ireland (1999-2010). *Service Imports and Exports Report* (Various Editions). http://www.cso.ie/releasespublications/documents/economy/2009/sei2008and 2009.pdf (accessed 9/10/2010).

Chung, H. (2004). An empirical investigation of immigrant effects: the experience of firms operating in the emerging markets. *International Business Review, 13* (6), 705-28.

Chung, H., and Enderwick, P. (2001). An Investigation of Market Entry Strategy Selection: Exporting vs Foreign Direct Investment Modes—A Home-host Country Scenario. *Asia Pacific Journal of Management, 18* (4), 443-60.

Combes, P. P., Lafourcade, M., and Mayer, T. (2005). The trade-creating effects of business and social networks: evidence from France. *Journal of International Economics, 66* (1), 1-29.

De Tona, C., Lentin, R., and Moreo, E. (2009). *Mapping of Migrant Organisations.* Migrant Networks Project, Trinity Immigration Initiative. Dublin: Trinity College.

Ducanes, G., and Abella, M. (2008). Prospects for Future Outward Migration Flows: China and Southeast Asia. The paper was submitted for the OECD workshop *The Future of Migration to OECD Countries*, Paris, 1-2 December 2008.

Dunlevy, J. A. (2004). Interpersonal Networks in International Trade: Evidence on the Role of Immigrants in Promoting Exports from the American States, *Working Paper.* Oxford, Ohio: Miami University.

Finfacts Online (2008) *Cowen heads for China: Irish-owned firms' share of Ireland's exports to China in 2007 was as low as 6.7%.* http://www.finfacts.ie/irishfinancenews/article_ 1015020.shtml (accessed 7/7/2008).

Flisi, S., and Murat, M. (2009). Immigrant Links, Diasporas and FDI. An Empirical Investigation on Five European Countries.In Emilia, Università di Modena e Reggio, editor, *Materiali di discussione*. Modena: Università di Modena e Reggio Emilia.

Frankel, J. A., and Rose, A. K. (2000). An Estimate of the Effect of Currency Unions on Trade and Output, *CEPR Discussion Papers*. London: Centre for Economic Policy Research.

Gao, T. (2003). Ethnic Chinese networks and international investment: evidence from inward FDI in China. *Journal of Asian Economics, 14* (4), 611-29.

Ghemawat, P. (2001). Distance Still Matters: the hard reality of global expansion. *Harvard Business Review, 79* (8), 137-47.

Girma, S., and Yu, Z. (2000). The Link between Immigration and Trade: Evidence from the UK. *Research Paper 2000/23*. Nottingham: Centre for Research on Globalisation and Labour Markets, School of Economics, University of Nottingham.

Gould, D. M. (1994). Immigrant Links to the Home Country: Empirical Implications for U.S. Bilateral Trade Flows. *The Review of Economics and Statistics, 76* (2), 302-16.

Head, K., and Ries, J. (1998). Immigration and Trade Creation: Econometric Evidence from Canada. *The Canadian Journal of Economics / Revue canadienne d'Economique, 31* (1), 47-62.

Heckscher, E. F., Ohlin, B. G., Flam, H., and Flanders, M. J. (1991). *Heckscher-Ohlin trade theory*. Cambridge, Massachusetts: MIT Press.

Helliwell, J. F. (1997). National Borders, Trade and Migration. *Pacific Economic Review, 2* (3), 165-85.

Hofstede, G. (2001). *Culture's consequences: comparing values, behaviors, institutions, and organizations across nations* (2nd edition). London: Sage Publications.

House, R. J., Hanges, P., Ruiz-Quintanilla, S. A., Dorfman, P., Javindan, M., Dixon, M. (2004). *Culture, Leadership, and Organizations: The GLOBE Study of 62 Societies*. London: Sage Publications.

Hu, Z., and Khan, M. (1997). Why is China growing so fast? *IMF Economic Issues*, Issue 8, Washington D.C.: International Monetary Fund.

Huang, R. (2007). Distance and trade: Disentangling unfamiliarity effects and transport cost effects. *European Economic Review, 51* (1), 161-81.

Irish Naturalisation and Immigration Service (2009). *Student Visa guidelines*. http://www.inis.gov.ie/en/INIS/Pages/WP07000018 (accessed 15/9/2009).

Jacobsen, M. (2007). Re-Conceptualising Notions of Chinese-ness in a Southeast Asian Context: From Diasporic Networking to Grounded Cosmopolitanism. *East Asia, 24* (2), 213-27.

Javorcik, B. S., Özden, C., Spatareanu, M., and Neagu, C. (2006). Migrant Networks and Foreign Direct Investment. *World Bank Policy Research Working Paper*. Washington, DC: World Bank.

Kugler, M., and Rapoport, H. (2004). Skilled Emigration, Business Networks and Foreign Direct Investment, *CESIFO Area Conference on Global Economy*. 10-11 December 2004, Munich.

Linder, S. (1961). *An Essay on Trade and Transformation*. Uppsala: Almqvist and Wiksells.

Murat, M., and Flisi, S. (2007). Migrants' Business Networks and FDI. *Preliminary*. Modena: University of Modena.

People's Daily Online (2010). *China's services trade deficit surged 160% in 2009*. http://english.peopledaily.com.cn/90001/90778/90860/6967924.html (accessed 3/2/2011).

Rauch, J. E. (2001). Business and Social Networks in International Trade. *Journal of Economic Literature, 39* (4), 1177-203.

Rauch, J. E., and Trindade, V. (2002). Ethnic Chinese Networks in International Trade. *The Review of Economics and Statistics, 84* (1), 116-30.

Ricardo, D. (1817). *On the Principles of Political Economy and Taxation* (2002 Edition). London: Empiricus Books.

Schrover, M., and Vermeulen, F. (2005). Immigrant Organisations. *Journal of Ethnic and Migration Studies, 31* (5), 823-32.

Smith, A. (1776). *An Inquiry into the nature and causes of the wealth of nations* (1995 Edition). London: W. Pickering.

Tadesse, B., and White, R. (2008). Do immigrants counter the effect of cultural distance on trade? Evidence from US state-level exports. *The Journal of Socio-Economics, 37* (6), 2304-18.

Tong, S. Y. (2005). Ethnic Networks in FDI and the Impact of Institutional Development. *Review of Development Economics, 9* (4), 563-80.

United Nations Conference on Trade and Development (2010). *UNCTAD World Investment Report 2010 Online Edition.* http://www.unctad.org/en/docs/wir2010overview_en.*pdf* (accessed 23/9/2010).

United Nations Statistical Division (2010). *Statistics of International Trade in Services and Tourism.* http://unstats.un.org/unsd/tradeserv/default.htm (accessed 14/10/2010).

Vernon, R. (1966). International investment and international trade in the product cycle. *Quarterly Journal of Economics 80* (2), 190-207.

Wagner, D., Head, K., and Ries, J. (2002). Immigration and the Trade of Provinces. *Scottish Journal of Political Economy, 49* (5), 507-25.

Walker, B. (2007). The Lost Tribes of Ireland: Diversity, Identity and Loss Among the Irish Diaspora. *Irish Studies Review, 15* (3), 267-82.

Wang, Y. Y. (2009). *The Chinese Earthquake Appeal Network in Ireland.* Migrant Networks Project, Trinity Immigration Initiative. Dublin: Trinity College.

Weidenbaum, M., and Hughes, S. (1996). *The Bamboo Network.* New York: The Free Press.

White, R. (2007a). An Examination of the Danish Immigrant-Trade Link. *International Migration, 45* (5), 62-86.

White, R. (2007b). Immigrant-trade links, transplanted home bias and network effects. *Applied Economics, 39* (7), 839-52.

White, R., and Tadesse, B. (2007). Immigration Policy, Cultural Pluralism and Trade: Evidence from the White Australia Policy. *Pacific Economic Review, 12* (4), 489-509.

White, R., and Tadesse, B. (2008). Cultural Distance and the US Immigrant–Trade Link. *The World Economy, 31* (8), 1078-96.

Xinhua News Agency (2004). *Premier hopes to learn Ireland's development experience.* http://news.xinhuanet.com/english/2004-04/29/content_1448487.htm (accessed 1/3/2009).

Xinhua News Agency (2011). *China's economy expands faster in 2010, tightening fears grow.* http://news.xinhuanet.com/english2010/china/2011-01/20/c_13699250.htm (accessed 3/2/2011).

Zlotnik, H. (1998). International migration 1965-96: An overview. *Population and Development Review, 24* (3), 429-68.

Zweig, D. (2006). Competing for Talent: China's strategies to reverse the brain drain. *International Labour Review, 145* (1-2), 65-90.

In: The Transformation of Asia ...   ISBN: 978-1-61470-873-5
Editors: B. Andreosso-O'Callaghan and P. Herrmann © 2012 Nova Science Publishers, Inc.

Chapter 10

HOW ASIA ACTED WITH THE REST OF THE WORLD IN DEALING WITH THE CRISIS – A GLOBAL INTER-REGIONAL PERSPECTIVE

Paul Gillespie

Asia's time has come. No one can doubt that Asia's economic performance will continue to grow in importance (The Economist, Strauss-Kahn 2010).

Asia spent the last 30 years building up the global supply chain to feed (Western consumption. Sheng 2009a).

If the 1997 crisis marked a key turning point in China's regional economic thinking and policies, so the 2008 global crisis might come to be seen as an event that facilitated a new phase in the consolidation of China's regional role. Breslin 2009: 834.

ABSTRACT

This chapter examines the changing international setting in which the 2008-9 economic crisis erupted and then at its consequences for the emerging more multi-polar world order. Comparative regionalism frames this analysis. The recent development of regionalism in Asia in examined in that light, particularly the expanding role of the Association of Southeast Asian Nations (Asean) and its overlapping and competing relationship with other regional organisations and fora. Three main reasons are proposed as to why these common responses are not as extensive as those flowing from 1997-8 in key functional areas such as trade, finance and monetary affairs, including significant initiatives in and between different Asian states. Potential lessons to be drawn from this comparison for our understanding of regional integration are suggested in conclusion.

INTRODUCTION

These quotations capture three important dimensions of Asia's role emerging from the 2008-9 global financial and economic crisis. In contrast to most of the rest of the world – and certainly its most developed western centres – Asia is a much more optimistic region about "its joint adventure, namely the pursuit of materialism based on rapid economic development" (*Economist* 2010: 46). That Dominique Strauss-Kahn, managing director of the International Monetary Fund, should acknowledge this so fulsomely, alongside an apology for his organisation getting it so wrong in the Asian financial crisis of 1997-8, was pleasing indeed to Asian leaders stung by that experience into developing closer regional cooperation in the following few years (Gillespie 2010a, Bowring 2010, Wheatley 2010). The question posed by their response a decade later is whether 2008-9 had a similar catalytic effect.

How that comparison plays out is constrained by the specific role Asia plays in the global economy. The region is closely bound up with the international division of labour, especially in manufacturing. This was outsourced first from Japan (and later from South Korea and Taiwan) to southeast Asia for onward exports to the United States and Europe in the 1980s; and then to China (along with manufacturing from the rest of the developed capitalist economies) from the 1990s for the same purpose. As a result Asian states are locked into a trading, financial and policy relationship with other world regions, and are more open to them than comparable areas. This makes their cooperative endeavours less autonomous and more competitive than elsewhere - and as a result less ambitious (Ravenhill 2009). Regional initiatives must also take account of the great unevenness between intra-regional interdependence in East Asia, where it is most developed, southeast Asia, less so, and south Asia which has hardly even begun this process (Sally 2010).

Given such differences it is widely debated whether we are speaking about the same region, allowing for these geographical qualifications within it, since a sense of common purpose and identity is so lacking. The perspective adopted here is that it does make sense to talk about Asia as an actor, partly because other parts of the world are now doing so. Regional identities are constructed by precisely such internal and external interactions – a fact appreciated by social constructivists (Acharya 2009). Regions are social constructions, "'given' by geography and 'made' through politics" (Katzenstein 2005: 10, 21, 36).

The story of how Asia has interacted with the rest of the world in dealing with the 2008-9 crisis must be told state by state as well in respect of the regional collectivity and identity gradually if unevenly being developed by its political and policy elites. Other chapters deal with state and regional policy in more detail than is possible here; this is less a narrative of the two crises than an analytical account of some of their major features. But since regional integration hinges crucially on whether key powerful states consider it is in their best interests to pursue such cooperation we must consider whether and how they saw such an opportunity in 2008-10. Inevitably China's role looms large in this respect. Its leadership faced strategic choices about their relationship with the United States in assuming more responsibility for managing the crisis - or decoupling from it (Bremmer 2010, Gillespie 2010). In making them the Chinese had to decide how to bring other Asian states along. Asian leaders also saw the advantage of developing greater cooperation in selected spheres, whether by bandwagoning on China (Ong 2009), encouraging its new regional outwardness (Breslin 2009), developing "omni-enmeshment" policies towards major powers (Goh 2007/8, 2008) or using the crisis to reduce dependence on the US (Beeson 2009).

The chapter proceeds by looking in section 2 at the changing international setting in which the 2008-9 economic crisis erupted and then at its consequences for the emerging more multi-polar world order. Comparative regionalism frames this analysis and can throw some light on how to understand the conditions in which greater regional integration occurs.

Section 3 examines the recent development of regionalism in Asia in that light, particularly the expanding role of the Association of Southeast Asian Nations (ASEAN) and its overlapping and competing relationship with other regional organisations and fora. Section 4 suggests three main reasons why these common responses are not as extensive as those flowing from 1997-8 in key functional areas such as trade, finance and monetary affairs, including significant initiatives in and between different Asian states. Section 5 draws some conclusions about the future of Asian regionalism and potential lessons to be drawn from this comparison for our understanding of regional integration.

1. THE INTERNATIONAL SETTING: REGIONAL INTEGRATION AND MULTI-POLARITY

The global financial crisis of 2008-9 occurred in a world already undergoing profound changes in its geopolitical order. The unipolar moment which gave the United States its global hegemony after the end of the Cold War proved to be relatively short-lived in political, economic and even in security terms. By the early 2000s power was shifting. This was symbolised by the sharp shock of the 9/11 attacks on New York and Washington in 2001, but was then disguised by the unilateral US response to them in Afghanistan and Iraq. Notwithstanding the US-led international alliance which invaded Iraq in 2003 the force conspicuously lacked participation by major European powers like France and Germany, showing that NATO no longer delivered unquestioning transatlantic allies to US leadership (Cox 2005). Equally, there was not a significant Asian participation in the expeditionary force. The gradual emergence of Brazil, Russia, India and China (the BRICs) as significant global players economically and politically happened during these years, a fact that was to be formally recognised with the enlargement of the Group of 8 to the Group of 20 in 2008 (Renard 2009).

By then the US had moved towards a net debtor position with the rest of the world, with China and Japan together holding half of the total US government treasury securities in July 2007, when foreigners also held 24 per cent of corporate and other debt and 11.3 per cent of total US stock market capitalisation. By 2004 the US had a net debtor position of 24 per cent of GDP - compared to a net 10 per cent creditor position in 1952, while the financial sector debt nearly doubled from 64 per cent of GDP in 1994 to 114 per cent (Sheng 2009: 3, 13). In 2008 the euro had surpassed the dollar as the most important currency for international bond and note issuance, making up nearly half the total international bonds and notes. The global financial crisis discredited the Washington consensus developed since the 1980s, based on neoliberal globalisation and financial deregulation – not least in Asia after the financial crisis of 1997-8, where alternative lessons were subsequently drawn from its traumatic impact in those years (Beeson 2009).

These trends should not be exaggerated, since US power remains relatively preponderant, however much it diminished absolutely. This was particularly the case in Asia, where its security imperium remained intact, despite these economic and political shifts. Although the precise role of that imperium is contested, few doubt it remains an essential factor in understanding the emergence of Asian regionalism before and after 1998, whether in terms of direct influence or competitive jostling for security position between different Asian powers

(Katzenstein 2005, Roundtable 2007). The most important change was the rapid emergence of China during these years as a regional and global power, founded on its remarkable economic growth and crucial position in the global supply chain after it became the main outsource for Western manufacturing companies. Talk of a G2 between the US and China (Bergsten 2008) proved overstated, partly because China was unwilling to become locked into such a limiting relationship since it also wanted to develop new patterns of cooperation with Asian partners (Breslin 2009, 2010). But it became clear in the spring of 2010 that its leaders had opted for a policy of sustained engagement with Washington on a broad canvass of issues, notwithstanding evident tensions over currency values, intellectual property and access to its markets, or continuing military/security issues in the South China Sea with US allies like Japan or Taiwan. Thus the talk of "decoupling" the US-China relationship proved ill-conceived - or at least premature.

Seen from Europe, these developments spurred on the EU's efforts to create a more coherent international profile and policy capable of dealing with the changes in world power. The Lisbon Treaty mandated the creation of a High Representative for Foreign Affairs and Security Policy and an external action service. These were implemented very much with the emergence of new regionalisms in mind. Several key assumptions ran through EU policy-making and analysis, among them that international politics is following a trend from the bipolar equilibrium of the Cold War, through the brief unipolar moment in the 1990s, towards a new multi-polar equilibrium. Unless Europe plays an active role in defining this new world order it was believed to risk being marginalised. A multilateral inter-regionalism based on multipolarity and interdependence should be a central value of the emerging system - which admirably suits the EU's exemplary self-image (Higgott 2010, Grevi 2009, Van Landenhave 2010, Renard 2009, Howorth 2010).

Such a worldview is tempted to extrapolate its own experience and values onto the rest of the world. Highly institutionalised regionalism is all too easily assumed to be a best practice towards which other world regions aspire and will evolve, so that "Europe's past represents Asia's future" (Higgott 2006: 18).This can create a "snobbery" about other parts of the world and unrealistic expectations about future inter-regional behaviour (Murray 2010a). Thus African, Latin American and most notably Asian regionalisms are understood in a teleological schema with Europe at its apex. That can lead to bad politics and misleading analysis (Sbragia 2008). Put differently, "Eurocentrism results in a false universalism" (De Lombaerde et al. 2010: 743). ASEAN's consensual approach towards protecting state sovereignty rather than pooling it arises from its members' history as subjects of colonialism, for example, whereas European integration originated in a collective effort to escape from the disastrous consequences of its own competing imperial (and anti-imperial) nationalisms.

Multi-Polarity and Comparative Regionalism

Such critiques of European assumptions have recently animated the study of polarity and regionalism in world politics – although the two approaches tend to run on different tracks without talking to one another. That comparison reveals differences as well as similarities between regions and the dynamics of their development is a salutary lesson for those expecting the emergence of a homogeneous or symmetrical pattern of regionalism (Warleigh-Lack and Van Langenghove 2010). Critics warn against substituting normative for empirical judgments in examining multi-polarity as well as regionalism (Higgott 2010). That polarity implies states being attracted to one pole and repulsed from another in a system of competing blocs is one typical realist account arising from US analyses and policy-making (Mearsheimer 2001). European accounts are more liberal internationalist, placing less emphasis on competition and more on interdependence and institutionalised inter-regionalism. But as Higgott insists, "rather than assume a multi-polar future, much more data and conceptual rigour are needed to document how and if multi-polarity are emerging. This includes thinking through multi-polarity as a contested term that has different meanings for those in different (political) contexts" (2010: 7). Instead of moving towards a new equilibrium of cooperating world regions, this transition may be towards a "'depolarised world' of fluid, unfixed and overlapping sets of relationships, alliances and attractions among states" (ibid: 6), a "non-polar" world of similar uncertainty (Haass 2008), or an "unbalanced multipolarity" in which potential hegemons (like China) are impelled to seek regional domination (Mearsheimer 2001, 2009) . Just as US policy-makers and analysts tend to prefer a regionalism based on bilateral relations and free trade agreements, so they see polarity more through the eyes of their own hegemonic experience than of an emerging system in which they must take much more account of other centres of power (Hettne 2007, Van Langenhove 2010).

Comparative regionalism addresses these changing realities of world politics and has the considerable merit of focussing on the inter-relationships between power, identity and geography in doing so. The renewed study of regions and regionalism has burgeoned in response to these international events and shifts (Warleigh-Lack 2006, Warleigh –Lack and Rosamond 2010, Warleigh-Lack and Van Langenhove eds. 2010, Hurrell 2007, Fawn ed. 2009, Murray and Rees eds. 2010). The central question posed is whether or not the changes are best understood from a regionalist perspective, since this is largely how globalisation has been encountered and managed. Some are sceptical about that emphasis (Acharya 2007), some say the two approaches should be combined with a continuing focus on US power (Katzenstein 2005), while others insist on the limited extent to which European integration sets an international trend (Sbragia 2008). There is tension between "old" and "new" regionalism, partly reflecting different approaches taken by specialists in politics and/or international relations compared to the more recent concentration of economics and/or international political economy on the less state-centred "open regionalism" of the 1990s (Vayrynan 2003, Söderbaum and Sbragia 2010). There are also renewed efforts to bring them together in a new synthesis taking better account of more recent changes in the international order (Hettne 2005, De Lombaerde and Van Langenhove 2005, Van Langenhove and Costea 2007, De Lombaerde *et al.* 2010).

The sheer disciplinary diversity in the study of regions across European studies, comparative politics, international relations, international economics, international geography and international political economy means it is difficult to create a common conceptual, theoretical and methodological approach towards comparison as well as the object of the exercise – although there is now an opportunity to do that (De Lombaerde *et al.* 2010). These disciplines give prominence variously to geography, identity, security, institutionalisation, intra-regional trade, interdependence, power asymmetries or optimal currency areas as determining factors. Methodologically, they variously emphasise realism, constructivism, qualitative, quantitative and comparative case study approaches. But despite the proliferation of studies describing and analysing differences and similarities, there is a paucity of well developed theory to explain the conditions under which particular types of regionalism can be expected to emerge, largely because of disciplinary fragmentation (Fawn 2009: 32-4). Interestingly there is no international journal devoted expressly to the subject - a definite gap in the market (although *Asia-Europe Journal* does some of this work).

"Regionalisation", "regionness" and "regionhood" have been suggested as supplementary terms to accompany "regionalism" in analysing the phenomenon (De Lombaerde et al 2010: 739). Regionalisation can be thought of as a long-term process of social or economic transformation, involving especially non-state private actors such as markets, private trade and investment flows and multinational firms, in which phases can be distinguished. Rather than comparing different regionalisation processes in the same historical moment, it might make sense to compare the cases in comparable logical moments or lapses of time – "regionness". An example would be to compare the conditions for monetary integration in the European Community in the 1960s and 1970s with the corresponding conditions for MERCOSUR in the 1990s - or for East Asia from 1998 or 2008 onwards. "Regionhood" sees regions as non-sovereign governance systems with (partial) statehood properties, and macro-regions as non-sovereign governance systems between the national and global level (De Lombaerde et al 2010; 740, quoting Van Langenhove 2003). "Regionalism" would then be reserved for the specifically political, regulatory and comparative decision-making process about such governance systems, "simultaneously a response to, and a dynamic behind, globalisation" (Higgott 2006: 22). These are not mutually exclusive processes.

Hettne and Soderbaum propose a five-fold schema in levels of regionness:

	Type of region Description
Regional space	A geographically contiguous area, but one capable of transcending national borders.
Regional complex	A regional space in which human contacts and trade patterns have begun to be shaped on a cross-regional basis.
Regional society	A regional complex in which cross-border regional transactions have intensified, become multi dimensional and made subject to new regional rules; non-state actors gain meaningful roles in regional governance, and regional institutions may be established.
Regional community	A regional society in which the region itself has become an actor, with its own collective identity underpinned by civil society mobilisation at regional level, with national identities becoming less important and a sense of shared culture and/or polity deepening.
Region-state	A new, heterogeneous state forms from the regional community, characterised by internal diversity, pluralism, and a multi-level distribution of power.

Source: Summarised by Warleigh-Lack and Van Langenhove 2010: 547ff , as adapted from Hettne 1993, Hettne and Söderbaum 2000.

Figure 10.1. The 'regionness' scale.

Although there is an implied developmental hierarchy from regional space to region-state in these five stages, Hettne insists that:

The five levels must not be interpreted in a deterministic fashion as a necessary sequence. Since regionalism is a political project, created by human actors, it may, just like a nation-state project, fail. In this perspective, decline could mean decreasing regionness; ultimately a dissolution of the region itself. (Hettne 2005: 548).

Drawing out the implications of this schema Warleigh-Jack and Van Langenhove emphasise (2010: 549-54): the dimensions of actorhood; the discursive relationship between regionness and statehood; the deepening relationship between regionalisation and globalisation; and the need in this global setting to link processes of intra- and inter-regionalism. They distinguish between the processes, projects and outputs of regionalism as proper objects of comparative analysis, taking account of differences and similarities. And they suggest that three major dimensions of actorhood are capable of being so operationalised: economics of a single space above or below the state; provision of public goods; and the relationship between actorhood and sovereignty. This is genuinely innovative comparative thinking; but it is too early to apply such distinctions mechanically to the development of specific regions.

This is still an emerging field, and there is no single methodological approach or theoretical framework to apply; looking at the work on other regions and comparative regionalism cannot provide an 'off the peg' set of concepts and tools that EU scholars can use without reflection. The same is also true in reverse. (Warleigh-Jack and Van Langenhove 2010: 554).

Nevertheless they can illuminate several of the elements determining the Asian response to the 2008-9 global financial crisis compared to the Asian crisis in 1997-8.

2. REGIONALISM IN ASIA

The close inter-relationship between regions and globalisation contains a central lesson on how we should understand regionalism in Asia. Regionalisation arising largely from private transactions, regionalism as state-led projects of cooperation, and regionness as an achieved level of integration take place within that context. As Higgott puts it:

Failure to recognise the dialectic between globalisation and regionalisation can mean that we impose a regional level of analysis on something that is actually global. We must consider the salience of extra-regional relations whenever we are considering regionalisation (Higgott 2006: 24).

Thus the characteristic pattern of regionalisation in Asia, by which economic integration developed through the relocation of Japanese plants in the late 1970s and 1980s and the related development of Japanese pan-Asian systems of production, came before institutionally coordinated integration through the signing of regional trade agreements from the 1990s (Andreosso-O'Callaghan 2008: 63). From Japan this relocation spread to South Korea, Taiwan, Hong Kong and Singapore; then to Malaysia, Thailand, Indonesia and the Philippines. Since 1997-8 the process has dramatically expanded on to China, Vietnam and Cambodia, orchestrated by the Chinese diaspora in Southeast Asia. But since the final goods arising from this intra-regional trade have to be sold somewhere, whether inside or outside the region, both regionalisation *and* globalisation are involved. The "processes of developing regional production networks are themselves driven by global process and are contingent on global markets" (Higgott 2006: 25).

That this is a key differentiating factor between Europe and Asia is confirmed by comparative statistical analysis of trade and investment in the two regions. It shows that economic regionalisation in Asia is largely orchestrated by multinational firms and their global systems of production, compared to the more intense European experience where there is much more regional production for regional consumption (Andreosso-O'Callaghan 2008: 64) – although that too is now being driven by similar market-driven and business-elite processes (Kriesi *et al.* 2008). The Asian experience of economic regionalisation is also far more uneven geographically between various sub-regions and countries than the EU's. The intensity of economic integration is higher for the Asia-Pacific region as a whole compared to ASEAN, for example. But although 55 per cent of Asia's world trade is intra-Asian, because non-Asian exports remain the Asian engine of growth, there is "still insufficient intra-Asian demand for Asian final goods to create a strong domestic Asian market" (Sheng 2009: 320). East Asia is also dramatically more integrated than South Asia. Intra-regional trade as a share of East Asia's total trade increased from 36.8% in 1980 to 54.5% in 2006. That is lower than the comparable share for the EU (65.8%), but higher than for NAFTA (44.3%) and much higher than for other developing-country regions (e.g. 15.7% in MERCOSUR). Intra-regional foreign direct investment has also become more important. Asia's industrialised economies account for 29.2% of FDI going to ASEAN and 54% of FDI in China (Sally 2010: 3).

Comparison thus reveals significant differences between the European and Asian regions concerning their respective openness to and dependence on the global economy. That is a significant finding in itself, from which some political conclusions can tentatively be drawn about their comparative evolution, the likelihood that they will have a similar future with regionhood, or reach contrasting points on the regionness scale in Figure 10.1. This framework of economic regionalisation and openness to the global economy drew the previously relatively distinct East and South-East Asian regions more closely together in the 1980s and 1990s. In terms of Figure 10.1 this represents a movement from a regional *space* to a regional *complex*. Geopolitically the process was accentuated by the end of the Cold War, which reinforced US hegemony in Asia and throughout the international system by giving economic globalisation and neo-liberal norms freer rein (Katzenstein 2005). It laid the ground for the decisive shift towards the political, albeit lightly institutionalised, development of the ASEAN+3 (APT) process after the Asian financial crisis of 1997-8, when Japan, South Korea and China were drawn into a relationship with their South-East Asian partners (Emmers and Ravenhill 2010: 4). That set the scene for the development of a regional *society* in East Asia as a whole - in that cross-border regional transactions intensified, became multi-dimensional and were made subject to new regional rules; non-state actors gained meaningful roles in regional governance; and regional institutions might be established, to use Hettne and Söderbaum's terminology. The next section will examine in more detail whether that process has reached its full potential; here it should be noted that this is contested in the scholarly literature, mainly because those coming from international political economy, regional security and social constructivist positions draw different conclusions from the evidence of loose economic cooperation, competitive proposals for regional architectures and diverse adaptation to and adoption of global trends involved (Breslin 2010, Murray 2010).

The significance of ASEAN's own development in the 30 years before 1997-8 has been similarly disputed and variously estimated in the literature (Ravenhill 2009, Morada 2008, Goh 2007/8). But the success of its founding members Indonesia, Malaysia, Singapore, Philippines and Thailand in creating a region of peace and stability by managing intra-regional conflicts should not be under-estimated. Nor should its ability to harness normative values of anti-colonialism, neutralism and nationalism and the abiding commitment to respecting sovereignty, inter-governmental methods, non-interference in domestic affairs and its consensual approach be forgotten (Acharya 2009). These characteristics allowed it expand to include Brunei Darussalam, Vietnam, Laos, Burma Myanmar and Cambodia despite profound differences in political and economic structure (Murray 2010: 599-600). They also brought ASEAN solidly from regional space and complex to societal status when the 1997-8 shock challenged it to create a new relationship with Japan, South Korea and China and then to decide whether stronger institutionalisation should be adopted in response.

If Strauss-Kahn is right that Asia's time has come we should be aware of how recently this is seen inside and outside the region and then how much its own definition and boundaries are still being contested. Its economic regionalisation and political regionalism depend more on global developments than elsewhere, because of the powerful external linkages in exports, security alliances and political relations with the United States especially. Such linkages are now competitive between Asian states, as China, India, Japan and the region's southeast jostle for position and allies. As a result the previously thin gruel of their regional partnerships is evolving into a confusing alphabet soup of varying organisations, a noodle bowl or lattice network rather than a more coherent supranational structure like the EU's, stopping well short so far of regional *community* that the EU has arguably attained (Ravenhill 2009: 216, Murray and Rees 2010).

But Asian states are not passive recipients of globalisation or the associated neo-liberal Washington consensus pushed by the International Monetary Fund since the 1980s. They adapt rather than adopt such models of development to their own needs in a "constitutive localisation" of world trends (Acharya 2009, Gillespie 2010). Just as South-East Asian cultures responded to Hindu and Buddhist influences from India and China by creating their own art forms and civilisations, so they bring their own political cultures of consensus and non-interference with sovereignty to bear on their regional cooperation. ASEAN's several major achievements over its 44-year history include having avoided wars between its members, creating peace between Cambodia and Vietnam and providing the essential framework for China's new relationship with them (Acharya 2009).

This last was achieved before and following the 1997-8 financial crisis. The Singapore analyst Kishore Mahbubani points out that during the 2008-9 crisis US and European policy-makers – and the IMF - "are doing the opposite of what they advised Asian policymakers to do in 1997-8: do not rescue failing banks; raise interest rates, balance your budget." The Asians learned valuable lessons then: "Do not liberalise the financial sector too quickly, borrow in moderation, save in earnest, take care of the real economy, invest in productivity, focus on education" (Mahbubani 2008).

ASEAN+3 (APT) was created to bring China, South Korea and Japan into a new political relationship with Southeast Asia. Together they developed new mechanisms on financial cooperation, currency swaps, regional trade agreements, disaster management, transborder crime, tourism, energy, avian flu, atmospheric pollution and the environment. Top national officials meet some 700 times a year in 55 bodies (14 ministerial and 19 senior official groups, two meetings of director-generals, 18 technical meetings and two track-2 meetings) and there is evidence that some common cognitive identity is evolving among them - if not among their general populations. An ambitious programme of development by 2015 and 2020 is under way, including plans for an ASEAN Economic Community, an ASEAN Security Community and an ASEAN Socio-Cultural Community. Critics say a lot of this is process not progress; weak because it lacks institutions, privileges consensus and is often bilateral; in practice makes economic, financial and trade relations sub-optimal compared to other world regions; and that future plans lack precision and operational deadlines (Ravenhill 2009, Morada 2009). The alphabet soup of Asian regionalism reveals profound disagreement on its boundaries, identities and relationships with the rest of the world. Japan and China jostle about whether to include India, Australia and New Zealand in regional fora – ASEAN+6. The East Asian Summit (EAS) includes them and in 2010 ASEAN states led by Singapore and Indonesia agreed to invite the United States and Russia to join the summit on issues ranging from security to trade and the environment, much to China's displeasure (ASEAN+8). China prefers a more exclusive club centred for the moment mostly on ASEAN+3, which others resist to balance its power, even though APT remains the anchoring basis for the EAS. India finds its new policy of eastern regional engagement frustrated by prior Chinese initiatives. The US links a stronger bilateral relationship with China to its declining economic hegemony and its continuing military super-powerdom in the Pacific (Gillespie 2010). However the Obama administration strongly favours a re-engagement with Asia. In her annual speech to the Council on Foreign Relations in September 2010 Secretary of State Hilary Clinton devoted a substantial section to Asian regionalism and the development of trans-Pacific partnerships, acknowledging that geopolitical change is taking a predominantly regional form (Clinton 2010). The speech contained 24 references to regions and 7 to Asia compared to 4 each to the EU and NATO (Acharya 2010). In October 2010 at the EAS in Hanoi she urged it to handle disputed maritime issues in the South China Sea, along with nuclear proliferation, the increase in conventional arms, climate change, and the promotion of human rights (Bloomberg 2010).

3. Regional Responses to the Asian and Global Financial Crises: 1997-8 Contrasted with 2008-9

Three factors arising from these distinctive patterns of Asian regionalism help us understand how the Asian financial crisis of 1997-8 was a greater stimulus for that process than the global financial crisis of 2008-9. *Firstly*, the focus of the first shock was specifically Asian rather than global, leading to a greater effort to correct regional shortcomings in response. In contrast the worldwide effects of 2008-9 had a less economic impact in Asia than the previous crisis, showing up its comparative strengths as a region of growth and surpluses – Asia's time had come. As a result this shock concentrated on drawing leading Asian states and to a lesser extent the region as a whole into the changing shape of world politics, notably through the Group of 20. *Secondly*, the worldwide interdependent nature of Asia's economic development exemplified by its role in the global supply chain to feed Western consumption stimulated it into regional action on the first occasion and global response on the second. *Thirdly*, China, as the emerging regional hegemon, had a greater distance to travel towards, and more interests in developing, closer regional cooperation in 1997-8 than in 2008-9, when it instead needed to consolidate relations already established in a setting of greater global influence than a decade earlier.

Asian Not Global

The 1997-8 Asian financial crisis had a dramatic if varied impact on levels of GDP, wealth and jobs and a traumatic effect on the region's social and political stability. After the collapse of the Thai baht in July 1997 caused a financial and currency meltdown elsewhere, output losses ranged from Japan (17.6%) to Malaysia (50%), South Korea (50.1%), Indonesia (67.95) and Thailand (97.7%) in 1997-8. Wealth losses were largest in Japan, where the crisis was the culmination of its asset price collapse since 1989. Stock market losses in the whole region averaged 66% of 1997 GDP, while land price falls were more varied according to national circumstances (Sheng 2009: 303-6). Riots, looting, strikes, student demonstrations and public protests registered the social distress caused in Indonesia, Thailand and South Korea where new governments emerged. Indonesia's real GDP per capita decreased by 14.4%, South Korea's by 7.5%. Asian currencies collapsed against the dollar. Unemployment rates increased by 63.7%, admittedly from relatively low levels. Migrant workers were especially badly hit. Inflation undermined wage rates, increasing levels of poverty (Sheng 2009: 307-11).

This was a genuinely East Asian crisis, not limited to the ASEAN states but extending to Japan, South Korea and China as well. In this way it created the conditions for the development of ASEAN+3 two years later. There was a common interest and perception that external international organisations like the IMF and governments like the United States had given very bad advice and offered far too little support when the crisis hit. A "politics of resentment" developed in response to this perceived indifference (which extended also to the Asia Pacific Economic Cooperation forum that included the US, whose policy orthodoxy dominated it) (Higgott 1998). Such deep feelings of vulnerability prompted a demand for change in regional institutions and "played a crucial role in fostering a stronger regional identity in East Asia" – "by far the most significant outcome of the crisis in terms of its impact on Asian regionalism" (Emmers and Ravenhill 2010: 3 and 9). There followed a period of institutional innovation to address these shortcomings in regional governance by a wider political cooperation, later extending to finance, trade and currency questions. It coincided with a rapid recovery from the financial crisis throughout the region, overlapping with China's decisive shift into a key position in the global supply chain and after Japan's initiative on an Asian currency zone failed because of US disapproval. It is important to recognise that ASEAN+3 was a political initiative, starting on the sidelines of the ASEAN summit in Kuala Lumpur 1997, beginning its institutionalisation in Hanoi the following year and formally launched at the Manila summit in 1999. Politics played through this process as "Japan ... felt compelled to respond to China's increasingly sophisticated and sustained attempts at cultivating good relations with its neighbours by utilising diplomatic overtures and offers of preferential trade deals of its own" (Beeson 2009: 78).

The subsequent currency swap, financial, trade, bond market and capital movement initiatives flowed from that political base, as have revived discussion of an Asian Monetary Fund and an ASEAN Economic Community (Sheng 2009: 312-16). The Chiang Mai

Initiative, agreed in May 2000, establishing a system of bilateral currency swap arrangements, was by far much the most ambitious of these, although in practice it has had a modest impact, notably in the 2008-9 global financial crisis. But with the associated "economic review and policy dialogue" the APT "assented to an unprecedented process of multilateral surveillance that had the potential to lead to a far more intrusive regionalism than ASEAN had hitherto been willing to accept" (Emmers and Ravenhill 2010: 12, 13ff).

Compared to 1997-8 the global financial crisis of 2008-9 had a far less traumatic impact on the political, economic and social lives of East Asian leaders and populations. Governments and regimes did not fall, national incomes did not collapse and jobs did not disappear on anything like the same scale. Even granting the region's open economic relations with the rest of the world and the truly global nature of the 2008-9 recession, the collective negative impact on East Asia was less than in 1997-8. The fall in growth rates was only slightly greater than in the dot.com bubble of 2001 and much less than in 1997-8 (Emmers and Ravenhill 2010: 2-3).

Looked at from the level of individual states in the whole Asian region, analysts discern differential impacts of the 2008-9 crisis on four groups: those highly dependent on exports (Hong Kong, South Korea, Malaysia, Singapore and Taiwan) experienced sharp falls in real GDP growth rates, exports of goods and services and fiscal balances, but the first two indicators recovered equally sharply in 2010. Their exchange rates and current accounts were stable (except for South Korea). Middle income countries like Philippines, Thailand and Vietnam with high export to GDP ratios had reduced trading and growth but recovered to less buoyant levels of both in 2010. The global crisis was not so devastating for China, Indonesia and India, the third group of large economies, which saw smaller dips in growth and exports, as their strong international reserves, internal demand and stimulus programmes insulated them. The fourth group of low-income countries with significant levels of poverty (Bangladesh, Cambodia, Lao PDR, Nepal and Sri Lanka) suffered large fiscal deficits and high levels of government debt as a result of the recession. (Dowling and Bickram Rana 2010: 58-79).

Emerging from this summary overview is a picture of a deeply diverse region locked in to the global economy, but most of whose states were able to withstand the 2008-9 shocks relatively quickly. In consequence they had less need to act together compared to 1997-8. The record shows they responded to the crisis at national and global more than the regional level. Most of the institutional innovation associated with the Asian financial crisis continued and was deepened in the period 2000-7, with more continuity than qualitative change. Thus the Chiang Mai Initiative was developed and multilaterised in 2007; the bond funds were brought on; the policy dialogue continues and is now joined by an ASEAN+3 research group on regional financial architecture and exchange rates; and probably most notably – but with more of a political than an economic domino effect - bilateral preferential trade agreements between states have proliferated from only one in 2000 to 45 in 2009, with another 45 under negotiation (Ravenhill 2010); these were also supplemented by more ambitious ASEAN trade agreements with China and South Korea. In November 2007 a blueprint for the establishment of the ASEAN Economic Community was adopted, building on accumulated commitments to create an ASEAN Free Trade Area launched in 1992. Goals of the free flow of goods, services, investment, skilled labour and the "freer" flow of capital were agreed. Topping this off politically ASEAN adopted its Charter establishing the grouping as a legal entity, also in November 2007, setting out its purposes, principles and decision-making procedures

(ASEAN Charter 2007); while the APT structure remained the core format around which the geopolitical jostling for more or less inclusive and open political dialogues in the whole Asian region were conducted.

That is a substantial achievement over a decade in such a previously diverse part of the world. But when measured against the actual use of these cooperative mechanisms, especially during the 2008-9 crisis, and the limited institutional innovation it has triggered – including its abiding flexibility on compliance and implementation - it is less impressive. While it always should be remembered that ASEAN originated as a form of political cooperation to encourage dialogue, build confidence and avoid regional conflict, and that its efforts to develop closer economic integration are relatively recent, these efforts must be subject to as much analytic criticism as was applied politically to its efforts by a succession of expert groups charged with further stimulating its closer integration (Eminent Persons Group 2006). The ASEAN Economic Community is, after all, one of the three main pillars laid down in the 2003 Bali Declaration on its development. In this light the following recent judgments on its economic record are instructively critical:

> An enormous distance has still to be traveled before ASEAN will have a set of agreements that are sufficiently specific that they could conceivably be legally enforceable – let alone mechanisms to provide this enforcement... Nothing in this pattern of agreements suggests that East Asia is moving in the direction of becoming a closed trading bloc ....Although substantial re-direction of trade within East Asia has occurred as China has emerged as the assembly plant to the world, East Asia continues to rely very heavily on extra-regional markets for its exports (Ravenhill 2009: 228, 231, 234).

Such judgments are reinforced by a detailed examination of how the global financial crisis affected East Asian regionalism. Thus the CMI was not in fact used in its first eight years. Confronted with the 2008 crisis it "failed abysmally. No country made use of this much-vaunted institution throughout the challenging period of 2008-9" (Emmers and Ravenhill 2010: 13). Key rules about how the CMI relates to IMF borrowing were unresolved, for example. Combined with the crucial fact that the Asian region as a whole emerged strongest from the crisis the attention of most Asian states concerned with changing world geopolitical and geo-economic power shifted towards the Group of 20 from the more Western-centred G8, including a reform of IMF voting and drawing rights, and away from making their own region more integrated. These developments address some of the most important concerns of Asian states at global rather than regional level, concentrating their attention there, "as the international economy is shifting to a new multipolarity" in which it "will need to manage a system of multiple major currencies" (Zoellick 2011). And furthermore, the "perceived shift in the global power distribution rather than any renewed or reinforced sense of regional vulnerability or common identity has given rise to competing proposals to strengthen the East Asia *security* architecture" (Emmers and Ravenhill 2010: 4), notably by China, Japan and South Korea, which also began to cooperate more among themselves than with their other ASEAN partners.

Global Response

This is the setting for the second major factor at work in 2008-9, which overlaps with much of the preceding discussion and may therefore be considered more briefly: the worldwide interdependent nature of Asia's economic development, exemplified by its role in the global supply chain to feed Western consumption, stimulated it to a global response, compared to the regional response in 1997-8. Economic statistics confirm this, in that ASEAN's trade interdependence increased only marginally between the two crises (although 55% of Asia's world trade is now intra-Asian), while China's export dependence on East Asia declined from 53% in 1996 to 36% in 2007 (Ravenhill 2010: 182). This brings us back to a central feature of Asian regionalism, its relationship with globalisation. In its economic manifestation Asian regionalism is defined by its openness. This openness is driven by its role in the world division of labour, the competing interests of different Asian economies within that setting, and the likely reaction of other world powers and regions towards any move towards a more closed economic space in Asia. There is still insufficient intra-Asian demand for Asian final goods to create a strong domestic Asian market. But as the currency question illustrates, global changes can stimulate deeper regional ones, so this is very much a moving target.

China's Role

The third major factor at play is that China, as the emerging regional hegemon, had a greater distance to travel towards, and more interests in developing, closer regional cooperation in 1997-8 than in 2008-9, when it rather needed to consolidate relations already established in a setting of its far greater global influence than a decade earlier. That interdependence and asymmetries of scale and power play a key role in regional integration is well established in the comparative literature (Mattli 1999, Laursen 2010). They are certainly important features of Asian integration, along with its openness. Sheng points out that compared to Germany which in 2006 accounted for 21% of EU GDP and around 15% of total EU financial assets, in Asia Japan alone accounted for 41% of total Asian GDP in 2006 and 53% of total Asian financial assets (Sheng 2009: 318). This Japanese dominance tends to be overlooked when concentrating on China, however justified that is in emergent terms. Seen thus, it is not surprising that the two states should combine competitive and cooperative norms during such a major transition.

These norms extended to Southeast Asia during the early 1990s. After the Tiananmen repression in 1989 China was grateful to find less criticism from there than elsewhere. It began to reinforce better relations individually with ASEAN states, building on "open door", "good neighbour" and "go global" strategies laid down in the 1980s (Ku 2009). This was "a crucial sea-change in not only China's thinking but Chinese policy" (Breslin 2009: 137), abandoning the view that ASEAN was an anti-communist alliance endangering China's security, and acknowledging that it was in its interests to find new regional allies. Diplomatic, political and economic engagements led to deeper social interactions as well during those years. China's decision not to devalue during the 1997-8 crisis was widely appreciated in ASEAN, easing the way for closer relationships with China in the following years through the APT.

China's differing motivations in the Asian and global financial crises can fruitfully be understood in a wider setting of how and when geo-economic and geo-strategic/geo-political considerations predominate in the development of Asian and other regionalisations and regionalisms. Breslin suggests that political economy tends to dominate when crises are most intrusive, as in 1997-8, leading to a shared demand for mechanisms allowing economic relations to flourish. Such considerations recede in the subsequent period of economic consolidation, when more political and strategic concerns come into play (Breslin 2010: 727-9). This was the case with China in the years 2000-8, during which its tremendous economic surge multiplied its political and global influence, even to the point that some commentators talked of a G2 between China and the US in a Pacific century (Bergsten 2008). However exaggerated this notion might be it highlights the predominance of high politics in such a major geopolitical transition. The rapid transformation of 'Asian' into 'global' power shifts over these opening years of the century does indeed help to explain why there was more attention devoted to global rather than regional economic issues by its leaders, especially when the impact of the global crisis was less pronounced that the regional one a decade earlier (Emmers and Ravenhill 2010). Since regional economic relations in East Asia are heavily dependent on global financial and trade flows Breslin believes the best way of categorising them is "globally contingent regionalisation" (2010: 729). That captures its openness very well, without necessarily concluding it will last indefinitely.

Within this, global setting debates continue about whether China will "decouple" from the US. The decoupling argument put forward by the global risk analyst Ian Bremmer says the Chinese leadership no longer believes US power is as indispensable as it once was for the country's economic expansion or the Communist party's political survival. Nor is access to US capital and commercial expertise so important for the next stage of its economic development. That development will depend more on its own resources than on US consumers. Bremmer argues this transition and unfolding conflict "is in many ways more dangerous than the cold war" (Bremmer 2010: 37). It heralds an emerging authoritarian state capitalism in which China inspires other parts of the world, including parts in Asia, to take a similar path, contradicting expectations that modernisation and liberal democratisation are organically linked. Those assumptions may not be correct.

In the longer term a "Beijing consensus" is set to compete with the Washington one so dominant for the last 30 years of globalisation in a more multi-polar world. Sovereign wealth funds, state-owned and directed companies and strategic alliances with emergent state regimes throughout the world are the economic hallmarks of this alternative model. Politically it is illiberal, state-centred and hostile to competitive party politics (Bremmer 2010, Gillespie 2010).

Given the currency of such ideas (together with countervailing ones by liberal internationalists like John Ikenberry (2009) who say China's relative underdevelopment will require an open engagement with the most developed states for a long time to come, along with a gradual socialisation into responsibility for stability and security in a setting of multi-polar world regions under continuing US hegemony) the outbreak of competitive regionalism in Asia outlined in section 3 of this chapter is not surprising. This is driven by the need to find balances and alliances which suit different states and interests in the region, and extends to the existential question of what Asia is. Breslin's conclusion is apt (2010: 729):

So while the debate in Europe might be on **consequences**, in Asia and elsewhere, the dominant issue for the students of regionalism is **causes** – what makes a region come into existence, cohere and have longevity? Or even more fundamentally, it is often on the prior question of 'what is the region'?

CONCLUSION

Compared to the East Asian financial crisis of the late 1990s, when the region suffered severely from a common shock, and (at least among its political elites) became a more coherent entity as cooperative action was taken to address that, the global financial crisis of 2008-9 had a less traumatic impact. The region was less seriously affected, partly because its leaders had effectively learned certain lessons a decade earlier which helped to insulate their countries. This learning process helped socialise them into the habits of selective regional cooperation, and thereby strengthened their role in the worldwide capitalist system. East Asia stood out as a region capable of withstanding shocks arising from the economic system hitherto dominated by the United States and Europe.

Suddenly East Asia was seen as a key to international recovery through the development of autonomous regional demand and investment cycles, notwithstanding its own more or less intense market, security and political rivalries. Paradoxically this outcome was achieved without an equivalent regional institutional innovation. Governments and economic actors responded more at national and global than at regional level. If this reinforced a picture of competitive rather than cooperative action, that would be a misleading impression, since there was a certain similarity in what was done by Asian leaders in their individual states and they had a common supportive approach towards the reconfiguring of geo-economic and geopolitical power through the G20. In the associated geo-strategic security sphere there was more genuine rivalry, for example between China and Japan in ASEAN+3 as they competed to encourage or resist deeper US involvement in the region, including by broadening its geographical scope and cultural identity to embrace India and Australasia as well as East Asia.

This chapter has suggested three main reasons why the 1997-8 economic crisis stimulated Asian regionalism more than the 2008-9 one: 1997-8 was more specifically regional than global, leading to a greater effort to correct shortcomings in response; its globally contingent regionalisation had a similar effect; and in the changed world setting of 2008-9 China had a greater interest in taking global than regional action, especially in securing a stable long-term relationship with the United States. So Asia interacted with the rest of the world more outwardly than before in dealing with the global financial crisis. This outward orientation should be seen as a relative strength - not a weakness because it was not accompanied by greater regional coordination. We are dealing with a major transition in global and Asian affairs: towards a more multi-polar world in which power will be shared more equally between different global regions, and towards a new configuration of power in Asia itself. These changes are dialectically related to one another, because regions are made by world politics as well as internal dynamics. Future cycles of economic and political change will alter the balances expressed in the 2008-9 conjuncture, including those concerning Asian regionalism.

Looking at that phenomenon in terms of the 'regionness' scale outlined in Figure 10.1 it was suggested that the developments discussed in this chapter have driven Southeast Asia and East Asia at least to the level of regional society. The failure to consolidate the definition, compliance and implementation of the new regulatory rules adopted in the 1990s a decade later, together with the renewed emphasis on national and global action, stop short of developing a regional community, even one that would be quite different from the European Union because of distinct historical and structural circumstances. It is impossible in the middle of such a transition to predict whether that will happen in the decades to come. There is ample room for conflict in the emergence of multi-polar systems, especially if they are unbalanced; and regionalism may not live up to the potential contained in convergent interests and values. However, Asia has come a very long way in two decades, so much so that it is now possible to talk about it as an actor where that would have been outlandish in the 1980s. Were we to revisit this subject in the early 2030s it would be foolish indeed to rule out the further development of its capacity to act, whether in terms of economic space, provision of public goods or in relation to sovereignty.

REFERENCES

Acharya, Amitav (2007), "The Emerging Regional Architecture of World Politics", *World Politics*, 59 (4): 629-52.

Acharya, Amitav (2009), *Where Ideas Matter? Agency and Power in Asian Regionalism*, Ithaca, New York: Cornell University Press.

Acharya, Amitav (2010), *East Asia Forum,* November 14th.

Andreosso-O'Callaghan, Bernadette (2008), "Comparing and contrasting Economic Integration in the Asia-Pacific Region and Europe", in Philomena Murray ed. (2009), *Europe and Asia, Regions in Flux*, chapter 4, pp 61-83, Basingstoke: Palgrave MacMillan.

ASEAN (2006), *Report of the Eminent Persons Group on the ASEAN Charter*, http://www.aseansec.org/64.htm (accessed 20.2.2011).

ASEAN (2007), *ASEAN Charter* http://www.aseansec.org/64.htm (accessed 20.2.2011).

Beeson, Mark (2009), *Institutions of the Asia-Pacific, ASEAN, APEC and beyond*, London and New York: Routledge.

Bergsten, C. Fred (2008), "A Partnership of Equals", *Foreign Affairs* 87 (4): 57-69.

Bloomberg (30.10.2010), http://www.bloomberg.com/news/2010-10-30/clinton-tells-east-asia-summit-to-have-active-agenda-for-maritime-disputes.html (accessed 9.2.2011).

Bowring, Philip (2010), "Welcome back, I.M.F.", *International Herald Tribune*, July 21st.

Breslin, Shaun (2009), "Towards a Sino-centric regional order? Empowering China and constructing regional order(s)", chapter 7, pp. 131-55 in Dent, Christopher M. ed. (2009), *China, Japan and Regional Leadership in East Asia*, Cheltenham: Edward Elgar.

Breslin, Shaun (2010), "Comparative theory, China and the future of East Asia", *Review of International Studies*, 36 (3): 709-29. *The Economist* (2010), "Leaving Asia's shade", July 24th p. 46.

Bremmer, Ian (2010), "Fight of the Century", *Prospect*, April: 37-41.

Clinton, Hillary (2010), "Remarks on US Foreign Policy", speech to the Council of Foreign Relations, New York, 8 September 2010
http://www.state.gov/secretary/rm/2010/09/146917.htm (accessed 20.2.2011).

Cox, Michael (2005), "Beyond the West: Terrors in Transatlantia", *European Journal of International Relations* 11 (2): 203-33.

Emmers, Ralf and Ravenhill, John 2010, *The Asian and Global Financial Crises: Consequences for East Asian Regionalism,* S. Rajaratnam School of International Studies Singapore RSIS Working Paper No. 208, August 16th.

Fawn, Rick ed. (2009), "'Regions' and their study: wherefrom, what for and whereto?", *Review of International Studies*, 35 (1): 5–34.

Gillespie, Paul (2010), "China and US still very much in it together", *The Irish Times* April 3rd.

Gillespie, Paul (2010a), "Asia plays new role as global power broker", *The Irish Times*, July 17th.

Goh, Evelyn (2007/8), "Great Powers and the Hierarchical Order in Southeast Asia, Analyzing Regional Security Strategies", *International Security* 32 (3): 113-57.

Goh, Evelyn (2008), "Hierarchy and the role of the United States in the East Asian security order", *International Relations of the Asia-Pacific* 8 (3): 353-77.

Grevi, Giovanni (2009), *The Interpolar World: A New Scenario*, Paris: European Union Institute for Security Studies, Occasional Paper 79.

Haass, Richard (2008), "The Age of Non-polarity: What will follow US Dominance?", *Foreign Affairs*, 87 (3): 44-56.

Hettne, Björn (2005), "Beyond the 'New' Regionalism", *New Political Economy*, 10 (4): 543-71.

Hettne, Björn (2008), "Regional Actorship and Regional Agency: Comparative Perspectives", *6th GARNET PhD SCHOOL* 9 - 13 June 2008, Brussels.

Hettne, Björn and Söderbaum, Fredrik (2000), "Theorising the Rise of Regionness", *New Political Economy* 5 (3): 457-72.

Higgott, Richard (1998), "The Asian Financial Crisis: A Study in the Politics of Resentment", *New Political Economy* 3 (3): 33-56.

Higgott, Richard (2006), "The theory and practice of region, the changing global context", chapter 2, pp. 17-38 in Fort, Bertrand and Webber, Douglas eds. (2006), *Regional Integration in East Asia and Europe, Convergence or divergence?* London and New York: Routledge.

Higgott, Richard (2010), "Multi-Polarity and Trans-Atlantic Relations: Normative Aspirations and Practical Limits of EU Foreign Policy", GARNET Working Paper No. 76/10.

Howorth, Jolyon (2010), "The EU as a Global Actor: Grand Strategy for a Global Grand Bargain?", *Journal of Common Market Studies* 48 (3): 455-74.

Hurrell, Andrew (2007), "One world? Many worlds? The place of regions in the study of international society", *International Affairs*, 83 (1): 127-46.

Ikenberry, John (2008), 'The Rise of China and the Future of the West', *Foreign Affairs*, 87 (1): 23-37.

Katzenstein, Peter (2005), *A World of Regions, Asia and Europe in the American Imperium*, Ithaca and London: Cornell University Press.

Kriesi, Hanspeter, Grande, Edgar, Lachat, Romain, Dolezxal, Martin, Bornschier, Frey, Timotheos (2008), *West European Politics In The Age Of Globalization*, Cambridge: Cambridge University Press.

Ku, Samuel C.Y. (2009), "China's Changing Relations with Southeast Asia: A Political Analysis", chapter 2, pp.23-47 in Yeoh, Emile Kok-Kheng (2009) ed., *Towards Pax Sinica? China's Rise and Transformation: Impacts and Implications,* Kuala Lumpur: Institute of China Studies, University of Malaya.

Laursen, Finn (2010), "Requirements for Regional Integration: A Comparative Perspective on the EU, the Americas and East Asia", chapter 13 pp. 227-38 in Laursen, Finn ed. (2010), *Comparative Regional Integration, Europe and Beyond*, Farnham: Ashgate.

Lombaerde, Philippe de, Söderbaum, Fredrik, Van Langenhove, Luk and Baert, Francis 2010, "The problem of comparison in comparative regionalism", *Review of International Studies* 36 (3): 731-53.

Mahbubani, Kishore (2008), "Why Asia stays calm in the storm", *Financial Times* October 28th.

Mattli, Walter (1999), *The Logic of Regional Integration: Europe and Beyond*, Cambridge: Cambridge University Press.

Mearsheimer, John J. (2001), *The Tragedy of Great Power Politics*, New York and London: Norton.

Mearsheimer, John J. (2009), "Reckless States and Realism", *International Politics* 23 (2): 241-56.

Morada, N. (2008), "ASEAN at 40: p5rospects for community building in Southeast Asia", *Asia-Pacific Review* 15 (1): 36-55.

Murray, Philomena (2010), "East Asian Regionalism and EU Studies" Journal of European Integration, 32 (6): 597-616.

Murray, Philomena (2010a), "Comparative regional integration in the EU and East Asia: Moving beyond integration snobbery", *International Politics* 47 (3-4), 308–323.

Murray, Philomena and Rees, Nicholas eds. 2010, "European and Asian regionalism: Form and function", *International Politics* 47 (3-4), special edition.

Ong, Bernard (2009), "Banking on East Asian Integration? Implications of Global Financial Crisis for Regionalism", *Asian Regional Integration Review* 2: 32-68.

Ravenhill, John (2008), "Fighting Irrelevance: An Economic Community 'with ASEAN Characteristics'", *The Pacific Review*, 21 (4): 469-88.

Ravenhill, John (2009), "East Asian Regionalism, Much Ado about Nothing?", *Review of International Studies* 35: 215-36, special issue.

Ravenhill, John (2010), "The 'new East Asian regionalism': A political domino effect", *Review of International Political Economy*, 17 (2): 178-208.

Renard, T. (2009), *A BRIC in the World: Emerging Powers, Europe and the Coming Order*, Brussels: Academic Press for the Royal Institute of International Relations.

Roundtable (2007), "Peter J. Katzenstein's Contributions to the Study of East Asian Regionalism", *Journal of East Asian Studies* 7 (3): 359-412.

Sally, Razeen (2010), Regional Economic Integration in Asia: The Track Record and Prospects, European Centre for International Political Economy, Occasional Paper No. 2/2010.

Sbragia, Alberta (2008), "Review Article: Comparative Regionalism", *The Journal of Common Market Studies Annual Review of the European Union in 2007*, eds. Ulrich Sedelmeier and Alasdair R. Young, pp 29-50.

Sheng, Andrew (2009), *From Asian to Global Financial Crisis, An Asian Regulator's View of Unfettered Finance in the 1990s and 2000s*, Cambridge: Cambridge University Press.

Sheng, Andrew (2009a), "From Asian to Global Financial Crisis", Indian Council for Research in International and Economic Relations, Third KB Lall Memorial Lecture 7 February 2009, New Delhi. http://www.icrier.org/pdf/AndrewSheng.pdf (accessed 10.5.2011).

Söderbaum, Fredrik and Sbragia, Alberta (2010), "EU Studies and the 'New Regionalism': What can be Gained from Dialogue?", *Journal of European Integration*, 32 (6): 563-582.

Van Langenhove, Luk (2003), "Theorising Regionhood", *UNU/CRIS e-Working Papers* 1.

Van Langenhove, Luk (2010), "The EU as a Global Actor in a Multipolar World of Multilateral 2.0 Environment", *Egmont Paper 56,* Brussels: Royal Institute of International Relations, 1-32.

Vayrynen, Raimo 2003, "'Regionalism: Old and New'", *International Studies Review*, 5 (1): 25–51.

Warleigh-Lack, Alex (2006), "The European and the universal process? European Union studies, new regionalism and global governance", chapter 29 pp. 561-75 in Knud Erik Jorgensen, Mark A Pollack and Ben Rosamond eds. 2006, *Handbook of European Union Politics*, London: Sage.

Warleigh-Lack, Alex and Rosamond, Ben (2010), "Across the EU Studies–New Regionalism Frontier: Invitation to a Dialogue", *Journal of Common Market Studies*, 48 (4): 993-1013.

Warleigh-Lack, Alex and Luk Van Langenhove (2010), "Rethinking EU Studies: The Contribution of Comparative Regionalism", *Journal of European Integration*, 32 (6): 541-562.

Wheatley, Alan (2010), "I.M.F. Turns on the Charm in Asia", *International Herald Tribune*, July 19th.

Zoellick, Robert (2011), "Monetary reforms for a multipolar world", *Financial Times* February 18th.

INDEX

D

E

F

G

H

I

S

T